THE PRIEST

Other Books by Don Gold

Bellevue
Letters to Tracy
The Park
Until the Singing Stops

THE PRIEST

Don Gold

HOLT, RINEHART AND WINSTON

New York

Published by Holt, Rinehart and Winston, 383 Madison Avenue, New York, New York 10017.

Published simultaneously in Canada by Holt, Rinehart and Winston of Canada, Limited.

Library of Congress Cataloging in Publication Data

Gold, Don.
    The priest.

    1. O'Connor, Brian, 1945–   2. Catholic Church—Clergy—Biography.   3. Clergy—New York (City)—Biography. 4. New York (City)—Biography. I. Title.
BX4705.O33G64   282'.092'4 [B]   80–22752

ISBN: 0–03–053981–1

First Edition

Designer: Robert Bull

Printed in the United States of America

10 9 8 7 6 5 4 3 2 1

THE PRIEST

Introduction

A Catholic priest is a man of God who must sustain his own faith and communicate it inspiringly to others. He is depended upon. The parish priest is on the front line: his life is devoted almost entirely to the spiritual and secular needs of his parishioners. To be effective he must be more than a believer. He must be part sociologist, part psychologist, part political scientist to deal with the longings and frustrations of Catholics who come to him for aid.

The parish priest is *there*, and the faithful know it. He baptizes their children, marries them, leads them from birth to death, brings them closer to God and offers them a sense of supportive morality. It is not easy on him. In the midst of a sexual revolution, he is a celibate. In a world where many live in contempt of God, he cannot waver. In an urban setting, he must deal with practical problems—poverty, unemployment, struggles against the bureaucracy, the ravages of age, unhappy marriages, neglected children, and more—that tax the faith of believers, priests and parishioners alike. He must understand the nature of our time, with all its moral conflicts, without succumbing to despair.

I wanted to know such a man well enough to write about him. I began my search, looking for a parish priest who would be neither saint nor drudge. I sought guidance from helpful priests, men who wanted their story told. I described my intention.

All sources indicated that the Catholic Church in America had changed. Older parishioners resented the changes; younger ones welcomed them. How did a young parish priest function within that changed Church? How did he differ from his older counterparts, and how did he sustain that faith so vital to his functions in the community? How did he help the people of his parish?

One middle-aged priest told me, "The Catholic Church today is not that Catholic Church of thirty or forty years ago. Forget about what you ever heard about priests and nuns implanting guilt in their lectures about sin, then sitting back in judgment. If you can tell the story of one young parish priest, you'll be telling enough, good and bad."

As a journalist, I listened. But as a non-Catholic, I could not corroborate his advice on first hearing. I had to find out for myself. I discovered that there were almost 50,000,000 Catholics in America and 1,825,000 in the archdiocese of New York, in 407 parishes. The numbers were impressive; yet I learned that attendance at mass was down, that the number of young men and women settling on a religious vocation was drastically diminished. The Church's grip on its members was slipping. In one national poll, 64 percent of Catholics believed that the right of a woman to have an abortion should be left entirely to the woman and her doctor—despite the Church's unambiguous opposition to abortion.

In another poll, more than half the Catholics surveyed felt that most Churches "have lost the real spiritual part of religion." They felt that the basic message of the faith, the solid, traditional theology, had been eroded by the Church's battle against the sexual revolution. They were in combat with the moral stand their own Church had taken over the centuries.

In the book *Human Sexuality: New Directions in American Catholic Thought*, commissioned by The Catholic Theological Society of America and attacked by the Vatican, it was pointed out that "there is a growing gap between what the Catholic Church officially teaches in matters sexual and what the faithful have come to believe and practice." The authors of that book asserted: "No physical expression of sexuality, including oral sex, provided it be mutually sensitive and acceptable, should be prejudged as morally wrong or perverse."

Checking back to Canon Law, I unearthed: "Clerics must be careful not to have in their houses nor to associate habitually with women who might be objects of suspicion. They may live in the same house only with women who are beyond all suspicion of evil by reason of close relationship, such as mother, sister, or aunt, or who are above suspicion because of irreproachable character or joined to a rather advanced age . . . the combination of two qualities makes the proximity of a woman relatively free from scandal or danger; namely: (a) an entirely irreproachable character, and (b) a rather advanced age. The canonical age in this connection has changed at various times. In this country today it is about forty."

The moral-sexual conflicts that have provoked priests and parishioners alike have plagued the Church in America since the upheavals of Vatican II, during the 1960s, when Pope John XXIII opened the doors and windows of his mammoth institution to the winds of change. At first, young activist priests were encouraged. But the new liberalism emerging from Rome began to fade as popes after John reverted to conservative doctrine. Priests who matured in the Church in the sixties were frustrated.

Today young men who might not have hesitated to enter the priesthood in another time often prefer to serve their God in the secular world. They reject the concept of celibacy. They are put off by the dogma and conservatism of the Vatican, offended by the Church's institutional rigidity. They want the right to dissent; they see little freedom to do so in the Church. They believe that one can have faith, and live by it, without becoming a priest. As a result, priests are in short supply; seminaries once crowded with eager students are barely populated.

The contemporary priest understands the system. The archbishop (in the larger dioceses) or bishop runs the show with subordinate bishops and priests to help him. On the neighborhood level, however, there are just the parish priests (and their supervising, resident pastors) doing the day-to-day work. What many younger priests find hard to understand is the lack of inspiring communication between the power structure and the priest on the street. Too often, they feel, grievances are left unattended, frustrations are not recognized, and support is withheld, forcing them to fend for themselves.

Many do just that. By living and working in the community, they come to know their parishioners. They continue to bring the Word of God to the people.

Mary Gordon, in her novel *Final Payments*, remembered an effective old priest: "I was impressed by the sheer amount of love Father Mulcahy had inspired in so many people. They had come to him in periods of astounding grief, in turmoil, in sickness, in unhappiness, in madness even. And he had understood the violence of their lives and their sorrows. He had sat with them for endless hours listening to them weep, listening to the catalogue of human suffering that is surprisingly varied, surprisingly limited. And, in their moments of success, at their daughters' weddings, the birth of their grandchildren, their fiftieth wedding anniversaries, he was there, carrying his shy festiveness around like a valise."

Such devotion creates stresses—not simply the stress of the celibate in a world painted in sexual hues, but also, for most urban priests, the stress of poverty that attacks many of the new immigrants in big-city parishes. Priests find they must defend the dignity of the poor against all odds. It is exhausting. Urban parishes have changed as new nationalities and new customs have been introduced. Today, many priests must speak Spanish, or they fail to communicate. They must survive the constant threat of loneliness; no man can spend his entire life helping others without helping himself, without having friends to console him.

Eugene Kennedy, professor of psychology at Loyola University in Chicago, has written: "The stresses experienced by priests may be greater than those experienced by any other professional group. The wonder is that good-hearted priests carry on as well as they do. They need support, understanding, and serious consideration by Church authority of the truth about their lives far more than they need criticism, false though hearty encouragement, or the benign neglect which they are now receiving."

Most young priests in America today, those between twenty-six and thirty-five, grew up in an era of change. They are antitradition and proconscience. They do not believe in blind obedience to the Church hierarchy. They tend to reason their way through issues, coming to conclusions that they believe support both the will of God and the needs of their community. And they tend to violate those regulations they feel to be inappropriate.

"Right-wing Catholics may insist that you are not a Catholic if you don't keep all the rules," Andrew Greeley, the priest-sociologist-author has written. "The majority disagrees. The majority may well be morally wrong. You don't make moral decisions by counting noses, but they don't think they are wrong. And herein is precisely the nature of the Catholic crisis: it is a crisis not of authority, but of the credibility of church leadership."

At once moved, intrigued, confused, and inspired by what I had learned about the state of the Church in America, I wanted to find an able parish priest whose life might personify the role of the urban Church. I wanted to find a young priest who still *believed*, and whose life was an extension of that belief.

There are 1,068 diocesan priests in the New York archdiocese, priests who serve their big-city parishioners from ordination to retirement. They are scattered throughout the boroughs of Manhattan, Staten Island, and the Bronx, and seven counties north of the city. Young priests among them are a distinct minority: only 175 were under the age of forty in mid-1979.

I talked to a number of these young priests in various parishes. When I told them what I planned to do, several of them mentioned Brian O'Connor and Incarnation parish. He was, they told me, a priest who believed in God profoundly and lived his life in terms of that belief. Incarnation, I was told, was a large, bustling parish that was ethnically varied —serving the Irish who had lived there for decades and newcomers like the Dominicans who had come to New York recently for a better life.

When I first met Brian I thought him a good, uncomplicated man. Large and bearlike, conspicuously overweight, he seemed calm and quite satisfied in his role of parish priest. As months passed, I became his shadow, his inquisitor, his friend. I realized that his mind was filled with knowledge and love. He had forgotten very little of what he had learned in classrooms, in the confessional, and on the streets of New York. Not conspicuously pious, he was conscientious. He did not shrink from the company of men or women. While careless about his appearance—about clothes, possessions, money—he cared about people, and not simply Catholics. His view of life, for the most part, was upbeat. He preferred superlatives—"superb," "excellent," "very good"—to words that derogated.

When I met him, he had spent eight years at Incarnation Church, his first assignment after ordination. In his work in the parish, he comforted the dying and their families with gentleness and understanding. He spent time developing religious-education programs for the children who attended Incarnation's elementary school as well as for those who went to the local public school. He led prayer groups, ran a religious outreach program, helped the poor and the troubled.

In the course of any given week, he would say mass frequently, deal with the problems of parishioners who came to the rectory door, visit parishioners in hospitals and nursing homes, conduct religion classes, meet with fellow priests, speak to the children at the Incarnation school, spend time at the neighborhood senior center, do baptisms and weddings, and hear confessions (also called "reconciliation" or "penance"). Through it all, he shifted from English to Spanish with ease.

He was a graduate of St. Joseph's Seminary in the Dunwoodie section of Yonkers, a few miles north of Manhattan. It was the seminary that produced diocesan priests for the archdiocese of New York. He had spent six years at St. Joseph's, getting his bachelor's degree after two and his master's in divinity after three more years of theology. After serving for a year as a deacon in a West Side Manhattan parish, he was ordained in 1971.

It had not taken Brian long, during his final year before ordination, to realize that the role of the urban priest demanded a knowledge of Spanish. He recognized the new wave of immigration: Cubans, Puerto Ricans, Dominicans, Colombians, Mexicans. It was a wave that was sweeping across the entire country, one that had changed the way the Church related to its parishioners. He spent time at a language school in Puerto Rico and lived with the people in the Dominican Republic and Colombia for months in order to learn Spanish the way the natives spoke it. When he arrived at his first post, Incarnation, he was ready.

After several years at Incarnation, he realized that he was spending much of his time with the elderly, the sick, and the dying. He could bring spiritual comfort to them; as their bodies betrayed them, their faith remained intact. Yet, he wanted to do more than that. He enrolled at Columbia University and, in 1976, was awarded a master's degree in public health, specializing in thanatology (the study of death and dying). Encouraged by that achievement, he served on Columbia-Presbyterian Hospital's committee on death and dying and taught the subject at a funeral school in Manhattan and at Montclair State College in New Jersey.

But now he was thinking about moving on; it was, he felt, time to do so. He didn't want to abandon his fluent skill in Spanish and hoped to serve in another parish in which it was spoken. He was waiting for such a position.

I began to follow Brian in the heat of July, and I concluded my work with him on Christmas Day. During those six months I became a presence in Brian's life; he sacrificed much of his privacy for my benefit. I followed him everywhere he went, taking notes. We sat for hours, taping his feelings on relevant subjects. He talked to me about his thoughts and responded to my probing. I was the witness to the events of his life, and he did not attempt to disguise reality for my sake. I talked to his family, his friends, and his associates; he did not attempt to muzzle or influence anyone. Out of a mass of accumulated material I attempted to shape a book that would accurately reflect the nature of his life and the strength of his faith. He gave much to me, and we became friends. That friendship enabled me to write about him beyond the scope of his own words and actions.

I have not tried to write a book about the Catholic Church as an institution. One volume would not be enough to accomplish that. I have tried to write a book about a man who is a priest, about how he lives his life and honors his God.

Early in my research I met an old priest nearing retirement. He told me, "If you are going to write about the Church, read this." He handed me the Nicene Creed, written in 325:

We believe in one God,
the father, the Almighty,
maker of heaven and earth,
of all that is seen and unseen.
We believe in one Lord, Jesus Christ,
the only Son of God,
eternally begotten of the Father,
God from God, Light from Light,
true God from true God,
begotten, not made, one in Being with the Father.
Through him all things were made.
For us men and for our salvation
he came down from heaven:
by the power of the Holy Spirit
he was born of the Virgin Mary, and became man.
For our sake he was crucified under Pontius Pilate;
he suffered, died, and was buried.
He was buried,
he was raised to life on the third day,
according to the Scriptures;
He appeared to Cephus
and afterward to the Twelve.
Then he appeared to over five hundred
of our brothers at once

most of whom are still alive, though
some have died.
Then he appeared to James,
and afterward to all the apostles.
1 Corinthians 15:3–7

Later I read Robert Daley's novel, *A Priest and a Girl*, in which a seminarian said, "I want to help reform the Church. To change it for the good." That seminarian was Brian O'Connor. In linking the faith of the Nicene Creed with a will to act, Brian defined his life. This book is an attempt to understand that life.

I

Summer

"Catholicism will persist. It always has, and the evidence suggests that it always will. Faith is not based on either the virtue or the intelligence of church elites. The Bridegroom is not to be judged by the spouse; she will be without blemish only when He returns. But in our current American Catholic manifestation, she has one hell of a case of acne."

ANDREW M. GREELEY
The Communal Catholic

"To place oneself before what seems to be bread and to say, 'Christ is there living and true,' is pure faith."

BROTHER CARLO CARETTO
Letters from the Desert

1

It was a fiercely hot July afternoon in Upper Manhattan. Along St. Nicholas Avenue, movement was slow. Aging air-conditioners sputtered. The neighborhood stores—a bakery, a grocery, a beauty salon, a restaurant, a furniture store—were all open for business, but were not busy. On the sidewalks, neatly dressed mothers pushed strollers with infants in them. A police car crept along; the driver waved at the pedestrians. One old Irish woman paused on her way shopping to exchange gossip with one of her neighbors; they had lived in the community for more than forty years. While they chatted they stared across the street at the McGonnell Funeral Home on the corner of 175th Street.

A group of mourners emerged into the heat, followed by six pallbearers carrying a casket. The entire group crossed the avenue, where they were greeted by a large, heavyset priest who escorted them into the Church of the Incarnation, the Catholic church on the corner.

The building stood there in a sea of urban concrete, dominating the scene. It had been there since 1930, when the neighborhood was 70 percent middle-class Irish-American, with a sprinkling of Germans and Italians. The architect had been inspired by the flamboyant Gothic style of the Church of St. Maclou in Rouen. He had built Incarnation of pale gray granite and trimmed it with carved limestone.

Its facade, tall and flat, ruled the avenue, adjoined by the simple, gray, four-story rectory on a block otherwise filled with stores. The corner, however, belonged to Incarnation. Its twin towers and long, narrow bulk were familiar to thousands of parishioners.

One of those parishioners, Maria Angotti, had just died at the age of ninety-seven. She had come to America as a teen-ager and had known poverty; yet she and her husband raised a family, earned a living, and eventually prospered. Most of her children left the neighborhood for suburban destinations, but Maria and one of her sons remained, even after her husband died. She had seen other immigrants, a new wave, arrive. She understood their plight and lived as a good neighbor with them. They spoke Spanish. She spoke Italian. It didn't matter. They got along. The neighborhood had changed, she knew that. Cubans, Puerto Ricans, Dominicans, blacks, joined the Irish, Italian, and German families that had lived there for decades. The poor and the middle class. For all the Catholics among them, Incarnation had been essential and would continue to be so. They relied upon their Church.

They brought Maria Angotti on her last trip into the church she had known for most of her life. The priest, Brian O'Connor, directed that final trip.

He felt the heat beneath his white vestments, but his mood was tranquil. He escorted the mourners to their seats at the front of the church; the pallbearers placed the casket before the altar and left. The vastness of the church dwarfed the mourners, the priest, and the casket. Beams of sunlight illuminated the bright colors of the stained-glass windows throughout the church, casting bands of blue and red across the pews. From the rose window facing in from the facade, the sunlight introduced more color. The simple altar was framed by a massive marble baldachino, pink and ornate, supported by four columns of red marble.

Brian began the service. He had seen Maria Angotti many times at mass, but had not known her well. There were too many parishioners at Incarnation for one priest to know them all. Now he worked his way gracefully through the service, moving from altar to pulpit and back, reciting prayers, commanding the rite. A few of the twenty mourners wept; most of them remained silent, whether respectful, devoted, or resigned.

A tenor sang from a loft at the front of the church, and an organist played. The seventy-five dollars the family had paid for the service included twenty dollars for each of them, twenty dollars for the Church itself, and fifteen dollars for the pool of stipends that the priests of the parish would share.

Brian urged the mourners to pray: "Let us pray with confidence to the Father in the words our Savior gave us.

"Our Father who art in heaven, hallowed be thy name, thy kingdom come, thy will be done on earth as it is in heaven. Give us this day our daily bread, and forgive us our trespasses as we forgive those who trespass against us, and lead us not into temptation, but deliver us from evil. . . . For the kingdom, the power, and the glory are yours, now and forever."

Behind the altar, with his arms outstretched, he was an imposing figure: six feet tall and 240 pounds. His blue eyes, behind his ever-present glasses, dominated his round, youthful face. There was conspicuous gray in his brown hair. As he looked over the mourners, the trace of a compassionate smile appeared on his face.

The sound of weeping stopped. Brian stepped down and approached the mourners, shook their hands. He did it quietly; the church was almost silent. The sun's rays highlighted the old oak pews; yet despite the afternoon heat, the church was cool.

At the rear of the church, a teen-aged boy wandered in, then out, his modest curiosity satisfied. A woman in tight red jeans and a low-cut blouse entered, made the sign of the cross, stood at the back of the church and listened, then left. The odor of incense filled the church, circulating from the altar where Brian had dispensed it to the open door facing the street.

The pallbearers, who had been chatting on the sidewalk outside the church, reentered, placed the casket on their shoulders, folded their hands in front of them, and moved slowly out of the church. They worked for the funeral home for a union-fixed fee of sixteen dollars per man; they had all done this before and knew that they must be somber.

The organ music again reverberated throughout the church. The mourners filed out to their cars for the ride to the cemetery. Brian walked them to the street, where the hearse and the mourners' cars were lined up.

Brian, at thirty-three, had conducted many funeral services in his eight years at Incarnation. There was a sadness about death that invariably touched him; yet he believed that life on earth was not the only life, that there was another joyous life to come. He tried to communicate both feelings to mourners.

As he stood in front of the church, Maria Angotti's son, an elderly man himself—tall, well dressed, and dignified —stepped up to him.

"Thank you," the man said simply.

"You're welcome," Brian said.

"She had a good life," the son said. "A long and a good life. When we were kids, there wasn't much money around. But they—my mother and father—found a way. And, you know, they got a great deal of their energy from their belief in God, from the Church."

"Yes, I believe that," Brian said. "They needed it when

times were bad, and when your mother was young, times were often bad."

The son told Brian that he was a doctor at Columbia-Presbyterian Hospital, the sprawling medical complex in the neighborhood. It provided a number of parishioners for Incarnation.

"She stayed in the parish and so did I," he said. "It has changed, but so what? We were a family of immigrants and so are these people." He waved his arm at nearby apartment buildings.

Brian nodded. "Some leave. Some stay. And new ones arrive all the time."

"My mother would not have been happy anywhere else. She could have moved to the suburbs with one of my brothers or sisters, but she wouldn't. This is where she settled years ago, and this is where it would all end for her."

"How did it end?" Brian asked.

"All systems were out, you might say. She was lucid almost to the last moment. Still telling us what to do with our lives. Then she simply died, quietly."

"In peace?" Brian asked.

"In peace," the son said. "I think her faith helped her do just that."

"We believe in that," Brian said.

"Sometimes I do, sometimes I don't," the son said. "When you're a doctor, your faith has to be put to the test."

"I can understand that," Brian said. "If you want to talk more about it one of these days, I'm easy to find. There are times when it isn't easy to deal with grief. If you want to talk to someone, give me a call or just drop in to the rectory."

"That's kind of you," the son said. "I've been in and out of the Church over the years."

"I won't give you a hard sell," Brian said, smiling. "We'll just talk."

They shook hands, and Brian gave him a gentle pat on the shoulder. The son joined the other mourners who soon entered their cars and followed the hearse up the avenue. The graveside service would be conducted by one of the parish deacons. Brian went back in, to the sacristy in the rear of the church—a spacious room with dark, weathered wood furniture where the vestments and various church objects were kept—to remove his vestments and return to the rectory.

On the sidewalk in front of the church, two teen-aged boys lingered. Their mammoth portable radio blared salsa music. Two priests, returning from a mission elsewhere in the city, glared at the boys and grimaced at the sound of the music. They paused in front of the rectory.

"You know what the Mafia does when they want to get rid of a body without a trace? When they don't want it to come floating up out of the East River?" the older priest asked.

"No, what?" the younger priest said.

"They take the body to one of their favorite undertakers and he slips it into another coffin, under a respectable corpse. He makes a sandwich."

"You're kidding."

"No. That's what they do. Can you think of a better way?" The younger priest admitted he could not. He had his own story to share.

"Did you hear about . . . ?" he asked, mentioning the name of a priest they both knew. "He's parading around with his mistress, hand in hand. The parishioners are talking."

"Obviously he didn't get the rule from his first pastor," the older priest said.

"What's that?"

"*Nunca en la parroquia,*" the older priest said. "Never in the parish."

"I always thought the rule was *nunca, nunca,*" the young priest said with a laugh.

"Who the hell was your first pastor?" the older priest bellowed.

They strolled into the rectory.

Slow-moving traffic continued: city buses, delivery trucks, gypsy cabs. Young mothers sat on a stoop on the side of the church and watched their children at play. A mailman, his shirt soaked with perspiration, waved at them as he passed. The odor of pork and garlic, blending in a pan, wafted from an apartment window across the street from the church. Two unemployed men leaned against a parked car while a neighborhood free-lance mechanic worked under its hood.

Inside the church everything was quiet. Several old women entered, walked slowly to the front of the church, knelt and prayed. The church could hold more than six hundred parishioners in its twenty-six rows of pews; it was almost empty again. One old woman arose from prayer and lit a votive candle, put some change in a receptacle for such donations, and walked up the middle aisle of the church. She looked up at the soaring, vaulted ceiling, imploringly, as if attempting to look beyond it.

Another old woman completed her prayers and followed up the aisle to the front door. Only a young woman and her two small children remained in the church, in a pew near the altar. They were kneeling in prayer. Softly, the woman's voice echoed through the open space, around the six massive pillars near the side aisles, to all corners of the church.

"Help us, help us, help us, Lord," she said.

"Help us," the children chanted.

They completed their prayer, eased along the row, and moved up the aisle. At the door, the woman stopped and stared back to the altar.

"We will get help," she said to her children. She grasped their hands and led them out of the church.

19

2

The next day was also hot, but Brian left the air-conditioned rectory to walk around the parish. It was too sweltering to lumber through all of it—the area stretched from 170th Street to 181st Street, from the Harlem River on the east to the Hudson River on the west—so he set out just to survey his more immediate turf.

He passed old tenements, once among the loveliest buildings in the area and now decayed. He paused to look at several brownstones, three-story houses maintained impeccably by proud owners; it pleased him to reflect that the decay had not become a terminal neighborhood disease. On the west side of the parish, stately apartment buildings still offered spacious, handsome apartments at reasonable rents. There were many stores, including several new ones. That encouraged him; where new stores opened, the neighborhood had to be alive and well. There was poverty in his parish, but there was pride as well.

Two blocks from the church he spotted Monique Brown, one of his favorites among the children of the parish. Monique was ten, black, small and thin, with glasses and a perpetually serious expression. She was a student at Incarnation's school; he saw all the children regularly when school was in session, but during the summer they were off on their own adventures. He was pleased to see Monique. He hugged her and she squealed.

"Are you glad it's summer?" he asked.

"I'm glad it's not winter," she said.

"Why?"

"Because in winter you pull off my hat and run off with it."

It was one of Brian's tricks. He would sneak up on her, pluck off her hat, and dash down the street with it. She would race after him and he would return it, amid laughter and mock anger.

"You're not wearing a hat now," he said.

"You bet. That's why I'm glad it's summer." She giggled. "You know what? On my report card last year, I got an M-1 in religion. M stands for good work, that I understand it good, and the one stands for ninety-five to one hundred."

"Terrific," Brian said. "You should be proud."

"I am. I am proud."

He patted her head and looked at her affectionately. She was immaculately dressed; her pale blue dress was freshly laundered and precisely ironed, her shoes were shiny, clean. He admired that.

"I read the Bible all the time," she told him.

"Good for you," he said. "That's what I like to hear."

"I like parts of it," she went on. "How God created man. And when God gave Moses, I think it was, the Ten Commandments. And when they showed how Adam and Eve disobeyed God. That the snake had told them to go and eat from the tree that God told you not to, and they did and they disobeyed God and God told them to leave the garden. I learned that you should behave good. And be kind," she said. "But it's hard sometimes."

"Sure, it is. It can't always be easy. Right?"

"Right," Monique said, looking up at him. Both were smiling.

"Do you pray?"

"Yes, I pray in the morning and in the night before I go to bed, then before I go to school. I have plenty of time to pray to God, and I believe that God listens," Monique said.

"He does," Brian affirmed.

"Good," Monique said. "I've got to go now." One of her girl friends was approaching. Brian gave Monique a final hug, leaned over, and kissed her on the cheek. As he moved on, Monique's friend caught up with her.

"Was that Father O'Connor?" the friend asked.

"Yes, he's my friend," Monique said proudly. "I think of him as my father, because he acts like a father to me and he plays with me and always talks to me. He plays with me more than my father does."

It was almost noon. His head throbbed under the warmth of the sun, unobstructed by clouds. A policeman on a motorcycle waved at him; Brian waved back. Although his clerical collar was tucked into his pocket, the rest of his outfit—black short-sleeved shirt, black pants, black socks and shoes—identified him. He often removed the collar because he disliked presenting a formal front.

He kept walking. When he got to the Fort Washington Senior Center, two blocks from the church, he went in. It was filled with old people, most of them women. Some, in wheelchairs, were bused to the building. Others, from apartments in the community, walked over. Inside the main room the men tended to sit in corners, alone or in pairs. The women sat around the long table in the center of the high room. The free lunch was the major event of their day. It brought them together, made them feel better than they would have felt alone at home. The center's primary mission was to combat loneliness.

Brian understood that. Whenever he visited, he came not

22

as the chairman of the center's board, the title he held, but to see his old friends—to talk, to console, to please. He listened.

Emily Flanagan, at eighty-eight, had barely slowed down. As soon as she spotted Brian, she rushed over to him.

"My sister is in a nursing home now," she announced to Brian.

"She'll get good care there," he said.

"Yes, it's good for her. She couldn't manage at home."

"And you, how are you doing?" Brian asked, gently gripping her shoulder.

"I keep going," she said. "I keep at it. I keep busy. It's very important. I don't want to give up, ever."

"If I know you, Emily, you won't give up," he said, smiling. "Your dancing days aren't over."

He walked around the center, shaking hands, greeting friends, touching people. He glanced at his watch and realized that it was time for lunch at the rectory. The hot weather had diminished his appetite; he hadn't realized it was time to eat. He left the senior center and headed back.

As he walked along 174th Street, past rows of old tenements, he saw a sign in the window of one apartment: *Donde esta Dios, No Falta Nada* (Where there is God, nothing is wrong). He heard Dinah Shore's voice from a blaring television set, explaining how to polish silver. *They can't pay their rent, but they're having Dinah Shore teach them to polish silver.*

Brian turned a corner onto Broadway. He passed store after store: fast food, jewelry, groceries, shoes, clothing, dry cleaning, flowers. They were all busy. There was life on the avenue, and that pleased him.

The weather remained unrelentingly hot the next day. Brian was grateful to be the priest on duty—the one who remained in the air-conditioned rectory on a given day to deal with the problems of parishioners. When the doorbell rang, he answered it. A bony, short, attractive young Hispanic woman looked up at him. She was, he concluded, approximately six months pregnant.

"Father, I want to arrange my wedding for next month," she said. She turned and introduced Brian to her future husband, a tall, skinny, reticent, boyish young man.

They went into one of the two private offices at the front of the rectory and Brian closed the door.

"Any problems?" Brian asked.

"Not really," the woman said. "Except my mother says I can't get married in white." Brian imagined the dialogue that must have ensued—the mother, a devout Catholic, proclaiming that her daughter had sacrificed her virtue; the daughter defending herself, more than willing to marry the father of the child.

"Relax," Brian said. "If we turned down every girl who wasn't a virgin, we'd be doing very few marriages here. Let's work out a nice, simple marriage ceremony and set the date."

The woman was pleased, and the young man nodded happily. Brian knew that she would come marching up the aisle with her baby along for the ride, and he wouldn't do anything to prevent that from happening. He helped them pick a date and suggested that they attend several premarriage conferences offered by the archdiocese.

After the couple left, the phone rang.

"Father, I'm depressed," a young woman's voice said. Brian had not recognized her name. "I want to talk to a priest," she continued. He made an appointment to see her.

He went into the kitchen and poured a glass of orange juice. He sat alone at the dining-room table and sipped the juice. He looked around the room at the sturdy old oak table and the paneled walls, at the fireplace and the mantle. Much of his adult life, he realized, had taken place in this room. And then he remembered Danny Kalb.

Danny Kalb was Jewish, a doctoral candidate in clinical psychology who had spent time in the rectory while researching the lives of senior citizens in the parish. Brian liked him. They became friends.

One afternoon the man who was pastor at that time took Brian aside and said, "I don't want that Jewish fellow eating at the same table with us."

"I don't believe you said what you just said," Brian exclaimed.

"I don't want to spend our money feeding that guy. That Jewish fellow," the pastor insisted.

They shouted at each other, and then the pastor said, "I am the pastor here and I don't have to listen to you."

Brian left the rectory, found Kalb, and told him the story.

"I don't want to be the cause of problems for you," Kalb insisted.

But Brian would not lunch with the pastor without Kalb being there. For days he ate at McDonald's, at other neighborhood restaurants. It lasted until the pastor was transferred—for other reasons. At that point, Brian arranged a banquet, with the rectory's rarely used gold-plated china and a tablecloth. The cook prepared a marvelous meal, and Brian and his friends tacked a sign across the dining room which read "Welcome Back, Jew."

Brian and Danny Kalb had remained friends ever since. Brian had gone to Danny's wedding, wearing his collar. *It was only fair that I be seen as a priest, after all that happened to Danny at Incarnation.*

The spirit of ecumenism prevailed, but there was more to it than that. No one could tell Brian how to choose his friends.

3

To the uninformed observer, Brian's life in the parish might have seemed to bear the characteristics of psychiatric social work. Day after day he helped troubled teen-agers, visited the elderly in their homes or in hospitals, counseled those who came to the rectory for help. Yet, in his own view, the core of his existence was spirituality. Among the sacraments, baptism and marriage, in particular, brought him joyously close to God. And the Mass was his own communion with Christ.

He celebrated mass almost every day. It was the sacrament that lent continuity to his love of God. At Incarnation there were four basic masses each weekday: 7 A.M., 8 A.M., and 9 A.M. in English, and 7:30 P.M. in Spanish. On Saturday and Sunday there were as many as thirteen (utilizing the main church and the smaller, lower church). Other masses throughout the week could encompass funerals and marriages.

For Brian, the Mass was a recollection of Christian tradition, a majestic mystery, a source of inspiration, an opportunity for prayer. In celebrating mass he reached back across the centuries to one of the pivotal moments in Catholicism.

The night before his death, Jesus celebrated the Last Supper with His disciples. He took the bread in His hands, broke it, and handed it to His followers, saying, "Take and eat. This is my body." After that supper, He passed a cup of wine: "Take and drink. This is the new covenant, shed in my blood. It will be poured out for you and for everyone so that sins may be forgiven. Do this in memory of me."

Eucharist is a Greek word for "thanksgiving." It is the term for the Mass, also for the bread and the wine (supplemented by the Word—by prayers, songs, and readings from the Scriptures) offered in Holy Communion. It is the Catholic ritual that depends upon a mystery that faith alone sustains: Jesus becomes the bread and the wine which nourish the believer. All sins except mortal sins are absolved through communion.

At Holy Communion Christ is present in the person of the priest, who assumes the role that Christ played at the Last Supper. Brian offered the bread and the wine—the body and the blood of Jesus—as an act of renewal that strengthens faith. It was vital to his life, a kind of spiritual heartbeat. At the same time, it was one of the most difficult sacraments to explain to non-Christians.

One evening, in his living room at the rectory, Brian entertained a visitor, a middle-aged rabbi who had lived in the community for years. Brian had met him six years ago at a senior center in an adjoining parish, and they had kept in touch. The rabbi, Max Isaacs, was involved in a variety of community activities and organizations, and from time to time he would drop by to chat with Brian, to compare views on the preservation of their neighborhood. He was a short, plump man and he always wore a suit and tie and hat, even on the hottest days of summer. Amazingly, from Brian's vantage point, Max never seemed to sweat.

On that July evening Brian had just returned from

celebrating the 7:30 P.M. mass. It had taken slightly less than an hour, and when Brian got back to his rooms, Max was resting in a large chair.

"Good to see you," Brian said. "Have a Coke."

"Better a Tab," Max said. "Thank you."

Brian went over to the bar in his living room, popped open a Tab, and poured it into a glass that he had filled with ice. He opened a beer for himself and sat down.

"Does the heat get you?" Max asked.

"Sometimes. But not in the church. It stays cool in there."

"You were saying mass?"

"Yes."

"Believe it or not, I've never been at a mass. I know it is important to your religion, though."

"Yes, it is. Central."

Max encouraged Brian to talk about it.

"It seems simple in structure," Brian began. "It's in two parts. The first is the liturgy of the Word, the reading of the Scriptures. On a Sunday, a reading from the Old Testament, one from the New Testament, and one from the Gospels. Then, there's the homily, the sermon. The second part is based upon the Last Supper, the consecration of the bread and wine, the reception of the body and blood by the disciples. After communion there's a closing prayer and the blessing to send people forth. There's more to it than that."

"What?" Max asked.

"Paul spoke about the fact that when we eat the body of Christ and when we drink His life, we proclaim His death until He comes in glory. The Mass is the sign or the mark of the people on their pilgrimage to God's kingdom. It is the food that sustains us on our journey through life. From the Scriptures, the follower of Christ is someone who gathers around the table and who shares in the bread of Christ. He . . ."

"When you say a mass," Max interrupted, "what do you stress?"

"When I celebrate mass, my preoccupation is with the sermon, because the rest of the mass is a performance, in the good sense of the word. It could become just repetition, doing the same thing day after day."

"I believe that. I have my own problems with doing services again and again," Max noted.

"What is important is to connect it to your own prayer life, so that privately you see the mass as a high point, as a source of the things that happen, spiritually, that day.

"Sometimes you may forget that the Mass is your own personal communication and the highlight of your own personal prayer life, the source of your own strength. It may become just communication on the human level—the gestures, the words, doing the right things. Instead of seeing that there's something beneath all that, beyond that. The other extreme is to treat the Mass as just a private communication with God and ignore the congregation. For me, the Mass is crucial. It brings me to God, even while it is bringing me closer to the congregation."

"When that happens, you must be moved. Profoundly moved," Max suggested. He sipped his Tab and leaned back.

"At its best, it is incomparable. Easter is the most important mass; the celebration of the Easter vigil is the most important celebration of the Church. We encourage people to come to it. In it, the basic mass is expanded. It can take two and a half, three hours. It takes place on the night before Easter, after darkness on Saturday, and most places have it at ten at night. There are many readings from the Scriptures. And there should be baptisms within the liturgy, especially adult baptisms. Some also receive confirmation, then First Communion—as part of the Easter liturgy. We bless the paschal candle, which is used for baptisms and funerals throughout the year, and we bless the water that will be used for baptisms. But at Easter, as during the rest of the year, the Mass is that central celebration, only more so."

"As I understand it, the wafer, the communion wafer, takes on a special meaning," Max said. "More than just bread."

"Yes. If the mass is a central sacrament, then communion is central to the mass. Gandhi once said that if he were God and he wanted to come to man, he couldn't think of a better way to come than in the form of bread. I know that I feel at unity with God during mass. It gives me strength. I can almost feel my spirituality deepening. It's true that I can remember going through masses where I felt it was almost like cranking up to feel emotionally what I knew intellectually. But most of the time I am moved at mass, about the kind of values we have and the way we can build our lives on those values. The liturgy of the Word, the readings, have a striking impact on me.

"The danger, as you say, is that celebrating mass can appear to be by the numbers. You forget that God wanted to reach us through the things of this world. In order to have the grace of God and in order to arrive at God, one has to use the senses. He chose simple elements of this world in order for us to communicate with Him: bread and wine.

"And the priest isn't someone who is different from us. He's an element of this world, too, an element God is using to give us a blessing."

"I have heard that the bread is a symbol of Jesus," Max said.

"That's a common way for non-Christians to look at it. But that's not the way it is. When one is receiving the Host and one is taking the Chalice, one is literally receiving the body and presence of Jesus. It is not just a symbol. One of the things that Catholics have tended to stress is the real presence of Jesus in the Eucharist to the detriment of the real presence of Jesus in their own lives—through the Bible or through prayer. Jesus is present to us in a very important way when we read the Bible, when we pray. It's true that a number of non-Catholics find it very difficult to understand the mystery, the real presence in the bread and wine."

Max nodded. He was one of those non-Catholics.

"Remember," Brian continued, "the core essence of being a Christian, in one sentence, is a belief that Jesus died and has risen from the dead, and that He came to save our sins and that one day we will share His life. You have the sacramental life in the Catholic Church and the presence of Jesus in the Eucharist. That's vital to the mass."

"Fascinating," Max said softly. "You know, I've never talked about all this with a priest."

"Am I preaching?" Brian laughed.

"No, no. Go on," Max urged.

"Well, the truth is that preaching is vital to the mass, too. In a parish you may not be the best preacher in the world, and yet you could be a very good priest if the things you say in the pulpit have content, if there is something there that people can grasp. And they can also see that the preacher lives it.

"There was a priest here a couple of years ago, a very good priest, who insisted on telling two jokes per sermon in order to keep people's interest. After a while you wondered if he was appreciated because of the jokes.

"Years ago most preaching was what we called 'thematic,' meaning the priest would decide on a theme that he would preach on a given Sunday. The problem with that was that the Vatican Council had said that it wasn't good because it did not often base the priest in Scripture. It did not lend itself to a consistent preaching on all the truths of the faith. The Vatican Council said that preaching should be based on the readings of the mass, on a three-year cycle. They contain most of the very important Scripture readings. But what's vital is the application of the idea. How do you take the transfiguration of Christ on the mountainside and apply it to modern times?"

"How?" Max asked.

"It was Christ revealing to His disciples in the midst of His suffering that He was the son of God. So that in the midst of our suffering we should not lose hope that actually this is the kingdom of God on earth, and that God is good. When we're sick or someone has died, or someone is being punished, we begin to say, how is it possible that God is good? We must believe that ultimately all the evil that exists will one day be conquered. In the midst of suffering, there must be the revelation that God is going to be victorious. One day we will see the complete victory. That, too, is at the heart of the mass."

"I understand," Max said. "Now, I understand."

"Good," Brian said. "You want to join our club?"

Max laughed. "No," he said. "I think I'll stay with mine." He finished sipping his Tab and got up.

"See you again one of these days, I hope," Brian said. Their paths did not cross frequently, but when they did they enjoyed themselves.

"Yes. One evening I'll tell you about Yom Kippur. The equal-time doctrine." He smiled.

"I've read a lot about other religions, including Judaism," Brian said. "They interest me. And we're not in competition. We're all in this together. I think it's a good cause."

"So do I," Max said. "And I'm still going to tell you about Yom Kippur."

"Good. And I'll listen."

"That's what I like about you," Max said. "You don't know it all."

"I never will," Brian said.

They shook hands, and Max went on his way.

4

Brian had to get out of the steaming city. He needed a respite.

For such moments he depended upon his family and his best friend. His brother John and his sisters, Maureen and Kathy, lived with their families in the suburbs (another sister and brother lived in California). His good friend Dan Cherico lived closer to Brian, in New Rochelle, with his parents.

John had invited Brian to his house; Maureen and Kathy and their children would be there, and Dan Cherico had promised to join them. It would be an afternoon of good fun with the children, good food, a splash in John's backyard pool. Brian could relax with them; the conversation would be lively and comforting, and he would not be summoned to a phone or hear the jangle of a doorbell.

He got into his car—a four-door Chevy Malibu sedan, which he prized for the mobility it gave him, even when he had to make the monthly payments—snapped on the air conditioning, and headed across the George Washington Bridge.

THE PRIEST

The facts of Brian's family life were not drastically different from those of many of his Irish contemporaries in the priesthood in New York—working-class families, many children, Catholic education from grade school to seminary.

He had grown up in Manhattan in an apartment at Ninety-seventh Street and Park Avenue. His mother was born in Scotland and came to America when her father, a miner, chose to search for good luck in the coal fields of Pennsylvania. At the age of seventeen she came to New York to work as a domestic. Brian's father was Irish, from a farming family in County Kerry. He came over when he was sixteen. Brian's parents were married in 1938 and his father spent most of his life as a bartender in a tavern a few blocks from home.

Brian was one of the six children the marriage produced, three sons and three daughters. Only Brian entered the priesthood; all the others married. His father died suddenly of heart failure in 1957. His mother died of cancer in 1975.

His father worked hard and his mother raised the children. His father was a quiet, gentle man who liked books and wrote poetry. His mother was a spirited and dedicated woman who worked diligently after his father died. She held the family together.

Both parents believed in prayer, but they were not conspicuously pious. Yet sensing a spiritual interest in Brian, they encouraged him. Brian remembered his father telling him "Priests are learned men." When Brian decided to become an altar boy, his parents were proud of him and expressed that pride to him. When he was in the sixth grade, he decided that his interest in religion demanded that he go to mass every day; no one else in the family did so. He went day after day, in all seasons, absorbing the message of the mass, coming closer to his ultimate realization. By the time he was in the eighth grade at the local Catholic school—Our

Lady of Good Counsel—he had moved toward the decision he was to make years later.

Fifty minutes after leaving Incarnation, Brian pulled into John's driveway, walked alongside the modest ranch house, and found a crowd in John's backyard, including a group of children bobbing up and down in John's circular above-ground pool.

His sister Maureen, trim and attractive at thirty-seven, was hugging her infant son. In jeans and T-shirt, with reddish brown hair free of gray, she looked younger than her years, not old enough to be the mother of six children.

"The other kids are over there," she yelled to Brian. She pointed to the pool and the backyard. Her older boys were busy playing baseball; the girls were in the pool, splashing and giggling.

"Ah, my brother the priest," his sister Kathy said. "Welcome." She was slim, tall, and stately, with blue eyes and graying short hair. At thirty-two, she could have passed for a fashion model. Her two children, a boy and a girl, did what she told them to do; Brian admired her sense of order ("She alphabetizes her cookies," he once told a friend). In her pale blue summer dress, she seemed totally at ease.

John was basking in the sun, reclining in a lounge chair, and he jumped up when Brian called his name. It was John's day off; five days a week he got into his vintage BMW and drove to the South Bronx, where he was a sergeant at the 42nd police precinct, a chaotic area largely evacuated by its weary residents. Five years older than Brian, he had joined the force when he was twenty-one; he could retire after twenty years in 1982. He hoped to take his Irish wife, Anne, and their preschool son, Brian, back to Ireland to live. Until then, he would do his job, count the weeks, and make plans.

"Get into your trunks," he urged Brian, "and get wet."

"Good idea," Brian said. He could feel his body relaxing in this setting.

John was wearing shorts, no shirt or shoes. He was solidly built, but despite that—and his occupation—he was a gentle man, soft-spoken and consistently helpful.

"Welcome to the O'Connor spa and health center," Dan Cherico called. "I may never return to civilization."

Dan wore brightly colored sneakers, baggy jeans, and a brilliantly striped shirt. Short, bearded, intense—with gleaming brown eyes and balding head—he was, in some ways, Brian's alter ego: an outspoken man, intellectual, informed, and occasionally belligerent. They had been friends since their seminary days; Dan had been tossed out of St. Joseph's. His belief in God had proved greater than his willingness to obey the seminary rules. He had been in open conflict with a number of influential teachers and had lost. After trying several other seminaries, he then decided to abandon the priesthood for a doctorate in human relations and behavioral sciences.

Despite the difference in vocation, they remained close friends. When Brian wanted to study thanatology, Dan joined him at Columbia. With money he had earned teaching and lecturing, Dan paid for Brian's tuition. The Chericos were a warm, generous family, and Brian often spent free time relaxing at their home. Likewise, Dan spent a great deal of time at the rectory. The other priests were entertained by him and were grateful for the way he volunteered his services. He bought new pots and pans for the kitchen, arranged for repairs around the rectory, and even provided counseling for parishioners in trouble.

For Brian, Dan supplied shampoo, cold remedies, clothing (Brian would never say he needed them, but Dan would check). He redecorated Brian's rooms. Brian depended upon Dan for such assistance and Dan was pleased to provide it. But neither Dan nor Brian was the subservient friend; they shared their problems and their triumphs, debated ideas intensely, accepted their differences.

Brian saw Dan more frequently than he saw John, Maureen, or Kathy, but he was pleased to see Dan in John's backyard, completing the roll call of people who were vital to Brian's well-being.

"Hello, hello, hello," Brian shouted to the children.

"Uncle Brian!" they shouted back, almost in unison. "Come into the pool," one group urged. "Play ball," another bellowed.

"I think I'll cool off first," he said. He went into John's house and put on the navy blue boxer swim trunks he had brought. When he returned to the backyard, Kathy stared at his girth; his belly was veering over the top of his trunks. Brian suspected that the clothes Kathy gave him at Christmas were deliberately too small, as a hint. But he was not intimidated. He returned her stare with a smile and dashed over to the pool, scrambled up the ladder, and plunged into the water. His descent created a wave that lapped over the edge. The children bobbing inside the pool giggled.

They dove and swam and Brian joked with them, tickled them, imitated a whale in the pool. Then he grabbed a towel, dried himself, and slipped into a chair. There was a comforting silence as Brian, Dan, John, Maureen, and Kathy all sat in peace, appreciating the sun.

"I bet you were always a good kid," Dan said. "Doing the right thing all the time."

Brian laughed.

"He wasn't an angel," Maureen said. "But he wasn't a bad kid. I wasn't surprised that he went on to be a priest."

"Why?" Dan asked.

Maureen cradled her infant son in her arms and stroked the boy's head as she resumed talking.

"I think it may have been an act of God. Let me explain. When he was little, say two and a half or three, it was in the winter and we were going across the street near our house. My mother was behind us, talking to some neighbors, and she said to me, 'Hold Brian's hand.' We were crossing and we had the green light and we got into the middle of the street and this cab driver started up before the light had changed. I left Brian in the middle of the street and I ran. I tell you, that cab bounced him halfway up the block in the air. Thank God in winter my mother bundled us all up. I thought he was dead. The driver stopped and took Brian to the hospital. You know what? He had only a slight shoulder separation. I think it was a statement from God."

She put her son on the ground and he began to walk stiffly away from her. She called to one of her older children to watch him.

"Actually, I thought from the time he was little that he'd be a priest," Maureen continued. "Didn't you, Brian?"

"I think so. It's hard to remember the entire sequence of events and influences right now, but I think so."

"You went to mass all the time. The rest of us just went once in a while," Maureen said.

"That's true. When I was a kid, I was moved by it. I don't know if I could have defined it then, that it was a serious spiritual experience, but I did know it was important to me."

"I remember when you were in the sixth or seventh grade, you talked about becoming a Christian Brother," Kathy said. "I remember one of your teachers saying to you, after Father died, why just be a brother? Why not think about the priesthood? You never said much about it, though."

"But I was thinking about it, obviously," Brian said.

"Yes, I remember that you were interested in it," John said. "You were the most passionate about religion in our family. You always were. I don't know if you could say it was a 'calling' back then, but you had it. You were an altar boy. You followed through. I started out to be one, but I didn't go through with it."

"Is this a serious conversation?" John's wife, Anne,

asked from the back door of the house. "I'm getting things ready for dinner."

"It's okay. Just heavy theological stuff," Dan said. "We need food, too."

"Okay," she said. "Go on with it." Her smiling face and blonde hair disappeared into the house.

"You used to get up and go to mass all the time, and the only way to get there was to walk," John said. "It must have been a twelve-block walk, in all kinds of weather, and at six or seven in the morning when the streets were deserted. You never refused to go. You wanted to go."

"Yes, I did," Brian said. "It may sound simple, but I felt good when I was at mass. Not that I felt bad with my family or with my friends. I didn't. I just felt especially good —spiritual is the word, I guess—when I went to mass."

"And there was Walter Birkle, too," Dan suggested.

One of the priests at Good Counsel, Father Walter Birkle, had been important to Brian. He had encouraged him to help in the church, and Brian had been both flattered and eager to do so. Father Birkle had taken Brian and other parish children on outings, trips, to baseball games, and, most important, on visits to Cathedral High School—a school that had produced many seminarians (including Birkle). When Brian was ready to go to high school, it was logical for him to attend Cathedral.

"He's still around," Brian said, "still someone I see. A good, gentle guy. He would talk to the boys when we were on a trip with him, or at a ball game. He would talk about the priesthood. He gave it dignity, purpose. That sounds lofty maybe, but to me, then, it was impressive. And genuine. He wasn't selling anything. He was suggesting that a life with God could be a worthy life. I listened."

Brian paused and seized a handful of potato chips. "But my experience wasn't like that of a lot of other priests. You know, a kid wakes up one morning, struck by religious lightning, and declares his intention to be a priest. It wasn't like that for me. I went to mass. I was an altar boy, working with the priests. Walter Birkle was there. I got a good Catholic education. All of that, I think, helped me make the choice."

"Mother must have been an influence," Kathy said. "In her everyday roaming, she always stopped into the church to say a prayer. You must have noticed that."

"Yes, I did," Brian said.

"You know, it's funny when I think about it now, but Mother used to tell me all the time about the night you were born," Kathy said. "Maybe it explains to a degree why she was so happy you became a priest. That night, she told me, Father wasn't home. It was snowing heavily. She had to go out into the snow in the middle of the night, and none of the cab drivers would stop for her. She finally got one to stop and he took her to the hospital. She had just got into the elevator when she had you. Maybe you wouldn't exactly call that a miracle, but I think she saw the hand of God in it. Something significant."

"There was more to her than the story indicates," Brian said. "Mother was a very good woman who worked hard, who knew how to laugh, who took care of us very well under difficult circumstances. We all learned something from her."

"She was a good mother," Maureen said. "She cared for all her kids. She expected a lot from us. I know what you mean, Brian. But she didn't really praise us much, now that I think about it. That's an old Irish trait: never saying you look nice or this or that. I even catch myself doing it. I find that the Irish, they're not warm. They don't express warmth. I have a lot of Italian friends, and they're so different."

Dan, from an Italian family, applauded.

"There's some truth to that," Brian said. "I have to work against that grain, too. Over the years I've tried to break free of all that . . . that reticence. It's not easy, but it's worth the effort. You get through to people. They can tell what you're feeling."

"I just thought of something," Maureen said. "Mother was honest, always. You got straight answers from her. That's the way you are, too."

Kathy looked a bit skeptical. "I can remember saying to Mother, 'Ma, please have some tact,'" she said. "You're not like that, Brian, but you did pick up that honesty Maureen was talking about."

John had been staring into space, enveloped in his own reminiscence. He broke out of it to join the conversation.

"When Mother died, we were all sad, but it didn't have as much of an effect on us as Father's death did," he said. "That was traumatic. Mother's death was unfortunate, but we were all living our own lives at that time. It affected you, Brian—more than anybody. You lived in the city then. We didn't. You took care of her. You called her every day. She was your tie to the old neighborhood. Your roots were there. You knew all the old Irish. When Mother died, it broke our ties with the neighborhood.

"But when Father died, we were all home. The whole family was thrown into an upheaval. We were all young. Why did it happen and how did it happen? Why did it happen to me? I remember asking those questions. You were small, Brian, maybe eleven when it happened. I often wonder how different things would have been for us if it hadn't happened. I don't know."

"I don't, either," Brian said. "You can't tell."

"I'm sure it changed everybody," John went on. "It changed Mother, because she had to go out and work. As for us kids, we didn't have our father's influence any longer, and you don't know how he would have influenced you. Would he have influenced me to go to college? I don't know. I was only in the second year of high school. Would he have influenced me to go into the police department? What would he have advised you to do, Brian, when you were eleven? To be a priest? I think he would have."

"So do I," Brian said. "We had talked about priests and he always said how smart they were and how good it was to be smart in this world."

"Well, you did it, you became a priest," John said. "I'm not sure I could have done it that way. As a priest you're putting up with somebody's problems constantly. So am I, as a cop. That's why cops become very thick-skinned. But I'm only a cop eight hours a day. I can walk away from it. But a priest can't. You have to do something about that individual in trouble. You get it all the time."

"Mom, we can't play ball when *he* gets in the way," one of Maureen's older boys shouted, clutching her toddler by the arm. "Please, Mom." Maureen got up, took the little one's hand, and brought him back to her chair. She lifted him to her lap, kissed his cheek, and resumed the conversation.

"You're just the way you were when you were a kid," she said. "I mean, when Mother needed you, you'd be there, the one to do anything or go anywhere. But I've seen you get mad, right?"

"Right," Brian laughed. "But not that often."

"You used to get mad during the civil rights time, when you first got out of the seminary," John said.

"We were all mad in those days," Dan commented.

"We'd go at it hot and heavy, as I recall," John continued. "We'd argue about civil rights and police brutality and things like that. You were extremely liberal in those days, very idealistic. I was on the conservative side, mostly because I was a policeman. And my wife, Anne, couldn't understand that. She has a very close family and they don't fight. But you and I both liked a good argument. You used to think everybody was decent. And you were a little bit against the cops. You thought we were extra tough on people."

"I did. And sometimes, even now, I still do," Brian said. "And you know what? The cops who are toughest on Catholics, in my experience, are the Irish Catholic cops. I don't know why."

"Never mind that," John said. "All I know is that you got to the point where you realized that not all those people were poor, downtrodden, and hopeless. That a lot of them got into trouble by their own actions or choices, and that a lot of them were crooks and thieves and liars, just preying on their own people. I think you can appreciate that now. But, you know, I don't think we've had one good argument in seven or eight years. I miss them, once in a while. But maybe I've changed in my thinking, too. Maybe there's common ground now for both of us."

"No doubt. I was an idealist once, and in lots of ways I'm still an idealist. I don't like cruelty. And, remember, I live with the poor. I know their problems."

"Okay, okay," John said, smiling. "A truce is declared, probably forever."

When Anne stuck her head out the back door, Maureen asked, "Need help in the kitchen?" Anne nodded. Maureen and Kathy got up and joined her. John, Brian, and Dan stayed by the pool. The conversation turned to the friendship between Dan and Brian, now thirteen years strong.

"A mutual friend introduced us," Dan said. "I was in between. I had done three years of college seminary and was thinking about going back. A year later, I entered St. Joseph's."

"I had just started there after my two-year seminary prep program at Cathedral," Brian said.

"Almost from that first time we met, we had a close relationship," Dan continued. "And you got involved with my family, too. You know, John, that he's free to come to our house—whenever, whether I'm there or not?"

"Yes," John said. "It's good for him."

"I remember that in those days in the seminary we had an awful lot of time to talk," Brian said. "You could sit down with people and really get to know them. I knew instantly that Dan was honest and forthright, very clear about his motives. After ordination was a difficult time for me because it was a logical time—like after any college graduation—for your friendships to slip away. It took an extra effort on both our parts to hang on to it. During the first two years after ordination, a priest tends to get swamped by his work, and then to rationalize that there is salvation through work. That's not so. And it was during that period when I really recognized the importance of our friendship."

"You made great sacrifices because of our friendship," Dan said. "The people you were close to in the seminary were people I despised. Yet they were the ones you could expect to work with for the rest of your life. Your colleagues, not mine."

"I realized that, then and now," Brian said. "Some of them are still my friends. You were as much opposed to that seminary system as you were to those individuals who offended you. I was able to share some of that with you."

"You still know the ones who got through it, but what about those who didn't?" Dan asked. "A goodly number of students were thrown out and never got any career guidance. For most of them, the priesthood was the only possibility of making it. And even worse, we never knew that we could have the same feelings as those outside had. We were told that the seminary was the voice of God. That's ludicrous."

"Sure it is," Brian agreed.

"I never felt that the seminary was speaking for God. They seemed to feel that you could be outstanding if you were just polished a bit. You know, lose a little weight and shine your shoes more often and speak less and listen more and nod your head. Be noncommittal. But that's not your style."

"Right," Brian said, smiling. He got up, stretched, and went into the house to get out of his bathing suit and into his clothes.

John and Dan went on discussing Brian as a priest.

"He has good Scripture background," Dan said. "And he has what the theologians call 'the consensus of the people of God.' The people in the parish respond to him. That's what Catholicism is all about. Not the consensus of the Roman curia, or the consensus of the higher view of the clergy, or poor exegesis, or poor Scripture study. He gives faith dimension. It makes him real. People don't see him as a goody-goody. Catholics expect priests to be men of faith. They see that in Brian, a healthy kind of piety, not the drippy kind."

"Where do you think he will go in the Church?" John asked.

"He is happy being a parish priest," Dan said. "Of course, eventually he'll likely have his own parish, as a pastor, running things. In the old days, when a priest got a parish—depending upon how good he looked, how friendly he was with the chancery office—he would get a parish that was not in debt, that had good income. They were called 'plums.' Unfortunately, there aren't any now. Every place in Manhattan, in the Bronx, is in great financial trouble. Yet that probably wouldn't matter to Brian. He wants to be a pastor someday—not to have the checkbook or run the administration, but to make decisions for the people. I know a lot of priests, and he is one who takes the priesthood as a way of life, not something you put on and take off."

Dan got up, tapped John on the shoulder affectionately, and headed into the house. As he entered, Brian emerged, dressed in his blue-and-green-striped Rugby shirt and dark brown pants, looking freshly washed and energetic.

"Time for dinner yet?" John yelled into the house. He was cleaning off two backyard tables.

"In a few minutes," Anne called from the kitchen window.

John set the table for the adults and a second one for the children, who were still occupied with the pool and the ball game.

Brian took a seat and was soon joined by his brother. Then he returned to his friendship with Dan.

"You know when Mother died, Dan's family was very supportive," Brian said. "His father told me to regard their home as my home. His father once said to me, 'If you want to stay here anytime, if you have some difficulty you want to think about, come to our place.' Dan didn't tell his father to say that. It was his father's natural reaction. That's the way it's been over the years. Sure, Dan and I don't always agree, and sometimes his style is a little too flamboyant and outrageous for me. But we're friends. We know what we disagree about—and we separate those issues from our friendship."

Anne announced that dinner was about to be served. With the help of Maureen and Kathy, she placed the dishes on the table. It was a feast, and everyone gathered around in anticipation and appreciation: a huge bowl of salad; a large roast beef; a sizable mound of mashed potatoes; several vegetables; an apple pie and a chocolate cake, with or without ice cream; tea or coffee.

The lively conversation continued throughout dinner, until Brian bounded up from the table to go play catch with several of Maureen's sons. The sun had begun to set and both Maureen and Kathy had to get home to await their husbands who were both working late that evening. The children loudly and playfully filed into the cars. After the final affectionate farewells had been said, Dan got into his and drove off, followed by Kathy and Maureen. Brian stood in the backyard with John and Anne and young Brian. He reached down, picked up his nephew, and planted a kiss on his cheek. His namesake smiled.

"Time to go," Brian said, and he put the boy down.

"Good to see you," John said.

"Yes," Anne agreed. Little Brian hugged big Brian around the thighs.

Brian extricated himself gently from the boy's grip and strode toward his car in the driveway. He turned back to wave to them, got into the car, and drove off.

It had been a rejuvenating day. Feeling good, he drove back to the eternally busy city and his work at Incarnation.

5

Brian's life, like that of most priests, was not dictated by a clock. He got up before 7 A.M. and often worked until late at night; circumstances, not a schedule, dictated his life. He was not allotted a day off; if he wanted a respite, he would have to arrange it.

For all that he did, he earned a salary of $250 a month, along with his share of the stipends the Church collected (at baptisms, weddings, funerals, etc.), which amounted to another $150 a month. He lived in the rectory and ate most of his meals there.

The rectory was more than a residence. Brian shared it with four other priests—and countless parishioners, visitors, and honored prelates from other countries spending a day or two in New York. For some it was a hotel and a restaurant. For those who found it at the core of their existence, it was a mental health clinic, a social agency, a center for theological discussion, an outpost of Catholicism in a New York neighborhood, and the headquarters of a small corporation.

In the two small private offices at the front of the main

floor, priests counseled parishioners with problems, planned baptisms and weddings and funerals, collected clothes for the needy. Beyond those offices, in a small foyer and adjoining office, a secretary handled the mail, answered the phone, kept records. In the foyer itself, at a small desk, various parish teen-aged girls worked in shifts, helping the secretary answer phone calls and greeting visitors at the front door. Beyond the foyer, down a dark hall, was the dining room, with its wood paneling and fireplace—giving it the air of a men's club—and its heavy, solid, well-preserved oak dining table and two matching chests for dishes and tableware. Beyond the dining room was a door to the church.

Upstairs, which could be reached by a narrow stairway or a small elevator, were the priests' rooms, including several single rooms for visiting dignitaries. One hardworking maid cleaned it all daily.

Brian lived in a suite at the front of the rectory on the second floor: a living room, with an orange-plaid sofa and matching comfortable chairs, a cocktail table, and bookcases filled with the books he had collected over the years—from John Updike to Hans Küng. It had a small bar, which was stocked with bottles of liquor, soft drinks, glasses and snacks to munch, and a television set. This room was the locale for the daily predinner social hour, attended by the priests and any guests they had invited. Here they would sip a drink and watch the early-evening news before the dinner buzzer sounded at 6 P.M.

Brian had the luxury of his own office adjoining the living room. It was sparsely furnished with a desk, chair, file cabinet, typewriter, and bookcases; however, he still did much of his work in the living room. His bedroom, off the living room as well, was comparably utilitarian, with a single bed, table, dresser, and large closet. His bath had the original tile floor and shower stall, and was but a few steps away.

When he was not out in the parish, Brian was usually to

be found in his living room, working: preparing the mass schedule for the priests (after conferring with them), helping to count collection money for deposit in the local bank, reading his mail, chatting with friends and fellow priests, or with representatives of the various community Catholic groups that met in the church, rectory, or school.

Incarnation was open to all religious and cultural groups that needed its space for meetings. Many Spanish-speaking groups met regularly. Some groups brought religion into homes; others, like those from the Dominican Republic, were intent on preserving their native culture. There were youth groups and charismatics, a demonstrative prayer group, as well.

Various English-speaking groups also met at the church to help immigrants adjust to the new life, to help the poor, to pray, or to disseminate the Word of God. The names were Irish and Italian—middle-class parishioners for whom the Church was as vital as it was for the Hispanics.

It was this mixture that encouraged Brian. The parish had them all: blacks and whites, poor and middle class, Hispanic and Irish, immigrants and established professionals.

To deal with them, the parish needed a structure; it had one which was clearly defined for staff and parishioners alike. Monsignor Tom Leonard, the pastor, was in charge. Monsignor Jack Barry (the title is an honorary one, granted by the Cardinal, not indicative of rank or power), like Tom Leonard and Brian, was permanently stationed at Incarnation; he served in the church at masses, weddings, penance, and baptisms, but spent much of his time with various Irish organizations throughout the city. Two other priests lived at the rectory, but they were classified as being "in residence" —they went to full-time Church jobs elsewhere in the city every day, although they helped at Incarnation when time permitted. Ken Smith, from Worcester, Massachusetts, and Sergio Torres, a "liberation theologian" from Chile who had fled that country when Allende's regime fell, were conscientious about their duty at Incarnation at nights and on weekends.

There were also three Hispanic deacons—laymen authorized to perform certain sacraments and a number of Church functions. All three were married. (Single men becoming deacons—a kind of subpriest—have to take the vow of celibacy, and married deacons whose wives die cannot remarry, according to Church rule.) They were permitted to dress as priests, in black with the traditional collar, but they remained laymen, not working full-time at Incarnation as Brian did, and held other secular jobs.

Everyone reported to Tom Leonard. At age fifty-two, he was ready for the responsibility of running a parish. A priest for twenty-three years, he had served in several parishes, been director of field education at the seminary, and for four years was director of priest personnel for the archdiocese, before becoming pastor of Incarnation in 1977.

A civilized, urbane man who spoke fluent Spanish, his interests were wide ranging; his library, which filled one entire wide wall in his living room, spilled beyond the shelves to the floor. A soft-spoken, pale man, he worked quietly, often privately; yet he knew he had to be a manager as well as a priest. He ran Incarnation as a small company. He worried about inspiring sufficient income to pay the parish bills—in 1979 that income came to $251,003, just $4,000 less than expenses—and he worried about the cost of the school, about the rectory expenses, about keeping the staff and the priests working happily.

He depended upon Brian's help in countless ways. Brian, for example, kept track of all the stipends the priests received; he divided the amount equally at the end of each month and distributed the money. He also helped to arrange for repairs around the rectory; a maintenance man was on the staff, but helpful parishioners donated their time as well at Brian's invitation.

Nevertheless, the parish was Tom's domain. He was

responsible to the hierarchy of the archdiocese for the efficient running of Incarnation. In reality, he heard little from the "executives" in the archdiocese tower in mid-Manhattan; they were concerned with the problems of the entire archdiocese and rarely intruded into Tom's realm. If the parish began to run a serious deficit, he would hear from them, but his intention was to avoid that, to run his own parish and forestall unnecessary attention from above. He had four priests to help him accomplish that.

Jack Barry was, at age fifty-one, like Tom, a native New Yorker. He had worked as a parish priest in Harlem, as a priest at St. Patrick's Cathedral, and as a fund-raiser for Catholic Charities before coming to Incarnation in 1978. Short, stocky, gray-haired, tough in manner, indisputably Irish, he entertained with jokes and terse indictments of vulnerable fellow priests. His was a misanthropic humor. According to rumor, something had gone wrong with his career.

Settling at Incarnation had not been in Jack Barry's plans. He did not delight in preaching. He did not speak Spanish. He was not fond of dealing with the problems of parishioners. When a stranger rang the rectory bell and asked for a drink or a meal, Jack would escort the person to the street, point to the door, and ask, "Does it say hotel? Bar? Restaurant?" Preferable to life in the parish was the company of friends outside, warm afternoons on the golf course, the solitude of his weekend house on Long Island, and trips to Ireland. But Jack was Tom's old friend, and Tom had agreed to have him stationed at Incarnation when a bishop at the chancery office had made the request to Tom. Tom was not blind to Jack's eccentricities, but he could not erase a friendship of more than twenty years.

Sergio Torres was fifty years old, the son of a shipbuilder in a small town in Chile, and a priest for almost half those years. He had come to New York to speak out for the radical view of Church-and-politics, to lecture at conferences, to write, to work for several worldwide Church organizations.

A short, dark, gentle man with a ready smile, his manner belied his politics, which were part Marxism, part Scripture. He had come to Incarnation in 1978. It was a natural step: he spoke Spanish and was willing to devote what time he could to parish work. When the director of priest personnel —Tom's successor—suggested that Sergio move to Incarnation, Tom readily agreed.

Ken Smith was pastoral coordinator for the Northeast Pastoral Center for Hispanics, with an office in the archdiocese tower. That job, coupled with his residency at Incarnation, enabled him to do what he most wanted to do—work with Hispanics. A priest for fifteen of his forty-two years, he had worked, at first, in a parish in Worcester, then came to New York.

He had survived a drastic operation for stomach cancer before moving to Incarnation, and the disease had been held at bay since then. The other priests knew about it, but they did not discuss it with him. A dark, thoughtful, moody man, Smith was not gifted at small talk, jokes, or kidding. He dealt with the facetiousness of others—comments about his hair, some of which was not his own—with stoical patience. He took himself, and his work, seriously.

Although these priests lived at Incarnation, their paths rarely crossed, except for meals and the late TV news. Tom had to manage the parish and know the people in it. Brian spent his time with the people of the parish. Jack was often away, leaving Brian with an added burden. Sergio and Ken went to their jobs every day.

They would all meet at meals. Breakfast was an expedient: juice, tea, toast prepared by each priest for himself. At lunchtime the robust Dominican cook arrived and sent up food in a dumbwaiter from her basement kitchen for those priests and visitors who were on hand. The true meeting of the priests' minds and wits took place at dinner, when all were home.

6

The dinners at the rectory were not elegant fare for gourmets to relish, but they were hearty enough for hard-working men to appreciate. A Weight Watcher would have blanched. Entrées included *arroz con pollo*, roast beef, fish patties, or roast pork. There were always potatoes, vegetables, salad, bread and butter, and dessert—always an assortment of cookies, in addition to Jell-O or cake or pie or ice cream —followed by tea or coffee. Wine rarely accompanied a meal; it was brought out only when a special guest, like a bishop from a Latin American country, was present.

The meal was served by several paid teen-aged girls, who set the table and cleared the dishes after dinner. With grace and skill they moved in and out from the pantry adjoining the dining room, seeming not to listen to the priests' conversation. However, the priests knew they did listen; when the girls were in the room, the conversation became noncommittal.

On a cool evening in late July—a break in the heat wave—the priests filed into the dining room for one such meal.

Brian had spent the day in the parish, on the streets, in apartments, at a hospital visiting a sick parishioner Tom had been busy at his desk, assessing the pain of various bills the Church had received that week. Jack had been out most of the day, on a mission he had not revealed to the others. Sergio and Ken had been at their offices. Now, they were reunited.

Brian and Jack sat at the heads of the long table. Tom was in the middle on one side; Sergio and Ken sat side by side on the other.

There was a unity about their attitudes at these dinners, a respect for the serenity of the meal and the setting. But that unity could be tenuous. The conversation might be profound —about theology or the state of the world or the serious problems of a parishioner—or it simply flowed according to the whims, the moods, and the relative happiness or unhappiness of those present.

The girls brought in the food: *arroz con pollo* and more. They put the platters on the table, and the priests immediately began serving themselves, passing the platters along.

"Oh, no, not again," Jack said. "Not that chicken again."

Brian laughed. "It's delicious, a good native dish." He helped himself to a large scoop of rice and a large chicken breast decorated with pimentos.

"I talked to one of the Dominican teen-aged boys last weekend," Ken said. "He is thinking about being a priest. I was encouraged by the way he talked about it."

"He's a good boy," Brian said. "Keep talking to him."

"I will," Ken said.

"It's a bit unusual to be so definite about it at his age," Tom said. "We don't hear that kind of talk too often these days. I wish we did. If we don't get more priests, we'll all still be sitting around this table twenty years from now."

"That's not such a bad idea," Brian said with a laugh. "The food is good, the accommodations are comfortable, the pay is adequate."

"You know, when I was in grammar school, I wanted to be a priest," Tom said. "But I didn't want everybody to know I wanted to be a priest. I guess I never talked about it, but I knew, someplace in the back of my mind. Once I got into the seminary, I knew that that's where I was supposed to be."

"It wasn't that way for me," Ken said. "I was an altar boy for eight years, from the time I was eight until I was sixteen. And even when I was in college, studying engineering, I went to mass practically every morning. Though I had girl friends, I did. But that desire to be a priest was there. I remember when I was in my third year in college, I went on a retreat at a Trappist monastery. While I was there I met a retired Episcopalian priest from New York. He died a few years ago at the age of 106. Anyway, I went and had a very long talk with him. He told me he was certain that I had a vocation to priesthood. Later on, he visited me, came to our house, went to church with me, encouraged me. He wrote to me every week. When I decided to enter the seminary, he came out every week and talked to me about my studies, about how I was feeling."

"For me, it was simple," Sergio said in his soft, soothing voice. "I didn't think about it much until I was in the last year of high school. Then I made up my mind and went ahead."

"That's the easy way out," Brian said.

"It *was* easy," Sergio said.

"I didn't figure I'd be a priest until I was about nineteen or twenty," Jack said. "The second year in college. I guess it comes into every little Irish-American's head. Hero worship, probably. I knew a couple of priests when I was a kid. The kind who played ball with you. Father O'Malley kind of stuff. But as a kid you think that being a priest makes you a big deal in the community. Hopefully, you could turn out to be just that."

"It was a more complacent time then," Tom mused. "No

one questioned things yet," he said, referring to the changes in the Church and in the world since his seminary days. "It was a much different way of life than it is now, much more joyous and happy. There was much more acceptance of you just because you were a priest. You were given the benefit of the doubt. Now you have to prove yourself. There was more respect for authority then, less dissent for its own sake."

Brian stared at Tom, a man and a priest he admired. Tom could be depressed by nostalgia, comparing the past to the present. Brian had heard the clerical gossip that Tom had come to Incarnation in a kind of fall from grace, a punishment for his failure to keep his younger brother in the priesthood. The brother had left and Tom had been blamed. For a priest who had worked in the archdiocese hierarchy, as Tom had, to be sent to a parish was thought of as a demotion. Brian didn't see it as that, but he knew how the bishops thought. It was not a matter that Tom often raised, but at times Brian could detect undercurrents in what Tom said.

"You know," Tom resumed, "after the Second World War, people saw the devastation and said, 'We've got to make something of this world.'"

"I don't really feel that we've stopped working on the devastation. It's just that the nature of it has changed," Ken said. "I still think there's much to be done in the parishes. I spent almost ten years in a parish in Worcester, and they were the most enjoyable years of my life, although they were the most difficult years as well. The Hispanics were coming to the diocese very rapidly. I was the only one working with them, the only one who spoke Spanish. I had to find nuns and priests and parishes where they could hang their hats. I had to get programs started. I had to get to know all the people."

"Exactly," Brian said. "I wasn't joking before. If I'm still a parish priest twenty years from now, having dinner with you, I won't be unhappy. That's what I wanted to do. We're out there in front, where the people want us to be. To help them."

Brian liked Ken, although Ken's intensity could frustrate Brian at times. He appreciated Ken's earnestness as a priest; Ken never apologized for, or disguised, his wish to help people.

"You don't get anywhere unless you listen to your parishioners," Ken said. "An old priest once told me, 'Be very strict with yourself and be very kind to the people you're serving.' If you're strict with yourself, then they have an example. You can lead people, gradually. You can't change a person overnight. It's preaching, week after week. It's the example of your life. It's your interaction with the people. They're pilgrims on the same road as you are. We're all walking together."

Brian smiled at Ken and applauded lightly.

"Sometimes I think that some of our parishioners are giving back zero," Jack snapped. "I'm not talking about money. I get a pulse feeling that there's not much loyalty out there. They might as well have a storefront community center. For them, the Church is free. There's a lot of takers out there. If you're going to take, you give." He stared at Ken, whose seriousness provoked him.

Brian looked at Jack, reflecting on how the man's hostility only masked a deeper sadness. Jack could be funny, clever, charming; he could be angry, morbid, offensive. He could help a friend; he could be a bigot. At meals Jack often made a statement simply to annoy Ken. Jack resented conspicuous piety. Brian did not, although Brian was not one to engage in it himself. It was not his style. But neither did he indict those who spoke sincerely of their mission or of God. He respected that.

Brian had not found a way to deal openly with Jack. He laughed at his jokes because they were funny. He knew that

Jack could be a good, loyal friend, as well as a persistent enemy. Beyond that, he understood that Jack was vulnerable; when criticized in the company of others, Jack withdrew and fell into a deep depression. Brian could never bring himself to that sort of cruelty. So he would listen to Jack without comment, unless the issue was serious, theological, or reflected upon Brian's own sternly held beliefs, in which case Brian would respond more intellectually than emotionally, and hardly ever at mealtime.

Tom did not have Brian's sense of reticence.

"No, that's not so," he said to Jack. "We have so often stressed the sense that the Church is people. Therefore, the welcoming Church ought to be the figure, the pastor, the shepherd. I know that in a large-city parish to know three thousand people and know anything about them, even to know their names, is in itself a great feat. One of the things about the charisma of the parish priest is his thereness. He is there for people in spite of his own sinfulness, in spite of prejudice, in spite of his anger. He's there."

"Exactly," Brian said. "It's not a question of give and take, some kind of equation. It's being there, doing what you can, helping when help is needed."

Through all the conversation, dishes were passed, food consumed. It was time for dessert, and the two teen-aged girls entered bearing Jell-O with embedded bits of fruit, cups of tea, and the ubiquitous tray of cookies. Sergio, particularly fond of cookies, seized several and passed the tray along.

There was silence for a few moments.

"Start any revolutions lately?" Jack asked Sergio.

"Not this week," Sergio replied, smiling.

As a "liberation theologian," Sergio spent much of his time attacking the evils of capitalism—as he saw them—in articles for Spanish-language political journals, in lectures and speeches, at seminars. He was part of a Latin American movement that was attempting to spread its influence throughout the world, to bring dignity and security to the poor of all nations.

Brian was fond of the man, if not the philosophy. But he respected Sergio's right to pursue his own belief. He knew that the parishioners of Incarnation were not likely to revolt under Sergio's banner. On several occasions when Sergio had spoken out from the pulpit about the decay in American life, parishioners had stood and shouted at him. They made it quite clear that they were pleased to be in America.

"He doesn't understand liberation theology," Brian said to Sergio, pointing to Jack.

"To understand liberation theology, you have to understand the meaning of theology," Sergio said. "Theology comes from the Greek and it is the study of God. More technically, it is the deeper understanding of the revelation that is in the Bible. Liberation theology is in continuity with that tradition, relating it to Latin America. Most of our people are poor. I say I'm not a Marxist, because for most people that means lack of freedom, lack of faith, not believing in God.

"But remember the Galileo experience. And Copernicus. And Newton. All condemned by the Church. And Darwin. Society is often opposed to new ideas. The Church has a mission to keep the faith and is always afraid of new ideas. Marxism is not always for violent change. But there is a struggle. Look at the poverty in Latin America, look at the small minority of the rich."

"You're pissing up a rope," Jack cracked.

Sergio did not acknowledge the barb. "Usually the Church is opposed to all the revolutions in history," he continued. "In Chile we tried to help the government, while hoping to criticize it from within. It didn't work."

"So what can you do now?" Tom asked sincerely.

"Introduce liberation theology to Christians in the United States. Raise the consciousness of liberal Christians here.

It's important to make them aware of what is really going on. Religion can play a role in that because this country respects religion. I would like to try to make the democratic system really work. The power is held by a small minority. Big business. It would be better to share the power, truly—to have a real democracy."

"You know, before you got here, I thought we had a democracy that didn't work badly," Brian said. "Even after listening to you, I still think so." While he was not receptive to the liberation theology argument for himself, for his time, his parish, his country, Brian realized that the movement was making progress in Third World countries where the poor were genuinely oppressed by government. He did not dismiss Sergio or his philosophy in that context.

"People think that I incite a revolution," Sergio said. "Well, if helping the poor win their dignity is a revolution, then I must believe in revolution. You know, if there was a true revolution in Chile or wherever, and I was there when it happened, and the revolution became violent and I knew who my enemies were and there was a confrontation in a plaza somewhere and I was there, I would have to act."

"How?" Brian asked.

"If someone handed me a gun at that moment and pointed to the enemy, could I pull the trigger? Yes, without regard, if the cause was just."

"I'm not sure I could say that," Brian said. "Yes, maybe, if the revolution were for real democracy. But if I pulled the trigger, I know I'd regret it. I can't easily link killing to freedom. I would rather do my work on the streets than on a firing line."

Sergio got up, announced that he was going to his room to work on an article, and left.

"I don't understand all that," Jack said. "I just don't understand it."

"It's not easy for us, with our background, to know what

it must have been like for him in Chile. I admit that," Brian said. "But he's a good man. Worth listening to."

"Maybe," Jack said. "But he's not my role model."

"Who is your role model?" Tom asked.

"My father, for one. The most fantastic guy that ever lived. For doing things for people. Humor. Knew everybody. Funny. He stood apart from the other Irish in our neighborhood. A snappy dresser. A straw hat, like that. He gave us tremendous support. And Joe Walsh, my first pastor, in Harlem. Joe was an unbelievable man. He was unique, in his humor, in his insight for humanity. The parish was all black; he was in black work all of his life. By his own choice. They loved him. Through all those things in the sixties, they still loved him. He transmitted a genuine feeling of love and concern."

Brian listened. *Something went wrong somewhere in Jack's life, something to make him unhappy, to keep him from relating to strangers, something a parish priest had to do—despite the lessons learned from his father and Joe Walsh.*

Jack stared into space. "You know, if you're not in sight, you're not in mind, as far as the power structure of the Church is concerned," he said.

Ken, Tom, and Brian awaited what was to come.

"I think a lot of guys, if they would admit it honestly, have let the thought of leaving not just pass over, but dwell on it. I think of getting out, at times. I'd be telling a lie if I said no. Sometimes you get very unhappy. Very lonely. I think there are a lot of priests who find themselves in that state.

"And boredom. A lot of priests are bored. It can be tough. One guy I knew left. He felt spent. He had nothing left. He said, 'I have nothing more to give.' I guess some of us have gotten old. God, when do you ever sort out all the problems? There are times when your faith seems less important to you than it did thirty years before. I don't

know, it just becomes less intense. At times all this seems
like a job. You know, when we were first ordained as priests,
we felt God inside. I don't know that the feeling exists
anymore. Something has eroded it. Consumerism. Secular-
ism. I don't know."

Brian did not comment. Jack seemed headed toward
despair, and he did not want to contribute to it.

"Someone will say, what's so tough about being a
priest?" Jack went on. "Some lady makes your lunch and
makes your bed and makes your supper. You're always
hearing that from some guy who's got a tough child situation
or wife situation. What I say is, remember we're out there in
the real world, too."

He pushed his chair back from the table and got up.

"I've got to meet a friend," he said, and headed toward
the door.

"We'll talk later," Tom said.

"Okay," Jack said, leaving.

Brian sighed. "Well, distinguished pastor?"

"Well, what? The pastor can't solve all problems. I'm an
initiator, the catalyst or choreographer of the many talents of
the people around here. Listen to their needs and let them
make their own foolish mistakes and get all the parts
working together and recognize that you have the baton, but
if the others don't do their share, the orchestra will sound
disjointed. Not rule by force, but rule by gentle persuasion."

"I don't understand some things," Ken said. "Here I am.
I don't need any more money. I don't need more clothes, or
a more beautiful room in the rectory. And the people I live
with are decent. What more do I need?"

"Thanks be to God," Brian said.

"Yes," Ken agreed. It was time for the evening Spanish
mass, and Ken got up to celebrate it. He went to the door to
the church and disappeared into the darkness beyond it.

Brian and Tom were alone. They trusted each other,

respected each other, shared a strong belief in God. They could talk to each other openly and honestly.

They sat in silence, sipping their lukewarm tea. Brian sensed that Tom wanted to speak, that he had something on his mind, so he sat there waiting. After a few minutes, it came.

"You know, Brian, my brother left the priesthood in 1975. It was a poignant time for me, although I was able to officiate at his wedding the next year. Those were difficult times."

"I know," Brian said. Tom had been held responsible for his brother's leaving by the Church hierarchy. That hierarchy, he knew, reflected the biases, hostilities, and motives of many large corporations. Resentments arose, festered, and were acted upon. It was not, he knew, the saintliest of structures.

"Some people, some priests tell me that I've been punished for my brother, my friend," Tom continued. "That doesn't bother me, really. It led me to the only experience I hadn't had: being a pastor. I had taught. I had preached. I'd been in parishes. I'd done administration. And when I got here, I thought I would be here just for a while, then move on. I haven't been spoken to in three years. I'm fifty-two. There's no place I can go, in our way of life.

"I think I could be the vicar general. I speak Spanish, I know all the priests. There's nobody in this diocese—this is not boasting—who knows the priests as I do."

"I know that," Brian reassured. It was true. Tom not only knew all the priests of the diocese, he even remembered the years in which most were ordained.

"But I can't spend my life saying isn't it too bad they didn't do this for me. That's not what life is about. So I go on. I may have some bitterness, but I don't think I show it."

Also true; Brian had not heard him speak like this often.

"You know, I grew up before you did. In another era. I'm not going to tackle the system. When I first came here, everybody said, 'What happened?' 'What did you do?' Because in their view I had gone from the third or fourth job in the diocese back to the ranks. Therefore, I had one of the problems: booze, money, or women.

"The truth is that I want to stay here. At least for six years. I've been here for two and a half, going on three. What I'd like to do is go back to preaching and running retreats. Not so much moving around.

"Eventually I'll die and face my eternal judge, and what then? Right now, I'm at one of the better places around. Lively. Maybe ten years from now I won't have the energy to do what I'm doing now. But what does ambition mean?"

"You're involved in this parish," Brian said. "You go to all those community board meetings. You are trying to get five or six buildings rehabilitated in the neighborhood. The people know that you work hard, that you care about them."

"I hope so," Tom said.

"It's true," Brian said.

Tom stood up, and so did Brian. They filed out of the dining room into the foyer. One of the teen-aged girls was manning the phone.

"Any calls for me?" Brian asked.

"Several," she said.

"As usual," Brian smiled.

Behind him, Tom laughed.

7

The next morning Brian stepped into the shower. The water was hot. It wasn't always hot. Weeks ago he had stepped in and turned on the water only to discover that it was stone cold. It turned out that the rectory water heater had gone off for lack of fuel oil; Tom had forgotten to reorder it. Brian had spoken sternly to Tom about it. Tom had responded at once, ordered fuel, and the problem was solved. Brian could not be angry at Tom for more than a few minutes.

They chatted at breakfast over spread-out copies of *The New York Times* and the *Daily News*.

The rectory phone rang and Brian got up to answer it. He returned to the dining room to report to Tom.

"A bricklayer who knew my father. He used to drink in my father's bar. I guess he hasn't stopped drinking since then. That was his son on the phone. The father's sick from drink and the mother's just plain sick, down to sixty-five pounds. Could I help? They're both in the hospital. I ought to go over. Will you cover for me if anything comes up that I ought to handle?"

Tom nodded, and Brian left by the front door.

The hospital was nearby, but too far to walk, so Brian took his car from the lot behind McGonnell's Funeral Home. He drove to the small hospital near the northern tip of Manhattan, a hospital that had seen better times. The receptionist knew Brian; she was one of his parishioners. She directed him to the old man's room, one he shared with six other elderly men. An aide was helping him into a wheelchair for a visit to his wife, in another ward.

Brian looked at the man from the doorway. He appeared weak, infirm. Although he saw much of that in his work, Brian had not gotten used to it. It saddened him. He walked slowly into the ward and shook the old man's hand.

"Well, Father, it's good to see you," the man said.

"It's good to see you, Charlie," Brian said. "How are you doing?"

"The best I can, I guess," Charlie said.

"Well, it would be good if you got better and got out of here," Brian said. He respected the medical profession, but he felt that unless people were seriously ill, they were better off at home than in a hospital.

"That's my intention," Charlie said. He was a thin man with combed blond gray hair, and he wore the usual long hospital gown.

"Let's go see Mabel," Brian said, referring to Charlie's wife.

The aide pushed Charlie down the hall and Brian walked along.

When they arrived at the wife's bedside, Brian barely recognized her. She was a modest indentation in the bed, astonishingly emaciated.

"How are you feeling?" Charlie asked her.

"Oh, not bad," she said softly.

"You know, both of you, you've got to take care of yourselves. Your old friends in the parish miss you," Brian said.

"She doesn't eat," Charlie said. "We throw out food."

"I just don't have much of an appetite," Mabel said.

"You know what *you* have to do," Brian said to Charlie.

"Yes, I know. Stop drinking. Look at my legs. They're all filled with water. And my liver isn't too good, either. I've got to stop."

"That's right," Brian said.

"You know, Father, it's getting more expensive to drink anyway," Charlie cackled.

"A good reason," Brian said. "Another reason."

Brian moved closer to Mabel, leaned over the bed.

"God will help," he said.

"Oh, yes, He will," Mabel whispered.

Brian placed his hand on her head and prayed:

"God Almighty Father, we receive all power and strength from you. Help your servant to regain the strength of her health and to have an increase of faith in your presence. We ask this as we ask all things through Christ our Lord. May your blessing come upon your servant in the name of the Father, the Son, and the Holy Spirit. Amen."

He repeated the prayer for Charlie. The other patients in the room, immobilized by tubes, medication, weariness, age, stared at him.

"I look forward to seeing you both back in the parish very soon," Brian said. "Let me know when you get home." He waved at them and headed for the door.

It was a common call, like so many he made week after week throughout the year. Often he was rushed; each day was packed with commitments to the people of the parish. He tried not to be abrupt, even when time was his adversary. He took the time to talk, to express his affection, to touch. His dealings with the elderly were an outgrowth of his interest in thanatology. He treated the old with patience and love, as they moved closer to death. He knew what a wrenching time that could be, those final years, months, days. It was his hope to ease the inevitable anxiety.

He left the hospital, got into his car, and drove to a nursing home not far away. It was a large, modern complex with bright, cheerful rooms and an attentive staff. The nursing home administrators had been helpful to Brian in the past, admitting several old women from the parish at his request, women who could no longer care for themselves. Two of them were awaiting a visit from Brian.

The first woman, Katherine Moriarty, was ninety. He found her sitting in the corner of a dayroom, staring into space. The others in the room were either watching television or sleeping in their wheelchairs, or bent over, babbling to themselves.

Katherine smiled, toothlessly, when Brian greeted her.

"Oh, Father, how good to see you," she said.

"It's good to be here," he told her.

She clutched a batch of letters from relatives; she wanted to share them with Brian. He took the time to read them; some were from people who had lived in the parish before he was born. He thanked her for letting him read the letters, and they chatted. Although her speech was slurred, Brian understood her. It was one of his talents, honed by many hours in such situations, hours of paying close attention to such women.

He said a prayer for her and moved on to another floor, where he found Margaret Touhy, sitting with a large group in front of a blaring TV soap opera. He wheeled her to a quiet corner. Margaret, a very old woman, at least as old as Katherine, stroked her silken white hair while they talked.

Cataracts had made her almost totally blind, but she told Brian that she didn't want to go through an operation at her age. She could see the outline of things, and she told Brian that she remembered what he looked like.

"Big fellow, right?" Margaret said. "Hair going gray, right?"

"Absolutely correct," Brian said, "but sometimes I wish I weren't so big."

"I remember you from the parish," she reminded him. "You were always there when I needed you."

For years she had lived in an apartment near the church. No one had ever been invited in. One day the rental agent decided to pay a visit. When she opened the door for him, he found the largest sea of garbage he had ever seen. He told Brian.

Brian went to see for himself. He could touch the ceiling without leaping. Appalled, Brian headed out into the parish to mobilize a clean-up crew. He found a group of neighborhood teen-agers whose respect for Brian inspired them to join the project. But Brian knew that the woman could no longer live there alone. He phoned an administrator at the nursing home and told him about Margaret's plight. It was *important*, Brian stressed, for her to be out of that apartment and in the nursing home. Brian did not abuse his influence as a priest, and the administrator knew that. The federal government would provide payment to the home, since the woman was penniless. The administrator agreed, found a room for Margaret, and Brian transported her, with a few of her favorite belongings, to the home.

He remembered all that as he held her hand.

"Do you like my new dress?" she asked.

"Yes, it's beautiful," Brian said. Margaret smiled and stroked the dress.

"Where did you get it?" Brian asked.

"I found it in my closet," she said. A social worker had gotten it for her, but she didn't know that. Brian did. The nursing home retained some of the woman's Social Security income for such purposes.

She spoke coherently to Brian, with a residue of both wit and determination. She had come to like the home, she said. The only thing that troubled her was the fate of her grandson, who was due to have an operation soon. He was just fourteen, she told Brian. Brian knew otherwise. The grandson had to be fifty now. Brian had tried unsuccessfully to locate him when Margaret first checked into the home.

Brian simply nodded while the woman told him of her concern for the boy. He knew that it was futile to explain reality to her. They sat, side by side, looking out a large picture window at the yard behind the home, with its trees and flowers. *The best thing I can do for such a woman is to listen to her.*

Brian got up and said a prayer for her. "Do you want me to move you to another part of the room?" he asked.

"No, no. I'm just fine here," she said, "just fine." They smiled at each other and Brian left.

He drove back to the rectory. The reason he appreciated his role as parish priest was its diversity. He comforted old people in hospitals and nursing homes. He listened to his parishioners tell him their problems, and when he could, he helped them find solutions. Children and the aged, black and white and Hispanic, the devout and the not-so-devout, the skilled and the unskilled. He was *there* for them. He could help them by simply *appearing* in their lives or by guiding them toward God, as he did in the sacraments of the Church, in the prayers he said for them in ceremonies, in private, and at bedsides. It was what he wanted to do. There was considerable satisfaction in that.

He got back to the rectory just before lunch. Tom and Jack were there, sipping cool drinks in Brian's living room along with Sister Helen, a lively, middle-aged nun who was visiting her old friend Tom. On such occasions, which were frequent at Incarnation, the conversation often dealt with the offbeat religious life, the eccentric happenings in the clerical world.

Sister Helen, a tall, thin, dignified woman, was wearing a simple white blouse and modest brown-plaid skirt; she rarely wore the habit of her order. She sat in a large chair sipping a gin and tonic.

"It won't be long before we hear the patter of little feet in our school," Brian said. Sister Helen had taught in several Catholic schools.

"Patter indeed." She smiled, then remembered a story she wanted to share with the priests.

"I was teaching in the sixth grade in an Italian neighborhood in Manhattan," she began. "I had one young boy who simply wouldn't do any work. He was lazy. I told him that I'd have to hold him back, that he wouldn't go on with the other kids. That was that, as far as I was concerned.

"Well, to tell the truth, I knew that his father was important in the Mafia, but I really didn't think much about it. Then, one day that summer, the father came to see me. He was all in black—black hat, black suit, black shoes. And we talked about his son. He didn't shout. He was a very gentle man. He wanted to know why I had done what I'd done to his son. So I told him. He listened. He kept listening. Then, when I was done, he just said okay.

"Months passed. The boy did repeat the year, and everything seemed to be going along just fine. Then, at Christmas, I got a present, beautifully wrapped with gold ribbon and Christmas ornaments all over it. I opened it with great care because I wanted to save all the trimmings. Inside the box was an expensive black negligee. I stared at it. It was lovely. The other sisters stared at it.

"In those days we would show all of our presents to the superior; so when the time came, I brought her the box with the negligee and told her who had sent it to me. She glared at it, and at me, and said, 'Well, this'll do just fine for our bazaar.' I never saw it again.

"But I did see the father again. He would come to our parents' nights, and whenever he saw me he would say, 'If you ever need anything, you just let me know, okay?' I never really knew what he meant. And I never did ask him for anything."

The priests smiled at the story. The rectory buzzer sounded, indicating that lunch was on the table, and Brian led the procession down the narrow and steep rectory stairway to the dining room. Having eaten a minimal breakfast, he was now very hungry. He was grateful for Sister Helen's presence; visitors always provided a brief and healthy relief from the unrelenting course of his parish work. He wolfed down his lunch—an assortment of rolls and cold cuts for do-it-yourself sandwiches, cole slaw, french fries, and iced tea. While the others continued to chat, he excused himself and headed for the door. He had promised to visit a parishioner in need who lived a few blocks from the church, and such calls always took priority over social pleasures.

The building in which Anna Morabito lived was once impressive, if not lavish, but the hallways had acquired a permanent coating of dirt and the elevator was rickety. Brian did not notice any of it; he had grown used to it. When he arrived at the door to the woman's apartment, he found it open. He poked at it and entered.

Anna, old and Italian, was seated in an aged wooden chair, but the apartment, almost miraculously, did not have the tarnished air of the rest of the building. The green floral wallpaper was not spotted. The furniture, old but solid, was not crumbling. She had moved in more than forty years ago; now, after her husband's death, she remained in it alone. She was well into her seventies, debilitated by failing eyesight and arthritis, unable to walk without the aid of a cane. She needed Brian.

"I get very lonesome," Anna said to him, "very lonesome."

"I understand," Brian said. "A lot of us have that problem."

"I can't get out to buy food," she added.

"Don't worry about that. We've got plenty of helpful kids around, teen-agers who are ready to give you a hand." He would ask one of the willing girls who worked in the rectory to do Anna's shopping for her.

"That would be just wonderful," Anna said. "I haven't been able to get out in four days. I just can't walk."

"Do your neighbors check on you?" Brian asked, knowing how vital that was.

"Oh, yes," she said, "I have very good neighbors. Three sisters live together down the hall and come in to see how I'm doing. I remember their father. That's how long I've been here."

"How about money? Do you have enough?" The Church had a fund to buy food for the needy; it could provide vouchers redeemable at a neighborhood grocery store. It didn't have the money to do much more than that, however, so Brian and the other priests had to be well informed on the various welfare benefits the city offered.

"Money? Oh, that situation's not so bad, thank you."

She made a list of the food she wanted, then handed it with some money to Brian. He stared at the photographs on the walls—one of a former pastor at Incarnation, others of her late husband, and one of her son. She noticed Brian staring at them.

"My son lives in another city in the Midwest," Anna said. "But he visits whenever he can, whenever he has to be here on business. I like to have company because I just can't go out much anymore. I need somebody."

"Don't worry about that," Brian said. "We're here whenever you need us. All you have to do is call the rectory."

She smiled, a toothless grin atop a frail body.

"You know, I don't see that social worker anymore," Anna told Brian. "She was a good woman, but she doesn't come here anymore. They send someone else."

"Yes," he answered. "She's not assigned to this neighborhood anymore. It's too bad. They come and go."

"Yes, they do, I suppose. But I miss her."

"The super here, is he okay?" Brian asked. "He takes care of things?"

"Oh, yes. Yes, indeed. He takes care of everything."

"When you have a good super, the building is taken care of. When you have a bad one, the building goes down fast."

"True, very true. I'm grateful for him. You know, I've lived here for so long that I wouldn't want to move out now. I wouldn't know where to go."

"Thank God you don't have to worry about that," Brian said, moving toward the door. "And, remember, we're here if you need any help."

"Bless you, Father," she said. As he went out the door, she called out, "Don't bother closing the door. Just leave it open. I get a breeze with it open." He respected her wish.

Some of the time, he realized, he was that social worker who didn't get transferred. When a parishioner needed such help—food, clothing, employment, welfare benefits—Brian could produce it, on his own or by intervening in the bureaucracy.

He didn't wait for the elevator to arrive. He walked down the old curving stairway and went out into the summer afternoon.

8

The children in the Church's day camp had been taken to the enormous swimming pool—actually two large pools side by side—in Highbridge Park, a few blocks from Incarnation. The park itself bordered on Amsterdam Avenue and hugged the edge of a high cliff fronting on the Harlem River. It was a busy place. Boys played baseball on the diamond. Teen-agers sat on benches, listening to their radios and tapping their feet to disco rhythms.

In the pool children splashed, cooled off, frolicked, yelled. Others sat against the surrounding fence, munching snacks, affectionately calling out to friends in the water. Incarnation's day camp spent time regularly at the pool; it was free and therapeutic.

The air was heavy and still, the temperature in the upper eighties. Brian removed his collar and tucked it into the pocket of his short-sleeved black shirt. It wasn't necessary to wear it all the time. Even without it, he was recognized.

He greeted a middle-aged Hispanic man, father of five, who was too proud to admit he was on welfare. He told Brian that all was well with his family.

At the side of the pool, amid the joyous screams of small children, a maintenance man came up to Brian.

"Father, look at these," he said, holding up a group of bottles containing pool water. "We're cleaning it up. It couldn't be cleaner."

"Good work," Brian said.

"Would you mind telling my supervisor that you're pleased?" the man asked Brian. He pointed to a man standing nearby. Brian strolled over and registered his approval. Often his opinion was valued in the parish.

He walked around the pool. At various points along the way, he stopped to say hello to the kids he knew, to the teen-agers who were working at the day camp for the summer, and to a few older parishioners getting some sun.

A tiny boy, four years old, scanty red bathing suit slowly falling in the rear, rushed up.

"Father, Father," the boy yelled.

Brian grabbed him, patted his head and cheek.

"Are you having a great time?" Brian asked, smiling.

"Yes, yes, yes," the boy said excitedly, and ran off to jump into the water.

Other small children spotted him and came running over, putting little wet hands on his thighs, leaving imprints of their meeting. Brian smiled at them, touched them, pushed them gently into the pool to their delight. As a child he had spent a great deal of his summer time in Central Park, and he knew how important it was for these children to have one another, and a park, to share.

He turned to leave. On his way out of the park he spotted Kevin Mulligan on a bench, his eyes closed, looking up at the sun, slowly acquiring a tan. Kevin, at sixteen, lived near Incarnation with his parents, a brother, and a sister. They had a pleasant, neatly furnished apartment; the father was a dentist and money was no problem for them, as it was for so many other families in the parish.

"Kevin," Brian called out. "Are you asleep or meditating?"

Kevin opened his eyes.

"Father, how are you?" he asked.

"I'm just fine," Brian said. "And you?" Kevin's red hair and freckles, his forthright manner, reminded Brian of several Irish boys he had grown up with.

"Good," Kevin said. "I've got a part-time job helping out in a grocery store. I'm off right now."

"So you're making some money?"

"Right. It's good to have it," the boy said, smiling.

"When do you finish high school?" Brian asked.

"Two years."

"And then?"

"I don't know."

"Think about college much?" Brian asked.

"Sometimes. I can't decide."

"It's a good idea, to go," Brian said. "Puts you in charge of your own fate. At least it does it better than if you don't go."

"Probably true," Kevin said.

"If you feel like talking about it, let me know. I'll be around."

"I will. I'll drop by one of these days."

"Good."

Brian tapped Kevin on the shoulder affectionately and moved on.

He walked out of the park, beyond the sight of sunbathers and the sounds of giggling children.

At the rectory he found a message from a woman whose name was vaguely familiar. He returned her call. She told him that her mother had collapsed at home, simply passed out.

"It could have been the heat or perhaps something worse," the daughter said. "She's at Columbia-Presbyterian and I know she would be pleased to see you, Father."

"I'm on my way," Brian said.

He walked along St. Nicholas Avenue toward the hospital. Along the way he greeted several young mothers pushing baby carriages, three shopkeepers standing in front of their stores, a pair of husky teen-aged boys carrying cartons into a supermarket, and the mother of a girl in the eighth grade at the Incarnation school.

He was struck by this marvelous quality of the parish, this wonderful mix of people. There was poverty, certainly, but the place was not a ghetto where despair reigned. The poor Hispanics were a proud people, eager to work, to make progress, to benefit their families. He remembered riding a bus up to Incarnation one day, a bus that wended its way through the affluent East Side. The children who got off to go to their schools near Madison Avenue were not as well dressed as those he saw in the parish, the kids who went to the Incarnation school and the local public school. He had been pleased about that. The parish had not become what the South Bronx had become: devastated, alienated, defeated.

At the hospital he stood in line to find out which room the woman was in.

"Patricia Morgan, please," he said to the clerk behind the information counter.

The clerk, weary of working in the hot office, did not acknowledge that he was a priest. She simply announced the room number and dabbed her forehead with a damp handkerchief.

Brian entered the ward and paused. There were twelve beds, most of them containing old women. There wasn't any air conditioning; a feeble breeze swept across the ward from an open window. All the patients were still, either asleep or too debilitated to move or speak.

He found Mrs. Morgan in a bed at the far end of the

ward. In the adjoining bed, an old black woman slept on her side, her hospital gown parted to reveal her backside.

Brian stood at Mrs. Morgan's bedside. He recognized her; she had been coming to mass almost every Sunday for years. They had not spoken much to each other; it was difficult to know all the parishioners, there were so many.

Mrs. Morgan looked up at Brian and smiled. The daughter had urged Brian not to be somber; the mother might get alarmed, think she was dying. It was a common reaction among old Catholics. Brian affected a manner of good cheer, despite the heat and the sweat that made his face gleam.

"It's good to see you again," he said.

She continued to smile. She clutched Brian's right hand in both of hers and stroked it gently.

"Very good of you to come, Father," she said.

"I hope you're out of here soon," he said.

"They're taking tests," she said. "A lot of them. I hope so, too."

Suddenly her smile deteriorated and she began to cry. Her speech became unintelligible. Brian stroked her hand. It was difficult for him to know exactly what to say to her. He kept stroking her hand and waited. She stopped crying and smiled again.

In situations like this, he felt he had to do *something*: listen, touch, pray, talk. He placed his hand on her damp forehead and quietly said a prayer. As he did, she began to weep again.

"Don't worry," he said when he was done with the prayer, "you'll be out of here in a few days."

"A neighbor is taking care of my dog," she said, wiping her eyes with the back of her hand. "And my daughter calls me."

"Yes, I know. She called me."

The room was silent. A nurse strolled up, stared at the priest, walked over to the black woman's bed, and rearranged her gown to cover her bareness. Across the ward, an old woman, propped up on one elbow, peered at Brian.

"Well, it's time to go," he said. "You be well."

"Oh, yes, Father, I will," Mrs. Morgan said, smiling again.

Brian went out into the midday heat and walked back toward the church. So many people needed a connection with someone else at times in their lives. It was hard to know just what to do at times, to provide that connection. Sometimes, he knew, it was enough just to be a priest and be *there*. Perhaps that fact would make Mrs. Morgan feel better. He hoped so.

Warm rain began to fall, and he ducked into a florist shop, where a policeman was cooling off.

"How ya doin', Father?" the policeman asked.

"Just fine. And you?"

"Fine, too. I wouldn't be a cop on a day like this if I didn't feel good about it," the policeman said. "It's like working on hot days goes with the job description."

As he walked back to the rectory, Brian thought that he might say the same about himself, if he composed his own job description. Saying mass, being on duty, being available to people coming in for help, administering, getting people trained to teach religion to the children, bringing communion to parishioners trapped at home by sickness or old age, hearing confession, conducting funerals and weddings, counseling, teaching in the school, coordinating.

He thought about the parish. In eight years he had seen it change. Some buildings were abandoned, but he knew that some would be renovated and others would be preserved. There was hope. The Church contributed to the stability as a sign to the people that it cared about them.

The most important thing he could do was to know the people. *When people are getting married, they're reassured if the priest has been with them all along, from baptism to that moment, has known the family, has been part of the events of their lives.*

9

It was another hot summer day and Brian could not get used to the annoying heaviness of the air. He had gone to a movie, *Breaking Away*, had liked the story of a young Indiana boy striving, achieving, on his way to maturity. Together with Dan and other friends, in and out of the clergy, Brian went to movies from time to time. It was one of his modest pleasures, along with visits to Dan's house for dinner (lavish, varied, irresistible Italian fare), an occasional swim at the seminary pool, and dining in Chinese restaurants throughout the city.

But such pleasures were the scattered punctuations in a life of work. At breakfast he thought about the film as he sipped his orange juice, recalling happily the sense of affirmation the movie offered. Then he got up and walked slowly to the senior citizens' center, two blocks away.

The center was important to the community and to Brian. It gave the elderly a place to go, friends to talk with, a destination for those who might otherwise feel isolated at home.

The center was in space leased from a Presbyterian

church with a dwindling congregation. It was run by Tom Schweder, a thin, energetic, chain-smoking man in his early thirties.

Tom had known Brian for eight years. They first met when Tom was looking for young volunteers. Incarnation had the only young population of any church around. Tom wandered into the rectory one Sunday night looking for help and found Brian, and help.

Together, they worked for the center to make sure that not only Brian's parishioners but everyone coming to the center was well looked after. When the city needed to be yelled at, or there was a demonstration, Brian was there. Once he had even picketed.

Tom's regard for Brian was epitomized in his memory of one of the center's old women, a parishioner of Brian's who was battling the pain of illness with drink and drugs. She lived near the rectory, and one evening Tom went to visit her. She was in a stupor.

"You've got to get yourself to a hospital," Tom insisted. She didn't comprehend what he was saying. Tom called an ambulance and she was taken to the hospital. Brian visited her there, talked to her about how self-destructive it was to drink and take drugs. She respected him and listened.

A few days later, late at night, she was released from the hospital. When she got home, she found Brian, Tom, and other friends waiting for her.

Brian told her to put on her favorite nightgown and get right into bed. He went around the apartment, checking to make sure there wasn't any liquor or pills in the place. He tucked her into bed, kissed her, and led the others out.

"God bless you," she shouted at them as they left. That, for Tom, was Brian, the man and the priest.

"You know, the center is really a replacement for what's missing in older people's lives," Tom had once said to Brian. "It's a substitute family when children are grown and gone.

Missing spouses. Missing jobs. Missing friends. We provide a sense of continuity for their lives."

Brian was one of the few in the center who knew that Tom planned to leave, to move on to another job. They talked about that and more on this summer afternoon, before attending a meeting of the center's board.

"We've got an attractive woman on staff. You know her," Tom said. Brian nodded. "Good-looking. Buxom. Well, we've got several old Hispanic men who want the pleasure of her company. It's tough for her to handle. She doesn't want to go out with them, and she doesn't want to hurt their feelings."

"So what can she do?" Brian asked.

"She could begin by wearing a bra, I suppose," Tom said with a laugh. He tugged at his moustache and lit a cigarette. "When she doesn't wear one, we get complaints from the old women as well." They agreed that it was more a matter of the undiminished sex drive of the Hispanic men than the woman's provocation.

"Reminds me of our former pastor," Brian said. "I once brought him over here for a visit, and when he walked in, a young girl was doing a dance, entertaining the older people. Something to see. The pastor glared at me and said, 'Does she belong to our youth group?' 'Yes, she does,' I told him, worrying about what he'd say next. 'Does she dance there like she does here?' he asked. 'Yes, she does,' I had to say. 'Well,' he said, 'the next time she does, invite me.' "

Brian and Tom laughed together.

They talked about other problems. A few old women were being disruptive at group activities. One drank too much; she had passed out at a recent meeting. Another screamed, threw things, and used the center as a place to do her laundry—in one of the center's cooking pots.

Tom introduced a familiar refrain: the difficulty of raising funds for the center.

THE PRIEST

"If we sponsor a trip, an outing," he said to Brian, "it's more expensive now than it ever was, and more difficult to get people to go." He suggested setting up committees to deal with such problems. "These people will work hard for themselves," he said.

He told Brian about a recent bingo game at the center. One woman had brought her young granddaughter and the granddaughter had won, which prompted cries of "outsider" from the bingo-playing regulars.

"It'll come up at the meeting today. Mark my words," Tom predicted, checking his wristwatch. It was time for them to join the other board members.

The large room adjoining the church chapel was as hot as the street itself. A large fan blew tepid air at those seated at the long table. Tom turned off the fan. The room became silent. "The thing's just blowing hot air at us," he explained.

Around the table, the board members inched forward. They were, for the most part, old people who had lived in the community for years and who depended upon the center for its daily hot lunch, its bingo games and other diversions, and as a place to see their friends. The board members were familiar to Brian, although they weren't all parishioners. He did know one Irish woman, complete with brogue, who came to mass every day and spent much of the rest of her time at the senior center. He knew an impeccably dressed Hispanic man in his seventies who came to church as well. There were others. Sarah Goldstein, a Jewish woman in her early seventies, attended the board meetings regularly; well dressed, articulate, and outspoken, she was involved in the center's work as both recipient and planner. Others present included a young social worker and several members of the center's staff.

"Hopefully, we'll make it through the end of the year," Tom announced. "Last year we ran out of money for food. We owed money. Brian's church donated six hundred dollars, and we made it by using that and by borrowing from our renovation fund. We're paying it back now." He lit a cigarette and asked a young boy who helped at the center in summer to go out and buy him another pack.

"The center is growing," Tom continued. "Our attendance isn't falling off. And we got approval for the renovation. We're going to tear up this place and rebuild it without closing it at any time along the way. There'll be complaints and problems, but when we're done, we'll have working johns, so you won't get your skirts or pants wet anymore. The toilets will have handrails."

"He means we'll be getting two brand-new mops," Brian said with a laugh.

"And more," Tom said.

The old Irish woman sat stiffly in her chair, prim in her clean, blue cotton dress, her hands clasped on the table. The old Hispanic man, dignified in his beige suit and dark brown tie, fondled his straw hat on the table in front of him. Sarah Goldstein, in a vivid print dress and with her bright red hair tied in a bun, paid close attention as well.

Tom brought up the matter of the disruptive people.

"That should have been taken care of a long time ago," the old Irish woman snapped, tapping the table with her finger.

Sensing that the subject might inspire a lengthy debate, Brian came to Tom's rescue. "We'll get to that, I promise," he said. "But, first, let's talk about something else that's important. Tom has been doing too much work; we need some committees to help him. We want you to be deeply involved in this place. We want you to help Tom make it the best center in the city." He suggested forming a program committee to rule on center activities; also a personnel committee, a budget committee, a fund-raising committee, a renovation committee, and a grievance committee.

"You're taking Tom off the hook, in other words," Sarah

said, laughing. She knew that Tom worked long and hard at the center.

"Right," Brian said with a smile. "We can take him off one hook and put him on six others."

"How about that child who was playing bingo?" the Irish woman interrupted. Tom knew that it was impossible to enforce an agenda at these meetings; people talked about what they wanted to talk about.

An old woman who had not yet spoken yelled out from the far end of the table: "Can a person be dismissed from the center?"

"Forever? I doubt it. But for a few days, yes," Tom replied. "There are limits, of course. But a committee could work out such problems before they get to the frightening stage."

"I have a gut feeling against committees," the young social worker said. She wore jeans, T-shirt, and sandals, and she gestured vigorously with her hands when she spoke. "You can't defend yourself at their meetings," she said. "There are rules for the center now and people should be asked to leave if they don't obey them."

A staff member loyal to Tom bristled. "A committee doesn't have to be a court," she said. "It is just part of a system to help us run this place. We need the support of our membership."

The old Hispanic man had been listening attentively. "I believe," he said slowly and deliberately, "that it is very rude to tell anybody you can't come into the center. This is a very serious matter."

Tom smiled and said, "We don't want the dirty ones to give us lice, that's all."

"That's something a grievance committee could deal with," Brian said. He knew that he should not interrupt the board members; their opinions were stoutly held. But he wanted to keep matters on track, to hold the rambling nature of such meetings to a minimum.

The old Irish woman broke in: "I could see nothing wrong with that darling child winning at bingo. She was with her grandmother, after all. And there was such a to-do about it. Is it against the law for a child to play?"

The old Hispanic man got up and started toward the door. "I have a doctor's appointment," he announced.

"Hope everything's well," Brian said.

"Yes. Just a checkup. I watch myself," the old man said.

The bingo game, Brian suggested, ought to be regulated by a program committee.

"Anyway, bingo is an evil institution," he added with a grin. He knew that it *was* illegal for the child to play, but he didn't want to raise that issue now. He opposed bingo, although he knew that Incarnation raised substantial amounts of money from it. It compromised the dignity of the Church for it to endorse gambling, even for a good cause. There was something incompatible between the Church and bingo. But this was his own feeling, and he chose not to apply it to the center's freedom of choice.

Tom had grown fidgety, and Brian knew that meant there was work he had to do. Brian announced that the meeting was coming to an end.

"Tom will send out a plan for using committees, along with the minutes of this meeting, to all of you," Brian told them.

"I'm going away on vacation tomorrow," Tom announced. He did not mention his plan to resign; it was not the right time.

The old Irish woman walked over to him, touched him lightly on the shoulder, and said, "God bless you, Tom, and have a good vacation." She turned to Brian and said, "Always good to be with you, Father." Brian smiled and nodded appreciatively.

10

Brian walked back to the rectory from the senior center. Along the way he spotted a twelve-year-old girl from the parish, a beautiful Puerto Rican girl who was one of the best students in the Incarnation school.

"*Que pasa?*" he asked.

"The boys are beating up the girls again," she said with a hint of a smile.

"You want me to come over and twist a few arms?" Brian asked jokingly; he never had to use force with the parish children. They had no wish to battle priests. "You want me to bring peace to the neighborhood?"

"Not really," she said coyly. "They're not really hurting us."

"Then, be nice to them. It's not easy to be a boy."

She giggled. He patted her head; she put her arm around his waist. They walked that way toward the rectory. In front of the church she broke away, waving happily, and went off to rejoin the boys.

Inside the rectory Brian had a visitor. Sonia, with one of

her children, was there to see him. He had seen her many times before. A few nights ago, when Brian was out, she had shown up without notice, clutching a bottle of sleeping pills that she had threatened to take. Brian was out and one of the other priests took the bottle, discarded the pills, talked with her, and walked her home.

Sonia was quite tall and thin, and her dark brown hair was unwashed and matted. She wore a tight-fitting T-shirt, soiled jeans, and sandals. Her child, gurgling on a bottle of milk, was unwashed. Brian escorted them into one of the private rooms at the front of the rectory and closed the door.

She was Dominican, in New York since childhood. Her English was flawless, yet she had not gotten the rest of her life in order. Brian knew that, and he had been trying to help her. He had not succeeded, but he was unwilling to give up.

"My mood jumps up and down," she said, crumpling a paper towel in her hands. "But more down than up. I am depressed so much of the time."

"Trouble with *him* again?" Brian asked. She was unhappily married.

"Yes. Maybe I should divorce him. But I don't . . . I don't know. We fight. He didn't want this baby. He wanted me to have an abortion. But I wanted the baby. When I had it, everything got worse. He wanted to have it all—to go with his lovers when he felt like it and to be with me when he felt like it. I didn't want that. He doesn't give me any money. He has it, I know. He has a good job."

Brian stared at her. There was something attractive about her. She had had six children, despite a marriage that had never been satisfying. Now she had begun to feel sorry for herself, to neglect herself, attitudes that Brian knew were counterproductive. She wanted to appear to be both sensual —she did not wear a bra under her T-shirt—and pious; her mood swung between those extremes.

"It's important to have a life with your family. A social

91

life of some sort," Brian said, knowing that the husband was not around much of the time.

"I try. But I'm thirty-two and most of the women my age have husbands or families or, if they don't, they go out looking for men. And I don't want to do that. But when I do go out at all, innocently, he accuses me of being unfaithful to him."

"Do you understand that you might be better off without him?" Brian asked.

"I understand, but I can't seem to handle things when I'm alone with the children."

"It's one thing to understand intellectually, but it's another to understand emotionally—and to act on that understanding," Brian said.

"I know. My relatives think it's all my fault, all of it. We fight about it. You know, I always tried to be a perfect daughter, a perfect mother, a perfect wife."

"Not even Christ could be perfect," Brian said.

She smiled at that, then began to cry.

"I've been in therapy," she went on after regaining control. "I know what it means to have supportive friends. But I don't seem to have enough support these days. It is good for me to talk to you, to a priest who understands me and my problems."

"I will try to understand, I promise you that," Brian said. "If I can help, I will."

Her nails displayed a flaking coat of polish. Her ankles were discolored by dirt. She scratched her foot aimlessly and resumed. Brian listened to her. He knew that her husband treated her in macho fashion. He knew, too, that she had a menial job, and a friend to take care of her children while she worked. It was a life almost out of control. One social worker he knew had recommended that the woman be hospitalized for psychiatric treatment. Brian had disagreed. She was depressed, not psychotic or even severely neurotic. And she was poor in a city that isn't always kind to its poor. She had a family to worry about; those children could not be abandoned.

They sat in silence for several minutes.

"I understand it isn't easy," Brian said. "I have a friend who may be able to help." When the counseling got complex, Brian often referred parishioners to Dan Cherico. Dan would see her, without fee, and if he couldn't help, he would refer her to a full-time psychiatrist; that is, if she felt ready again for that.

Brian had no more to say. Simple solutions, he knew, would not help her.

The woman shrugged.

"I'm not sure I want to talk to anyone else about it. I can talk to you," she said.

"Yes, of course. And we'll talk again, soon. But think about seeing my friend. He's here often. Just come into the rectory and ask Dan Cherico to call you. That's his name. If you leave your name and number, he'll call you."

"Maybe I will," she said, smiling.

He watched her push the stroller to the sidewalk and head for home. A good-looking woman, smart, she spoke English like a native, but somehow she was trapped.

Brian heard a familiar wheeze in front of the rectory. He spotted Jim Doyle passing by. Doyle, at eighty-two, was dying of lung cancer. He saw Brian staring at him and shouted, "I haven't got long to go."

"Don't say that," Brian said, shaking his head. "We need you around here."

Doyle was a short, thin, tough parishioner whom Brian admired. He had spirit, the wish to prevail against cancer; his faith had helped him sustain a stalemate. At least so Brian believed. Doyle was a man who felt close to God.

"You know, when I was a kid, I was tough," Doyle said to Brian. "A rowdy. I ran away from home, went around the country riding the rails. Joined the navy. Good thing I did. I never knew it would come to this. Now I can get treated at the veterans' hospital."

Doyle had lived in Incarnation parish since the 1930s. Ten years ago he got married for the first time. He and his wife lived near the church.

Doyle and Brian met often. They shared jokes, chatter, an Irish heritage, a belief in God.

"At my age, what more do I want? I've lived my life. I go to church. The truth is, I don't feel pain when I'm praying," Doyle said to Brian. "You know, the first time I ever went to church, I was about twelve years old. When I saw the crowds, I thought, if they believed, I should believe. But I didn't have a strong feeling for it until after I got married, late in life. Now I'm here, in church, every day.

"The Church taught me that I'm not afraid to die. The way I was raised, we had a conscience. Because we knew we weren't in the clear, we were always afraid to die. But now my conscience is sort of clear."

"You pray every day?" Brian asked.

"Every single day," Doyle responded. "Most of my prayers are not just for myself, but for my mother, my father, sisters, brothers, friends, relatives. The whole family."

"It's helpful, isn't it?" Brian said.

"Very, very helpful," Doyle said. "And I pray for you, too."

"For me?" Brian was pleased.

"There's a reason for that. Your mind is on all of us. Some people may be thinking of something else while they're talking to a person. But not you. You help. You haven't given me a nickel. I don't need money. You've given me something spiritual. You're the top man to me."

Brian was moved. True, he had known Doyle since first coming to Incarnation, and had always been fond of him, and he had been saddened by the decay of Doyle's health.

But he had not realized that his affection for Doyle had meant so much to the man.

He didn't know exactly what to say to Doyle in gratitude. Words were insufficient. He put his arm around Doyle's frail shoulders and hugged him gently. Doyle smiled and moved along toward home.

Brian went into the rectory, feeling good about himself and his work.

11

July vanished in all of its steaming intensity. August arrived with more of the same. On the morning of the first Friday of the month, Brian went out to bring communion to those parishioners who were too old or too sickly to come to mass. He took the long, wide stole from a drawer in his room. One side was white, for use in communion; the other side was purple, for use in confession. He went to the Blessed Sacrament chapel in the church, to the left of the main altar, and opened the tabernacle. Inside he found a small gold container with the Host—communion wafers—and removed it. He took one Host for each of the people he would visit. Four small children were playing and praying in front of the main altar. They did not pay attention to him, nor he to them. He moved down the center aisle of the church and into the street. It was 9:30 A.M., and he had fourteen stops to make before lunch.

He did not like to rush through communion calls. He knew that the people he would visit would welcome him, would want him to stay and talk, but it wasn't possible to oblige them; there was so much work to do, he couldn't allot more than a morning to these calls. But receiving communion, he knew, was what mattered most to these people.

He went along the street two blocks to an old, large tenement. He entered the elevator, sniffed, and leaned against the wall. *After a while, you become oblivious to smells.*

Brian found his first call, an old woman, in bed. She had left the door open for him. She looked weary.

"Have you been getting out at all lately, Mary?" he asked.

"No, no, it's too hot," she murmured.

"We've been through a bunch of these summers together, haven't we? Well, before you know it, there'll be snow on the ground."

"God willing," she sighed.

He put the stole around his neck and looked at her. He had been coming to bring communion to her every month for four years; he could document her deterioration. The deacons made such calls, but most old parishioners preferred to see a priest. The room was intolerably hot, and Brian performed the service rapidly.

Next he stopped at the door of Charlie and Mabel, the couple he had visited in the hospital a few weeks earlier. The husband drank too much; the wife, declining for months, had been eating little.

"Charlie, you're looking much better than you did in the hospital," Brian said to the husband. "That's good."

"I've been taking care of myself, like you said," Charlie responded.

"Have you been staying off the stuff?"

"Well . . ." Charlie began.

"Have you been behaving?" Brian asked.

"Not bad, not bad."

"And Mabel, how's she?"

"She's eating now. Eating better now."

"Good, very good," Brian said.

Mabel sat in a chair and Brian stood in front of her; Charlie retreated into the kitchen.

"And you, Mabel, how are you?" Brian asked.

"A bit better," she said. "Yes, a bit better."

"That's good. I hope you continue to feel better, and better."

He bent over toward Mabel and recited: "Give us support and encouragement. . . . Have mercy on us. Happy are we who are called to this supper." His voice echoed throughout the apartment.

"Now that you're feeling better," Brian said, "keep an eye on Charlie, too. He gets a B-plus for not drinking so much, but he should be off completely."

"Right you are, Father," she said, smiling.

"Well, it's good to see you home again," Brian said, "both of you."

She maintained a frozen smile.

Brian left. She isn't getting better, he thought; she will get worse, and Charlie will drink more and more. He wished he could have the power to cure all the ills he encountered. He knew he couldn't, but some of these people haunted him. The best, perhaps all he could do for them, was to visit them, to be a factor in their lives.

An immaculate old woman in an immaculate old apartment was next on his list. She had put on makeup for his visit and was pleased to see him. She moved with the aid of a walker, after having broken her hip months before.

"How's the hip?" he asked.

"It gets better all the time. At my age, it takes a while," she said, smiling.

He began the communion service and the woman joined in. His voice boomed, hers was frail.

"This is the lamb of God who takes away the sins of the world," he chanted.

When it was over, he strode toward the front door. She handed him a five-dollar bill for the Church.

"You don't have to do that," he said.

"I know I don't have to, but I want to," she said.

Brian felt ambivalent about such donations. The Church could not survive without such generosity; yet he knew that some of those who gave were depriving themselves in order to do so.

Two sisters from Colombia were next. When Brian arrived, he noticed three lighted candles on the dining-room table. One sister greeted him, the other remained in bed; the small table beside her was covered with medicine bottles. Brian went to the bedside and offered communion in Spanish. Despite the heat, the old woman in bed was covered by a blanket. When Brian finished, she said, *"Muchas gracias,"* and he said, *"Buena suerte."* Good luck. The healthy sister escorted him to the front door.

"I think she wants to die," she said.

"It is sad, but I can understand that," Brian responded. "Some of these people I visit wish they had died years ago. They are sick of suffering." He did not believe in euthanasia, deliberately bringing a life to an end. He did believe in allowing a person to die in peace, without medical intervention, if that was the choice. The sight of someone kept alive by medical devices, lingering in despair, offended him. There was, he knew, a life after the one on earth. Life did not end when the heartbeat stopped.

In the next spotless apartment, Brian greeted an old Irish couple. The man was in a chair in the bedroom, next to the window, his leg propped up. He was thin and pale.

"How are you doing, Jack?" Brian asked.

The man waved his arm. "So-so," he said.

"Well, you've got a good woman to take care of you," Brian said. "Right, Emily?"

"I want to put on the air-conditioner, but he won't let me," Emily said. "Doesn't want it. Has bad circulation.

99

Gets up every fifteen minutes during the night."

She was short, energetic, in charge of the household. *He's lucky he has her; she can be depended upon.*

Brian brought them communion.

Afterward, he looked around the apartment. It was well maintained, clean, with attractive furniture.

"How are you holding up in the heat?" Emily asked.

"Not bad. Maybe I'll lose some weight," Brian said with a laugh.

"There's been no relief from it," she added.

"When we get winter, we'll get relief," Brian said, heading for the door. He stopped, turned toward the husband, and said, "No dancing for you, understand?"

Jack laughed and said, "It's good to have the pleasure of your company, Father."

Emily followed Brian toward the door and handed him thirty dollars, a stipend to say six masses for her son, who had died a few years ago.

"We miss him," she said.

"I know, I know," Brian said sympathetically.

At his next stop, Brian discovered a tiny old Italian woman. He hadn't met her before.

"Mrs. Esposito, do you speak English?"

"A little bit," she said, smiling.

"Do you need anything? Can I help you?" he asked.

"No, Father, no, thank you. I got my family," she said.

On her living-room table there were copies of Italian magazines, cookies, medicine, a well-worn rosary. As Brian recited in English, she prayed aloud with him in Italian, creating a contrapuntal chant.

When he was done, he touched her head lightly. "Anything else, Mrs. Esposito?" he asked.

She clutched his hand. "I pray to God that I want to die. I got a lot of things wrong. The head. The eyes. My husband dead forty-three years. My son no marry. I need operation on neck, on stomach. I pray to die."

Brian was unprepared for the outburst. He touched her arm. In thanatology he had learned about allowing people to die with dignity. It made sense to him. And here was such a person. Yet he could not easily *want* her to die. He did not know her, but he liked her instantly on this their first meeting.

"I will pray for your life," he said. "And for your soul."

"I pray for you, too," she said.

        Brian walked to a tall apartment building, modern and spacious, one of the few high rises in the parish. The apartment he visited was sunny, handsomely furnished. A mother and daughter shared it, middle-class Irish who had led reasonably happy lives until illness struck them both. While Brian spoke, they sat on a velvet sofa, their canes beside them.

"May we be guided and strengthened by His power. Happy are we who are called to this supper," he intoned. He placed the Hosts on their tongues; older Catholics preferred that to having the Host placed in their hands.

There was a check for ten dollars for the Church on a table near the door.

"Take it, please," the mother urged. He did, thanked them, and left.

He found an eighty-six-year-old Cuban woman in an apartment just beyond the parish border, really in neighboring St. Elizabeth's parish. He tried to explain to her that priests preferred not to cross each other's lines; it was better that way. She did not seem to care. Her children had once attended the Incarnation school, she told Brian, but now they were no longer Catholics. She didn't want to be like them.

She wore a blue gingham housedress and fondled a rosary with one hand while clutching a cane with the other. Two candles glowed on a table.

"You speak Spanish very well," she said. "I am glad."

"Shall we begin, Josefina?" he asked.

"Si," she said.

She folded her hands in front of her as Brian prayed in Spanish. *"El cuerpo de Cristo . . ."* He placed the communion wafer in her mouth; he did not bring wine on these calls because it was not required. Eventually that might change, but for now the Host was sufficient.

"Okay, senora," he said when he had finished. *"Buena suerte."*

She offered him a few rumpled dollar bills. "For you," she said in Spanish.

"No," he said. "Not for me. For the Church, okay?"

"Okay," she said. "You know, Father, I'm trying to discover how to leave this life," she added solemnly.

"Josefina, everything is taken care of. It will happen according to God's plan," he said.

"Yes, you are right. It will," she said.

As he left, he thought about what the woman's children would say when they realized that a priest had been in the apartment. If they had left the Church, as their mother said, they could be harsh in their anti-Catholicism. He was aware of such bigotry, but was not intimidated by it. Fortunately, he did not have to face it often in his parish. And when he did, he rarely felt the need to rage against such idiocy.

He moved on. An old Italian couple, middle class and comfortable, greeted him at his next stop. As Brian escorted the woman into her living room, the husband retreated into the kitchen—he was not as religious as his wife and did not wish to receive communion.

The wife, a gentle woman with a ready smile, was pleased to see Brian's familiar face.

"Are you melting away in the heat, Father?" she asked.

"Nina, if I could melt in the heat, I would be very, very grateful," he said, laughing.

"Oh, you're not that heavy," she said soothingly.

"Let's say a good meltdown of about twenty pounds wouldn't be a bad thing."

"I stay in when it's hot," she said. "We've got a nice place here and there's no point in sweltering when I can be cool right here."

"Smart, Nina, smart," Brian said.

She told Brian that she wanted him to hear her confession, as well as give her communion.

"Of course," he said.

She sat in a chair, with Brian on another chair facing her. They recited the Our Father together. "Have mercy on us," she said, accepting the Host, making the sign of the cross.

Brian heard her confession. *Her sins are nonexistent. She simply wanted to talk to a priest.*

She handed Brian a twenty-dollar bill and leaned forward to whisper in his ear.

"Tony's cheap," she giggled, pointing to the kitchen, where her husband sat, waiting for them to finish. "I'm not."

Brian laughed, but did not comment.

"Thank you, Father," she said, raising her voice to alert her husband. "Thank you very much."

Brian headed for the door. As he reached it, the husband approached and handed him two dollars. Brian smiled, thanked him, and left.

Along the street, Brian moved rapidly; there were other matters to tend to on this Friday, and he had to complete the communion calls by lunchtime. This was, as well, the day that the Church's bingo game took place at a neighborhood bingo parlor.

His next call was at the apartment of an old Puerto Rican couple, the Mendozas. The wife had cancer.

"How are you feeling?" he asked her.

"I have no pain," she said, smiling at him. Husband and

103

wife, their hands clasped, sat on their sofa while Brian stood in front of them, bringing communion in Spanish.

Next, a ninety-two-year-old Italian woman—thin, white-haired, and regal—awaited him in a spacious, oak-paneled apartment not far from the Hudson River. In years past it had been a splendid home, and its quality survived.

Another priest had warned Brian that the woman said the Our Father in Latin. Brian knew he would have to fake it; he hadn't used Latin since his seminary days, but he was determined to do his best. He entered the dining room, where the woman sat waiting for him.

She recited the Our Father in Latin; Brian moved his lips, speaking a few words in Latin and many more inaudibly. The woman was deaf; she did not notice the difference.

"Only say the Word and I shall be healed," he chanted. She accepted the Host and sipped from a glass of water, an ornate crystal glass she had put on the table beside her.

"Father, will you offer a mass for my husband?" she asked, handing Brian an envelope, a donation for the Church.

"Certainly, I will," he said. "And you keep cool in summer and warm in winter."

On a wall outside the building, Brian saw some incremental graffiti in Spanish. CHRIST IS COMING, in blue print. NOT HERE, in red. YES, BUT HE'S GONE AWAY, in yellow.

He walked along the street, sweating, past children he greeted in English and Spanish, to the apartment of an old bedridden Irishman who had lived in the parish for decades.

Above the man's bed there was a poster: Notice—Six Persons Per Bed Limit.

"Where are the other five, Reilly?" Brian asked him.

"These are tough times, Father," the man said. "I'm having trouble finding them."

Brian laughed. "If I run across any volunteers, I'll send them over," he said.

"That's the kindly parish priest for you," Reilly said.

The room was intensely hot, and the sweat dropped from Brian's forehead onto Reilly's bed. Brian rushed through communion.

Brian went quickly to another apartment in the same building. A crippled old Irish woman in a wheelchair was ready for him.

"How are your spirits? Good?" Brian asked. Her name was Fogarty, but he couldn't remember meeting her before.

"Not bad, but my body won't cooperate," she said. "Sometimes I pray to die. You know, Father, I've always been a shy person. And now I don't like people to see me looking like this. Oh, dear. I haven't gone to confession in weeks because of that."

"Don't worry about it," Brian told her. "God is forgiving."

He glanced at his wristwatch. It was 12:20 P.M., almost time for lunch. He offered communion, patted Mrs. Fogarty on the head, wished her good luck, and headed out into the street.

He arrived at the rectory as lunch was being served. Tom Leonard was alone at the table.

"You shouldn't have to eat alone," Brian said to him.

"I'm not. You're here," Tom responded.

"Be grateful," Brian said, smiling.

"I am, I am," Tom said.

"A hot day for communion calls," Brian said. "Hot streets. Hot buildings. Hot elevators. Hot rooms. Thank God it's cool in here."

He ate a hamburger on a bun, french fries, salad, cookies, and tea.

"That's a high-calorie meal," Tom joked.

"I need the energy," Brian said with a laugh.

12

Brian was on duty, the priest who would deal with the problems of the day—answer the phone calls, advise the visitors, arrange baptisms, weddings, funerals. On a sweltering day, it kept him inside, close to the air conditioning. It was, he thought, a fair exchange. There was one funeral that he had to do, but he had time to prepare for that. He sat in his room and waited.

The front doorbell rang. He responded. It was Alfred Warner, a respectable, meek, middle-class businessman who had been coming to see Brian once a week for months. Warner didn't worry about money; he had a responsible job in a large corporation. Living alone in a grand old apartment in the parish, he devoted considerable time to his stamp collection, maintained meticulously in many volumes. Short, thin, and restrained, he found Brian one of the few people he could discuss his problem with.

It was a common problem. A psychiatrist Brian had met at a Foundation of Thanatology conference had told him, "If we could find the proper man for every woman, the proper woman for every man, psychiatry would collapse."

Alfred could not find a woman.

"Welcome, Alfred," Brian said.

"Good morning, Father," Alfred said. His manner was formal and old-fashioned.

"How have things been going?" Brian asked.

"Troubling," Alfred said. "Troubling. I feel like a relic from another age."

"We've talked about that before," Brian said, "and you're not. You are a man with standards. You are polite. You treat women with respect. There is a woman out there who will appreciate that."

"I suppose. But I haven't found her yet. Last weekend I went out with a woman I met right here in the parish, after church on Sunday. Handsome woman, young and lively."

He mentioned the name of a woman Brian knew. She had a reputation for being "aggressive," for racing immediately to bed with any man she met. She could not achieve a sustained relationship, either. Dan Cherico had attempted to counsel her, but without notable success.

"How did it go?" Brian asked.

"Badly. That night, the first night we ever went out, I took her to dinner, then we went back to her apartment. She wanted to go to bed with me."

"And you?"

"I just wasn't ready to move so quickly," Alfred said. "I wanted to get to know her first. I went home."

"That's the reverse of what often happens," Brian said. "Are you aware of that?"

"Yes, I know we're the ones who are supposed to be the aggressors," Alfred said. "But I like to take my time."

They talked quietly for twenty minutes about Alfred's frustration. Brian continued to assure him that there would be a woman with whom he would get along. Alfred needed that support and got it from Brian regularly. Brian couldn't "find" that perfect woman for him, but he could endorse Alfred's search for her.

"I appreciate your time," Alfred said. "I know how busy you are and how frustrating it must be for you to listen to me."

"Not at all," Brian said.

"I believe in God," Alfred said. "I believe He will help me."

"You're right about that. Your faith will keep you strong, no matter what troubles you."

Alfred smiled shyly.

"I've got to get to work now," he announced, getting up. "I'm a bit late already."

"See you next week?" Brian asked.

"Definitely," Alfred said, heading out the front door of the rectory.

As he left, Joan Robertson entered. She had been a parishioner for years. She was sixty-five, but looked eighty. Well dressed, neat, respectable, she followed Brian into the rectory office and sat down. He sat beside her and listened.

"It is so difficult, Father. I've always gone to church. I've gone to church here for forty years. I've known them all, all the priests and sisters who ever worked here. I've prayed. I still pray for the strength to get through," she said, wringing her hands.

"What is it, Joan?" Brian asked. "Tell me."

"My sister's husband died a few weeks ago and she is much older than I am and she is very nervous. She expects me to take care of her. Lord, how can I do that when I'm all alone myself, with two daughters to worry about, one who lives with me and one who's unhappily married."

Brian recalled that her husband had died several years ago. She had some income—his pension, her Social Security —and a comfortable apartment in the parish, but that wasn't enough to make her happy. It never was.

"I don't have a man to turn to, Father. That's why I'm

here. My husband passed away. You know that. He would be away on business for five or six months at a time and my daughter, the one who's married, felt that he was not a loving father and when he came home and found out that she felt that way, he couldn't understand. That's what he did for a living, you know, what else could he do? Well, she was a smart kid in high school, but she tried to take pills to kill herself. I didn't know what to think. It was terrible. Then she went off and got married, but that didn't work out, and then she got married again and he beats her up and now she's drinking too much.

"I said to her, 'Drink milk,' and I asked her if she had milk in the house and she said she did but that she just poured Scotch into it. Oh, Father, I have high blood pressure and I'm not well and I'm at the end of my rope. I pray to God every night for the strength to go on, but I am so tired of all this. It is more than one person can handle. I mean that."

She continued wringing her hands, alternately dabbing at her red nose with a tissue. Brian did not interrupt her.

"God, she had the whole world ahead of her. She could have had it all. But she had this trouble about her father and then the pills and now drink. Father, I can't decide what to do. I can't do it all. I can't take care of my sick sister and worry about my daughter."

Her face was getting redder. Blotches appeared on her arms. She did not pause.

"You're the only man I can turn to, Father. My husband is dead and I don't have any sons. I have to turn to you for help, Father, because I don't know what to do and I don't know how much longer I can deal with all this. My daughter was beautiful, smart, and did well in everything in school. Then, it all fell apart. Help me, Father, please."

Brian listened sympathetically. Her life was in crisis. Even though she was religious, he realized she didn't need Gospel quotations at this moment in her life.

"It's not easy," he began. "You can't tie up these people

and bring them in for help. Your daughter has to want to be helped. If she does, and if she'll come in to see me, I'll arrange for her to talk to someone who might help her." He had Dan Cherico in mind.

"What about A.A., Father?" the woman asked.

"I don't think that this is just a drinking problem. I think your daughter needs more than that."

"Oh, God," the woman said.

"If she really wants help, we can get it for her. But she has to want it. And follow through."

"Can she call you?"

"Of course. Give her my name and the rectory number and we can make an appointment."

"I pray every night," the woman said. "I pray for strength."

"I'll pray for you, too," Brian said. "Have your daughter call me soon."

"I'll tell her," the woman sighed. "You know, Father, she had every opportunity. She was the star in her school plays. She had a good mind. And she was beautiful. Now, she's just slipping away. Just slipping away."

"I'll do whatever I can," Brian said, escorting her to the door. "Whatever I can."

As the door clicked behind her, Brian sighed deeply. He looked at his watch; it was time for the funeral.

The deceased was Mary Shea, an old Irish woman. The Irish were the people whose traditions he knew best. When an Irishman died, it was like having a relative die. He could comfort them out of his own experience, both as Irishman and priest.

At such funerals he could recite one of his favorite Irish blessings:

May the road rise up to meet you,
May the wind be always at your back,

May the rains fall gently upon your fields,
May the sun shine brightly upon your face,
And until we meet again, may God hold you
In the hollow of His hand.

He recited it to the small group of family and friends who attended. Their names were names out of his own childhood: Shea, O'Reilly, Sullivan. Outside the church after the mass, the mourners clustered; they chatted and laughed. For some, the funeral had been truly reuniting; for others, the sorrow had linked them only in momentary affection.

Brian changed out of his vestments and joined them on the sidewalk in front of the church.

"Father, that was a lovely mass," an attractive, chic young woman said. "I'm Mary Shea's granddaughter, Emily."

"Yes, I remember. I think we met once before," Brian said. "You were younger then, with braces on your teeth."

"That's right," she smiled. "Look at the fruits of the orthodontist's labors."

"Good work," Brian laughed. "Good work."

"You know, my grandmother depended upon this church," she said. "She came to mass every day, if she could, even though she was in her eighties at the end."

Brian thought of his own mother, who would walk through the old neighborhood daily on her way to shopping or visits with friends, and he remembered that she would always stop into the church to pray.

"Yes," he said. "I understand that."

"Meet my dad," the woman said, introducing Brian to a middle-aged, dapper Irishman in a dark green suit.

"Good to meet you, Father. Wonderful mass," the man said.

"You're wearing the green, I see," Brian said, smiling.

"Whenever possible," the man said happily.

The funeral procession was forming in the street: the hearse, then a string of cars carrying mourners. Brian got into his car and followed the hearse for the twenty-minute ride from Incarnation to Calvary Cemetery in Queens, one of the largest cemeteries in the world. Graves were placed side by side for acres, with little open space.

At Calvary the pallbearers removed the flowers from the hearse; the gravediggers took out the coffin and placed it on supports over the grave. A disinterested jogger raced by without pausing. In the sunlight the gravestones gleamed: Donovan, Flanagan, Sheehan, Caruso, Kelly, O'Leary, Lupo. Each mourner picked up a flower and placed it on the casket.

Brian's voice boomed out, underlined by the steady hum of street traffic. "Our Lord, Jesus Christ, conquered death . . . comfort us in our sorrow—give our sister eternal life." He recited an Our Father.

After it was over, he lingered briefly to say good-bye to the mourners. The casket remained aboveground; in most Catholic funerals it wasn't lowered during the ceremony, unless requested by the family.

One of the mourners had a familiar face; Brian recognized him as a former parishioner.

"Tommy Warren," Brian said. "It's good to see you again. Where have you been?"

Warren was tall, muscular, and well dressed. "We moved, Father. We had to. My wife got mugged. Not badly, but she was scared," he told Brian. "So after all those years up there, we moved to New Jersey. Believe me, Father, we didn't want to go."

"I understand," Brian said. He had heard the story before, this urban lament—the wish to do better, to have a better home, a response to fears both founded and unfounded, driving people out of the city. There were reasons to stay, as he chose to do, as others did—to keep the neighborhood alive. But, for some, it was not possible. They wanted to be "safe." He never felt unsafe in Incarnation parish, but he could understand those like his own sisters and brother who chose to abandon the frustrations of life in New York City.

Warren moved on to his car.

Mary Shea's middle-aged daughter walked up to Brian. "Thanks, Father," she said, trying to put an envelope with money in it into Brian's hand.

"No need for that," he said, "really."

The mourners returned to their cars and drove off. So did Brian, steering past the rows of graves toward the exit.

There's so little one has to do as a priest at a funeral to make it a good experience for the mourners. The mass itself is simple and effective, so people respond to it. The most frustrating funeral is when there is no response, no grief, when they're angry about taking a day off from work to be there. I wonder what happens to the love, the caring, at times like that.

He directed his car through heavy traffic, back to the rectory.

13

Sonia was back to see Brian again. She had brought three of her six children; they played loudly while she and Brian talked in the rectory office. Brian noticed that her hair had been washed and her nails were newly polished. She allowed a sandal to fall to the floor and moved her toes seductively.

"How are things going?" Brian asked, peering at her leg.

"Right now, it's better," she said, "but not really good."

They talked for an hour, about how Sonia could deal with her errant husband. Brian reminded her that Dan Cherico was available to talk with her. She was thinking about it, she told Brian.

As she left, he could see the outline of her breasts challenging the confinement of her T-shirt. He dismissed a fleeting lascivious thought.

Brian was not devoid of interest in women. He enjoyed their company and was at ease with them. He rarely failed to peer at attractive women he passed on the street. But his admiration for them was limited, by choice. He had taken the vow of celibacy and he had not, as an act of convenience, reinterpreted it. Yet, he refused to deny his heterosexuality.

He was aware of the chatter about priests and sex. He had heard that the priesthood was a safe refuge for homosexuals, for the sexually naïve, for men who feared sex, involvement, and intimacy. He did not accept that view.

It was a subject that he and Dan Cherico talked about. When Dan arrived at the rectory later that day, Brian mentioned that he had seen Sonia.

"Did she try to seduce you?" Dan asked, laughing.

"Not exactly," Brian said. "And apparently she doesn't want to seduce you, either. She's thinking about calling you for help."

"But she hasn't called yet."

"Right. And maybe she never will," Brian said.

"Maybe she thinks that priests are sexually naïve."

"Well, we're not."

"I know that. You don't have to convince me." Dan smiled.

"Seriously, I really don't think there's a quality of sexual naïveté among priests. No, not among the ones I know best. Some of the older priests, maybe. And I don't think that violations of celibacy are rampant."

"We know a few cases, don't we?"

"Yes, a few. But not that many. And I don't think that the priesthood is filled with gays, either. Not in my experience. I've looked at our attitudes toward sex. I've read books in the field. How can I talk to people with sexual problems if I don't know what they're talking about?"

"Absolutely right," Dan said. "And in this parish, there's a lot of open behavior with sexual connotations."

"That's true," Brian said. "There's freer expression among Hispanics. It's expected of everyone. Hugging. Kissing. Saying to someone that you could be attracted to that person. You can kid around to almost any extent and they are delighted."

"But if you actually started to go after one of the women . . ." Dan began.

"She would be ready to be carried away on a stretcher," Brian completed. "I can even say to women in the parish that the one thing I need is a woman. They laugh. Remember that Fellini movie where the guy climbs a tree and keeps yelling, 'I want a woman'? Well, I stood at the top of the staircase in the rectory one day, yelling like that, and the women were all laughing. In other cultures, people might think that I was stepping over the line, but I don't think so. I think it's a good way for me to handle it."

"But there are some women who set out to compromise a priest. Right?" Dan said, stroking his beard.

"Sure, some women do try to either trap the priest or compromise him. Nuns have mentioned to me that it's the same thing with them, in their relationships with men. Some people say about us, 'They've never even had a sexual thought.' Those same people are intrigued by the fact that it can't possibly be true. It's a challenge."

"But you don't permit yourself to be challenged that way, do you?"

"No. I don't allow myself to be in a situation that would lead to not being celibate. Don't play with it, I say. Don't taunt it. Don't hold the rope halfway out the window. Just say to yourself, I have willed this, this is the way I envision my life.

"After all, I have chosen to be celibate. Ten years ago, if I could have chosen to be a priest and to be married, I'm not sure I would have. Speaking about it from where I am now, if the Pope said tomorrow, you could get married if you want to, I wouldn't see my life changing. I wouldn't act differently."

"I seem to remember that there were a couple of women you were attracted to when we were in the seminary," Dan recalled.

"Yes, there were one or two special women in my life then, but that was before I'd taken the vow. One of them was not very intense at all. The other was a little bit so, but not that much, not overwhelmingly. It just seemed to me, then, that I could marry someone like her. It was possible then. But I haven't had a moment as intense since then. Before ordination, I suppose I had the conventional view—getting married, having a family, settling down. I'm more sophisticated now. You can have a relationship with a girl that doesn't involve having a family. On the other hand, you can get married and be much more spiritual and much more moral than a lot of priests who are celibate."

"I know that. But I'm not ready to get married," Dan said with a laugh.

"Your father keeps telling you to get married and get out of his house, doesn't he?" Brian joked.

Dan smiled. "I like it there, at home."

The lunch buzzer sounded, and Brian and Dan moved on to the dining room. Tom Leonard was at his seat. Jack Barry came rushing in, along with Ken Smith, who had taken a day off from work.

"We were talking about sex," Dan announced.

Tom looked at Dan and smiled. There was a spontaneous, perceptive quality about Dan that inspired good conversation at the table, and Tom appreciated that.

"I was saying that I didn't have any trouble being celibate." Brian smiled, anticipating a barbed comment from Jack. Ken spoke before Jack could make it.

"I believe very solidly in celibacy," Ken said seriously. "It's one of the signs of the kingdom that is to come. I don't believe that everyone who is ordained to priesthood is called to celibacy. I do believe that married men should be ordained priests."

"They are," Dan pointed out.

"I know that. We have thousands of married men who

are ordained Catholic priests today," Ken noted. "And we've always had them. There are several rites with the tradition of married clergy—Ukranian, Ruthenian. And since World War II, all married Protestant ministers who have become Catholics—and there have been scores of them—and who wish to become priests are ordained. But they must work in Germany. There are many of them there."

"Brian and I were talking about the cliché that if you are a celibate, you can't understand sex," Dan said.

"Foolish," Ken said. "I know, speaking for myself, that I am flexible in regard to a person who's having a sexual problem. I don't condone behavior, but I understand the humanity of it. The difficulty, the temptation.

"Let's take the matter of masturbation," he continued. "Someone comes to me to talk about it. I say, 'Well, if you didn't have the problem, we'd send you to a doctor.' The person laughs and feels at ease.

"All this talk about sex these days. Yes, we have to understand it, when our parishioners have their sexual problems. But let's not forget something important. We must forgive. The Eucharist is a forgiving sacrament. Confession is a forgiving sacrament. Communion is a forgiving sacrament. What we call mortal sin—completely turning your back to God—if you haven't done that, stop worrying, for God's sake."

They passed the platters around. A huge mound of scrambled eggs, surrounded by bacon and Italian sausages, bread and butter, salad.

"You know what I think?" Jack said. "It would probably be a very good thing to forget about celibacy, a very good thing. You know what? Don't think the doors would be deluged with a crowd running to find somebody, either. On the other hand, when there's a real happy marriage, imagine the depression when one of the partners dies. That's real loneliness, too. But in my opinion, most priests could handle sexual freedom. Some would marry, certainly, if they could. Maybe more than once. But marriage is no piece of cake, either, you know."

"I feel that there will be married clergy," Tom said. "I think they will be married first, then clergy, not clergy who will then get married. Traditionally, in the orthodox churches, you can get married and then become a priest, but you can't marry after you become a priest. I think that strong tradition will persist, so the Church of Rome might allow married men to seek priesthood."

Most of the food was gone, consumed by hungry priests. Dan ate delicately; he was on a diet. He had a peach and a pear and a Tab.

The secretary stood in the doorway. "A call for you, Father O'Connor," she said.

"Right," Brian said, and got up and left the room.

"Why the talk about sex, today?" Tom asked.

"No special reason," Dan said.

"I don't worry about Brian," Tom said. "I just wondered."

"Well, the truth is, I suppose, that he's been challenged over the years. There have been several women who have thrown themselves at him. I think he's honest enough to admit that he was tempted. That's healthy. Not to admit it is crazy. He has told me that he has never acted upon it. I believe him. If he never said, 'I feel like getting laid,' I think there would be something very wrong. What he's really saying is 'I want an escape.' And he gets that in travel, movies, dining out."

"Someone here to see you." The secretary had appeared again, for Tom.

"On my way," Tom said, getting up. The others joined him in filing out of the dining room.

14

Brian returned to the seminary at least once a week; it was just a few minutes from Incarnation by car. When he went back to swim in its pool or bake in its steam room, he went directly to the gym and came back directly, without pausing to stroll through the seminary itself. He felt little nostalgia for the place.

On one hot August morning, when there wasn't pressing business at the rectory, he decided to drive up to the seminary for a more leisurely visit. The place would be quiet, with few summer residents, and he could attempt to revive his feelings about it.

As he drove through the gate of St. Joseph's in the Dunwoodie section of Yonkers, he spotted the familiar statue of Christ he had passed so many times before. He remembered that in the turmoil of the late 1960s, it was not unusual to see it draped with a handwritten sign that read "Get Out of Vietnam."

He parked the car and entered the main building. It was an impressive place, dark, built of stone from a quarry on the property, with an abundance of marble, mosaic tile floors, wood panels, and statues. He walked slowly through the main floor, pausing at a figure of a saint, noting that it had been a source of great amusement in his time there to point out that it had two right feet.

He entered the chapel and stared up at the domed ceiling, then all around at the stained glass, the main aisle with seats facing in, the immense pipe organ in the loft, the large paintings behind the altar and on the dome itself. He walked into the cloister with its garden, tucked within one wing, created to encourage meditation and prayer.

In the main hall, he met a classmate he hadn't seen in months; they exchanged greetings. The classmate, like Brian, drove to the seminary occasionally to use its swimming pool. He joined Brian for his nostalgic tour of the building.

There were statues everywhere. "When Spellman became Archbishop of New York, he wanted the statues removed from St. Patrick's and brought here," Brian recalled. "The rector of the cathedral at the time told Spellman, 'Over my dead body you will.' The poor rector died not long after that—he's buried under the altar at St. Patrick's, as is Spellman—and the statues were shipped here. Not the best art."

As they walked through the halls, peering into familiar classrooms and student rooms, Brian wondered rhetorically: "How did it go from being a place for scholarship to a place for the training of anti-intellectuals?" He resented the low academic quality and what he felt to be the inadequate compassion and skill of the teachers in his time.

They passed the rare-book room, donated by Major (Edward J.) Bowes of radio fame; Brian noticed peeling paint on the walls. "In our time, at least the place was sparkling. They never would have let it go like this. And in those days the classes would have forty students. Today they have five." The shortage of priests was acute; young men were not tempted to attend the seminary any longer. They had other alternatives for service and status.

They entered a parlor, studded with portraits of popes. Brian sat down in a frayed chair, while his classmate stood nearby, staring at the paintings.

"I didn't like those years," Brian said. "The rules. But I never associated that feeling with the place itself, just the people. During the first two years, remember, we weren't allowed to use the elevator. You could use the phone only on Wednesday morning. No television or radios in the rooms."

"I remember," the classmate said.

"We'd get up at five-thirty. And you weren't allowed to speak after eight at night. The only time off was on Wednesday afternoon. I think I got by just by taking every course I could take. One semester I took twenty-eight credits, including a course on sign language for the deaf. I took that on Saturday mornings."

The classmate didn't respond.

"You haven't said a word," Brian noted.

"You've said it for me," the classmate said, smiling. "But I do remember that there was a full-time psychologist on duty for group sessions and individual counseling. He kept busy."

"He sure did," Brian said.

"I've got to be going," the classmate said. "Enjoy your visit."

Brian proceeded alone through the stately building. The halls were empty and dark. He encountered an old priest. Brian recognized him: the man had retired, but lived at the seminary.

"How are you?" Brian asked.

"I'm ninety-three," the old priest said, "and you have to say that you don't believe it."

The man had once befriended a destitute Mexican priest,

stranded in New York. That priest had become a cardinal; he had named the New York priest a "canon," an honorary title.

Now the retired priest had to fend for himself. He got a pension, but out of it he had to pay for his room and board. Diocesan priests had to take care of themselves after seventy-five; order priests were more fortunate—they could be taken in and cared for in their order houses.

The canon stared into space. "I feel alone in this immense building," he told Brian. "Last week I got sick and there's nobody here to give you a pill. The professors have their own interests, their own worries. But I'm keeping up now. No aches, no ailments."

Brian wondered whether anyone would know if the old man got sick, badly sick. He wished him good luck and continued his stroll.

He found a student room unlocked and went in. Bed, desk, desk chair, lounge chair, sink, and closet. Shutters to darken the room. He recalled feeling claustrophobic in his own room here. Not because of the room itself, but because he felt trapped, unable to release the tension.

He entered a classroom. Behind the raised platform there was a painting of Christ being cared for after the Crucifixion. Brian and his classmates had called it "Safe at Home."

He went outside, out of the main building, past a convent no longer used to house nuns. They were Carmelite nuns in his time, dedicated to caring for the sick and the infirm. Appropriate in those days, as Brian recalled.

The building had a checkered history. In the 1920s the charge had been made—and denied—that a tunnel connecting the convent to the main building had encouraged trysts between nuns and priests. The building had been renovated recently to house college students planning to attend the seminary after graduation. Brian stared at it, then kept moving.

He passed an old building now housing computers for the diocese. He glanced up at a high tower beside the diocese's TV station, which transmitted programs to Catholic schools.

That had been known in Brian's time as "Spellman's phallic symbol." One of his classmates had insisted that Spellman put it up to make them all sterile.

He walked by the gym and the tennis and handball courts, across a large lawn speckled with burned-out grass. Three hundred people used to take the loop around the whole place after dinner. *We used to cut the grass, take care of the place. When they got fewer students, they lost a work force, too. So the grass is dying out. They really need a brain trust to save this place.*

He arrived at the parking lot, stood beside his car, and looked back at the seminary. He was silent for several minutes.

So few students in this massive place now. Where will the new priests come from?

When Brian got back to the rectory, he found Dan Cherico in his rooms, rearranging furniture, throwing out useless old mail that Brian had tossed around.

"Where were you?" Dan asked.

"At the sem," Brian replied.

"Why, why, why?" Dan protested.

They talked about the seminary, Brian in his favorite rocking chair, Dan sprawled on the couch.

Despite what both remembered of the rigors of the seminary, the severity of its rules, the limited contact with the outside world, Brian had sustained his faith and had not buckled under the pressure. Others had—more than 70 percent of Brian's class had dropped out, Dan among them.

"The thwarting of the personality is inevitable in a seminary structure," Dan said, patting his beard, generating energy for one of his frequent assaults on the institution. "For example, historically in the seminary people could not drink. So rather than teaching someone how to drink, they did not permit drinking. A fellow gets ordained, lives on his own in a rectory, maybe with one or two other guys, and it becomes much easier to drink. In the seminary you couldn't date or have any real contact with women, either."

"If they caught you, they would throw you out," Brian said. "If it were reported that someone was seen at a dance, or obviously on a date, in our time he would have been expelled."

"Right. We saw people getting booted out for that just before ordination," Dan added. He got up and began to pace. "The booze and the babes are the clearest to see. But what about other maladies? Some people have caustic personalities, or are vicious, or lazy. That kind of thing was tolerated in the seminary. But it's not going to be tolerated in a parish."

"That's very true," Brian said. "What the seminary tried to do was simulate its own version of reality, which did not work. You were told that you had to get up at five-thirty in the morning because as a priest you would have to get up for the seven o'clock mass. The idea of getting up at five-thirty and praying because of the intensity of your belief was never a factor. They just didn't prepare you for what you would need later—not just external discipline, but your spiritual strength. The ones who got through best were the ones who were superficial guys, who responded to the rules but were not necessarily very religious. And some of us who found the rules meaningless were the ones who now do very well in the parishes."

"A lot of good people were weeded out," Dan said. "I would say I could name dozens off the top of my head."

"You don't have much on the top of your head," Brian interrupted, smiling.

"This is a perfect tonsure," Dan snapped, patting the

bald spot atop his head. "Let's not talk about it. Remember that fellow George who had a keen interest in psychology, who had taken some courses in it, but who really had a street-wise sense about counseling, very interested in working with dope addicts?"

"Yes. And runaways and orphans, that type as well," Brian added.

"Right. He worked with prostitutes. He worked with organized crime people. And he had an interest in sex—sexual theory, sexual development. Very quickly the seminary pegged him. They picked him to head the psychology club because it looked good to have student participation in those things. That became a focal point to attack him. They said that his interest in psychology was really detrimental to his priestly or spiritual formation. He got thrown out because he wanted to talk about development. He saw so many of his confreres in the seminary suffering from arrested development with adolescent kinds of personalities. He wanted them to grow. He was very open about it. And although he did all the Mickey Mouse things—got up on time, went to class on time—he didn't believe in any of it. And he said so. So he got thrown out."

"He never found himself after he left the seminary," Brian noted.

"I can remember two other fellows who were in the seminary with us and who didn't stay long," Dan continued. "They were Italians, and their attachment to family was something that the seminary was bent on destroying."

"In a very subtle way. They didn't say they were doing it," Brian pointed out. "They'd say that the Gospel injunction required that you had to leave your father and mother and follow Jesus. The seminary was your community. You belonged to your parish."

"So there they were, in the seminary," Dan said. "They were from upper-middle-class families and both drove sports cars. They came to the seminary with every intention of being priests. They wanted to serve. Once, they got tickets to an off-Broadway play. And one of the leading theologians of the seminary thought that was one of the most disgraceful things he had ever heard. Why would anyone want to go to see such an obscene play. Those two guys just couldn't handle being treated like little children. They lasted about ten days.

"Yes, a goodly number of guys were thrown out of Dunwoodie," Dan continued. "Very fine people, who would not give up so easily. They went on to other seminaries in other dioceses, where the rules were less important than the faith. Seminaries differ, after all, the way the archbishops differ. But at Dunwoodie, the faculty gave you the notion that if you couldn't be a priest in New York and you went someplace else, you would be inferior. Nonsensical. A lot of people who were thrown out of Dunwoodie went on to become good priests."

It was almost lunchtime. Brian was getting hungry. He got up, went to the small bar, and popped open a can of Tab. He returned to his rocking chair.

"Part of what we were trained for we did not meet in the reality of the parish," Brian said.

"The realities of a parish can destroy your spirit if you're not ready for them," Dan offered.

"Definitely. All of a sudden you're in face-to-face contact with your parishioners. Human contact. A lot of guys who get through the seminary aren't prepared for that."

"You were ready," Dan said.

"Not really. But I do remember that last year in the sem happily. Going out to a parish and serving as a minister."

He had spent his final year at the seminary as a deacon at Blessed Sacrament parish on the West Side of Manhattan. Bustling and with a mixed population, the parish provided the experience he needed, the transition that would make his assignment to Incarnation easier. But first came ordination.

"Ordination was wonderful," Brian said. "The ceremony itself, with the Cardinal there. The mass can be long and tedious, but I remember the bishop laying hands on us, calling the Spirit down on us. Walking into the sanctuary, kneeling down. I felt, in some way I can't quite describe, transformed. I was a new person."

"And a new priest," Dan said with a smile.

"I was very nervous. I remember that," Brian said. "Nervous and excited and anxious. Saturday morning at St. Patrick's. All our families and friends were there. And they would come to us to receive our first blessing as priests, a very special thing.

"You know, you're together as a group in the seminary. You're together as a class on retreat. You're together as a class at ordination. Then, all of a sudden, each man is on his own. You have your own mass in your own parish the next day—in your home parish, where you were raised. Then, three or four weeks later, you're on your first assignment."

"And here you are. The life of Brian," Dan said.

The buzzer sounded; lunch was ready. Brian bounded up and went down the two flights of stairs to the dining room. Dan took the elevator.

It was a happy time. The woman, Sheila Mack, had come to the rectory to arrange the baptism of her newborn son, Jeremy. Trim, young, and bright, she ran her fingers through her long brown hair and told Brian how delighted she was to have a new life as a mother.

"I thought about not having a child, not right now anyway," she said. "But then I realized how our lives—my husband's and mine—would be better with one."

Brian was refreshed by her opinion.

"We're going to have a party to celebrate, with as many of our relatives as we can assemble and with Jeremy as the guest of honor," she said. "But first tell me what I have to know about baptism."

"When I was baptized," Brian began, "I was baptized according to the rite the Church has used for hundreds and hundreds of years, the rite for the baptism of adults. There was no child baptism until around the year 315 or 320, and then, in those early days of the Church, it was usually done in a very perfunctory way."

"I didn't know that," Sheila said.

"It's true. But now the emphasis is much more on the community celebration. Many parents feel that baptism is to take away original sin, from the doctrine that we're born in a world where, without Jesus, we would be doomed, we would not be saved. At the Vatican Council the emphasis was placed on becoming a member of the Church and receiving the spirit of God.

"Traditionally, a child's baptism is a month after birth. A parent brings the child, after the parents and godparents have gone through a series of conferences—and then you have the baptism. There is emphasis now on the presence of the parents at the baptism."

"Terrific," Sheila said. "We want it to be one of the high points of our life."

"It can be. Baptism, after all, is the foundation of the other sacraments. You cannot receive the others unless you've been baptized. It is the entrance into the Church, the receiving of the Holy Spirit."

"I remember that from school," Sheila said.

"Good. You were paying attention," Brian said, laughing.

They picked a date for the baptism.

"Do come to our party afterward, if you can," Sheila said.

"I'll try, but this is a busy life. I don't get to many parties," Brian said. It was true. His work prevented him from attending many celebrations, even when he had officiated at the reason for the celebration.

After Sheila left, Brian sat in the office and remembered a day when another young mother, one of the neighborhood radicals, showed up to arrange for the baptism of her new son. Brian had asked her various prebaptism questions, explained the sacrament, then asked, "What do you plan to name the child?"

"Yashica," she said.

"Yashica?" Brian asked.

"Yes."

"Where did you find that name?" Brian asked.

"I'm naming him after my brother's camera," she said solemnly.

"Your brother's camera?"

"Yes."

"I see," Brian said. "It's good that he didn't have a Hasselblad."

The memory delighted Brian. People were often wonderfully and eccentrically naïve. The recollection stirred another.

A woman wanted to name her son Stalin. Brian asked her if she knew who Stalin was and she said she didn't, but her husband had read a lot of history books and he loved Stalin.

"Stalin was a Russian who ordered the murder of millions of people, probably more than the Nazis murdered," he told her.

"I never heard about that," she said. "He's a hero to my husband."

Brian refused to baptize the child Stalin. She went home and discussed it with her husband, then came back to Brian.

"We decided to name him Joseph," she said.

Brian went ahead with the baptism.

He got up and moved toward the sacristy at the rear of the church to put on his vestments. It was time for a baptism.

This was a moment of spiritual rebirth, a uniting with Christ, but Brendan William Duffy was not aware of any of that. The one-month-old boy attempted to sleep through it all on this warm day in August.

Brendan's parents eyed him proudly. His father, William

Duffy, was a young corporate executive. His mother, Patricia Gilhooly Duffy, was a resident in surgery at Columbia-Presbyterian. They attended mass at Incarnation regularly.

When Brian entered the church to begin, Brendan was asleep in his godmother's arms. Brian, dressed in white with a long white stole with embroidered red crosses, stepped toward the front pews and spoke.

A small group of family and friends was sitting in the first two pews. Everyone was smiling, including Brian.

"What name do you give your child?" Brian asked.

"Brendan William Duffy," the parents responded.

Brian continued: "You have asked to have your child baptized. In doing so, you are accepting the responsibility of training him in the practice of the faith. It will be your duty to bring him up to keep God's commandments as Christ taught us, by loving God and our neighbors. Do you clearly understand what you are undertaking?"

"We do," the parents intoned.

Brian traced the sign of the cross on the baby's forehead. The godmother, holding Brendan, looked ecstatic.

"My dear brothers and sisters, let us ask our Lord Jesus Christ to look lovingly on this child who is to be baptized, on his parents and godparents, and on all the baptized."

Brendan stirred a bit, but Brian went on without pausing, speaking of the birth of God's spirit in Brendan. "Life isn't what we can feel or see," he said. "It is motivation—love, charity, forgiveness—or life is meaningless. We can't touch the spirit of God, but we know it is there."

Brian prayed for the child, and those present chanted, "Lord, hear our prayer." He invoked the saints, listing them to the accompanying chant of "pray for us."

The family moved forward from the pews to the baptistry located beside the main altar. A few people were praying in the far reaches of the church; one man approached to watch the baptism.

"My dear brothers and sisters, we now ask God to give this child new life in abundance through water and the Holy Spirit," Brian intoned. The baby, in his little white gown, remained asleep in his godmother's arms. Brian poured water from a gold pitcher into the marble font.

"Dear parents and godparents: You have come here to present this child for baptism. By water and the Holy Spirit he is to receive the gift of new life from God, who is Love. On your part, you must make it your constant care to bring him up in the practice of the faith. See that the divine life which God gives him is kept safe from the poison of sin, to grow always stronger in his heart.

"If your faith makes you ready to accept this responsibility, renew now the vows of your own baptism. Reject sin; profess your faith in Christ Jesus. This is the faith of the Church. This is the faith in which this child is about to be baptized."

Brian questioned the parents and godparents. Did they reject Satan? Yes. And his works? And his empty promises? And sin? And the glamour of evil? Yes, to all. "Do you believe in God . . . in Jesus? In the Holy Spirit, the Holy Catholic Church, the communion of saints, the forgiveness of sins, the resurrection of the body, and life everlasting?"

The voices echoed throughout the church: "I do."

The godmother held the baby; the mother took his hand. Brian gently poured water on the baby's head. The baby stuck out his tongue, then went back to sleep. Brian made the sign of the cross with oil on the baby's forehead. The baby squealed, tried to open his heavy-lidded eyes, then dropped back into sleep.

Brian passed a lighted candle among those present; when it had made its round, Brian handed it to Brendan's father to keep. Brian's crucial words hung in the air: "I baptize you in the name of the Father, and of the Son, and of the Holy Spirit."

Brian led the family and friends in a recitation of the Our Father. Then, placing his hand first on the mother's head, then on the father's, he prayed that "they may be the best of teachers." When it was over, Brian turned to Brendan, still asleep, and said, "There, that wasn't too hard, was it?"

He handed the baptismal certificate to the father. Flash-bulbs popped around them, relatives preserving the moment. Brian held Brendan, who yawned widely as the camera carriers took more photos. As Brian chatted, the baby awoke, crying. It was time to go.

Brian went to the sacristy to remove his vestments, then joined the family outside the church.

"That was wonderful," Brendan's mother said to Brian.

"It is a special moment, even for us," he said, "especially when the parents are involved."

"Aren't they always involved?" she asked.

"Now they are, yes. But in the old days, the priest did it all. The parents weren't involved, only the godparents. The mother stayed home and cooked for the party afterward and the father sat in the car and smoked. Fortunately, all that changed eight or nine years ago. I like it this way, with the water, oil, and white dress for Christian dignity, the active participation of the parents in the ceremony, and the presentation of the candle as a lasting reminder of the occasion."

"So do we," she said.

Brendan, in his father's arms, cried out.

"He's saying he wants to go to the party," Brian said, smiling.

"Well, off we go, then," the mother said.

They disappeared down St. Nicholas Avenue, and Brian headed into the rectory. He extracted an envelope that the father had given him. It contained a twenty-dollar donation to the Church and twenty-five dollars for Brian. Most parents couldn't afford to give that much to the Church, and hardly ever was there anything for him. He was glad to get it. It would buy him a dinner out and admission to a movie, or help meet one of the payments on his car.

He went back to his rooms in the rectory. He had been working on a prayer for use at mass on the Feast of the Assumption of Mary, and he reread it. He liked it:

". . . That Christians may be known more for honest, humble service than for adherence to power or prestige, let us pray to the Lord. . . . That we, the parishioners of Incarnation, will do all in our power to make this a better community, let us pray to the Lord. . . ."

A few days later Brian was off to another and quite different baptism. He headed toward Columbia-Presbyterian Hospital. A young mother had asked him to baptize her premature baby.

He found her in a maternity ward, recognizing and immediately assessing the situation. Diane Corrigan was unmarried, sixteen, a sweet, innocent girl he remembered from her time at the Incarnation school. She was flanked by her mother and by the mother of the boy who had fathered the child. The girl's mother was neatly dressed, fashionable, in her late thirties. The boy's mother, her hair piled high in rollers, sat on an adjoining bed and wept.

Diane seemed numb.

"It's rough to have a baby at your age," Brian said. He knew the Church's stand on artificial birth-control methods, but he was not in favor of unwanted pregnancies.

"I'm sixteen," Diane whispered.

"Did you plan it?" Brian asked.

"No, it just happened."

The child was there, he thought, and that had to be dealt with. He discussed the baptism with Diane, and she agreed to postpone it until the baby was older and healthier; it weighed only two pounds. But Diane wanted Brian to say a prayer for her new son. He agreed.

With the girl and her mother, he went to the neonatal intensive-care unit. Diane, in a long pink robe that contrasted with her long, straight, bright red hair, sat in a wheelchair pushed by her mother. Brian walked alongside.

The baby was smaller than most of those in the busy unit: he was breathing with the aid of a respirator, and his mouth opened and closed to the rhythms of the machine. Brian peered in; his shadow almost put the baby in total shade. He said a prayer for the child's well-being. When he was done, Diane's mother attempted to hand him an envelope with money in it. He refused persistently as she followed him around with it.

"Are you going to marry him?" he asked Diane as they went back to the ward.

"No," she said sternly.

"That's my advice," Brian said. He knew the boy. "Wait for two or three years. See how it goes."

"I intend to," she said.

He held her hand and touched her head. She returned to her room with her mother, who tucked her into bed and came out into the hall to talk to Brian before he left.

"Well, how's that for a problem?" the mother sighed.

"Everything gets solved, somehow," Brian said. "But I know what you mean. Did she know anything about birth control?"

"No," the mother said. "And the Church doesn't want us to use it."

"Yes, I know," Brian said. "I know what the Pope said. And yet there's a whole understanding about conscience that supersedes anything that is a rule."

"Is that what you tell the kids?" she asked.

"I've been known to raise it, yes. It's one of the elements of Christian faith—recognizing responsibility and living with the consequences of our actions. I don't advise kids to have sexual relations. I say no to that. But if a girl tells me that she can't help having them, or she's going to have them no matter what, that's the reality of it. Then I am tempted to mention birth control—as the lesser evil."

"What about abortion?" the mother asked.

"It's the worst of the two evils, of course," Brian said. "It's seriously wrong. Yet when a girl comes to see me after she's had one, I'm torn. Do I make her feel guilty by being very doctrinaire about it? And then urge her to work toward forgiveness? Or do I make it easier by saying that we've all committed sins? It's tough."

"They grow up so quickly these days," the mother said with a sigh.

"Yes, they do. Girls at twelve or thirteen already see themselves as potential mothers. It's part of the Hispanic culture. You're Irish, and so am I, but this is a rapidly mixing community. The kids' peer group will say, you're lucky because you were able to have a child before we did. How do you deal with that?"

"I don't know, I don't know," the mother said, dabbing the corner of her eye with a handkerchief.

"It will all work out, somehow. It does," Brian said. "You'll help her take care of the baby because you're a good mother and you know how. Diane will grow up more rapidly, and then she'll take care of her own child. And you'll have your life again."

"I hope so."

"You will," Brian stressed. "But between now and then, if you need any help from me, let me know."

"Thank you, Father," the mother said. She turned to go back to her daughter's bedside. Brian headed out of the hospital.

16

On a Monday in August Brian celebrated the 9 A.M. mass and, after an abbreviated breakfast, drove to Beth Israel Hospital on the Lower East Side. One of his parishioners had told him that it would be good if he would visit Maria Flores, who was a member of a charismatic renewal group at the church. According to his source, Maria's condition was *grave*, a Spanish word that Brian knew could mean anything from slightly injured to terminal.

He found Maria in a four-bed room. He looked at the three other women and concluded that they would not leave the hospital alive. It troubled him. Maria, in her late twenties, was in the fetal position, but awake. She was quite short and plump, with a pleasant round face and large brown eyes. She was wearing a new pink-and-white quilted robe, and there were red roses on the table at her bedside. She smiled at Brian.

"I bring you greetings from all your friends in the parish," he said to her in Spanish.

"Thank them for me," she replied, smiling.

"When did you come in here?" he asked.

"A few days ago."

"Have you been sick before?" Brian asked. He didn't know her medical history.

"Yes," she said. "I had cancer of the womb and I got chemotherapy and it was taken care of."

What did she mean, "taken care of"?

"That was two years ago," she continued. "Then, a doctor came to my house and gave me an injection and it made me sick and dizzy, so now I came back to the hospital."

"Did they tell you what you have?" Brian asked. He pulled up a chair and sat down beside her. He knew the answer to his question, but he would not introduce the subject, would not say the word. His knowledge of thanatology had given him a keen perception of the dying, what they wanted to hear, what could be said to them safely.

"No. But I still get dizzy," she replied. "As soon as they find out about the dizziness, I'll go home."

There was a husband and a six-year-old daughter at home, Brian knew. He felt depressed, but he did not show it.

They chatted about the church, the parish, their mutual friends. Brian wanted to bring her some cheer; he made her smile simply by encouraging her own good nature.

Brian offered a prayer for her. As he left, she wished him good-bye.

In the corridor Brian searched for her doctor and found a young resident who knew the case. At first the resident chose to be uncooperative, not responding to Brian's questions.

"I'm her parish priest," Brian said firmly. He was not wearing his collar, but was in proper black attire without it.

The doctor seemed annoyed; he was making rounds with a group of other residents and did not want to discuss the case. Brian persisted.

"Is it a panic situation?" Brian asked.

"Panic? No, it's not a panic situation," the resident replied. "But she is terminal."

"Terminal?" Brian asked, his voice rising.

"Yes, terminal. Cancer of the breast that has spread to the bones." The doctor moved on. Brian headed for the elevator; he would take the time to see Maria again.

He returned to the rectory for lunch; the other priests were out, so Brian had his run of the food available. He sampled cold roast beef, salami, and ham, along with bread and salad, Jell-O, cookies, and tea.

After lunch he went to visit an old Irish couple who had lived in the parish for thirty-five years. The man, retired, served as an usher at mass; the woman was sickly and rarely went outside. When Brian arrived, the husband greeted him cheerfully; the woman was waiting for him in the living room. The apartment was spotless, the furniture preserved beneath clear plastic covers.

"How are you doing?" Brian asked her. So many of the people he visited had health problems that at times he felt like a doctor.

"Well, I get very bad attacks of breathing and very bad pains in my chest," she said.

"Angina and emphysema," the husband said. "She's got those nitro pills."

"And my nerves aren't too good, either, staying in the house all the time," she said.

"Maybe you ought to cut out all that Saturday-night dancing," Brian joked.

She cackled. "You know, Father, if you don't get better, you get worse," she said.

They retired to the bedroom, where Brian heard her confession, then returned to the living room for communion.

Brian recited an Our Father with her. After communion, Brian said a blessing: "Bless all who dwell in this house. . . ." He turned to the woman and said, "Feel better.

Use your air-conditioner. Thank God you have one."

"Yes, indeed," the woman said. She told Brian that she could use some household help, a maid and a cook, but she didn't have the money.

"No trouble. Contact the Seventh Day Adventists. They're good people. And cheap. You'll have to pay something, but not much. They're in the phone book. Their social agency has nothing to do with religion, by the way."

The couple thanked Brian for his advice and he headed out into the street, toward the senior citizens' center. He had promised to attend an important board meeting. Most of the board members did not know why it had been called, but Brian did. Tom Schweder was announcing his resignation.

The board members, six women and one man, were patting their brows with handkerchiefs. It was another hot day. Brian opened the meeting by noting that there would be a need to hire a new program director—the previous one had quit—and a bookkeeper to keep track of the center's funds. Then he turned the meeting over to Tom.

"Well, I have to say it," Tom began. "I've taken another job. I'll be working with an organization that supervises a number of senior centers, and I'll be leaving in three weeks." He seemed breathless.

The others responded instantly.

"This place will collapse without you."

"You should have a lot of happiness."

"Oh, no. Not you, too."

"Well, you don't have to keep it a secret," Tom said. "Let me read my letter of resignation, so you'll know how I feel." He began to read—about the six years he had spent at the center, the love and respect he felt for those he had come to know there, how he would never forget the center and its people. He could not get through it. He started to cry.

"Tom, we feel the same way about you," one of the women said. "We hope to get someone with a lot of patience, like you have."

"We're very sad that you're going," Brian said. "But I know there are times when you have to move on."

"You did so much for everyone," said the old Irish woman with a pronounced brogue.

Brian tried to change the subject to the choice of Tom's successor. He and Tom had discussed one candidate, a young man with solid experience at other senior centers; it was their hope that they could convince the board to approve the man. Brian mentioned the candidate's name.

"I know him," a dignified black woman in a wheelchair said. "He's a very helpful and understanding young man."

"With luck, we can get a director on hand soon," Tom said. "To mind the store. I'm going to need your help to get it all done."

An air of forced gaiety prevailed, and Tom picked up on it.

"I'll show up a few times a week," he said, "to check on the renovation."

"And the personnel committee can do the interviewing job," Brian reassured the others.

"How can you tell in an interview if a person has patience?" Sarah Goldstein asked.

"You can tell," Tom said.

"Especially if a person pounds the table and insists that he has patience," Brian joked.

"I'm still shocked," Sarah sighed. "It's the shock of my life. But I'm happy for you, Tom."

"Any other bombs, Tom?" Brian asked.

"Oh, dear," the Irish woman said softly, "I won't sleep tonight."

"I haven't slept in two weeks," Tom said.

"I guess as long as we can make a good transition, without too many hitches, it'll be okay," Sarah said.

"Maybe Tom will come back in five years," Brian suggested.

"Just remember, whoever we get won't be Tom," the black woman instructed.

The meeting adjourned with hugs and kisses for Tom. Brian walked back to the church.

Brian was tired. The optimism that carried him through his long days was constant, but at times it showed signs of wear.

He wanted to sip a cool drink and relax. When he got to the rectory, he discovered that he would have to postpone that respite. There was a woman waiting to see him, a Puerto Rican woman.

They had talked before. She was not attractive: very large in size, overweight, sluggish in manner, a notorious neighborhood gossip. She stopped him on the street constantly, offering bad news about assorted parishioners.

He escorted her into the office. As he sat down, she began.

"I think my husband is having an affair," she said intensely.

"Why do you think that, Conchita?" Brian asked. He was very thirsty; he thought about a glass of lemonade.

"Well, he invited me to have dinner at the apartment of a woman he said he worked with."

"So?"

"I got there and she seemed like a nice woman and we all sat down to dinner."

"Uh-huh."

"She asked him to get the salt and he knew where it was."

"I see. But he *lives* with you, doesn't he?"

"But he's away a lot. He sells ties."

"I know."

"So I don't know where he is half the time. He could be with her."

"What do you think you ought to do about it?"

"I don't know. I haven't worked in years, since before we were married. I'd have to get a job if I asked him to leave. I'd have to take care of the kids. They're old enough to take care of themselves, but I'd have to watch over them, you know. I don't look old enough to have those kids, you know. I still look good."

"Are you sure he's having an affair with that woman?" Brian asked.

"I think so, because of the salt."

"Well, it could have been worse. You could have found his underwear in the bathroom."

Sometimes, when he was very tired, things seemed absurd.

He knew that the woman wouldn't take his advice if he gave it; he had given it before to no avail. She went her own way, being unkind to others in petty ways, flaunting her problems to get attention.

"I didn't mean to be sarcastic," he said. "But you've got to figure out what's wrong and what you might do to correct it all to make your life better. You've got to look at alternatives and choose the one that's best for you and the children."

"I'm an attractive woman," she said, preening. "I don't really need him."

Brian remained expressionless. He needed that lemonade.

"I am," she insisted. Brian remained silent.

"What should I do?"

"Think. Think about it. Weigh the alternatives. We can talk again about it." He had to postpone any advice he might offer. He didn't want to appear to be uncaring, but there were moments when his capacity for good cheer was eroded.

"Okay, I'll think about it and I'll be back to see you again, soon," she said.

"Fine," he said.

She got up and went out the door. Brian went to the kitchen, poured a tall glass of lemonade, and drank it without removing the glass from his lips.

Brian hadn't slept well. He had thought about Maria Flores, the young woman with cancer at Beth Israel. He knew, when he awakened, that he would have to see her again. She had a daughter, and he worried about what would happen to the girl if Maria died. The woman's husband, he had heard, was not preparing himself for her death. It was common; denial was one of the early stages in the grief associated with dying. He drove to see her.

"How are you today?" he asked in Spanish as he entered her room.

"Better," she said. "Better."

"What does that mean?" he asked.

"I asked the doctor when I could go home and he said soon."

"Good, good," Brian said. He touched her arm gently.

"I am feeling much better," she said.

"And you could take your medicine at home. And be more comfortable there."

"Si," she said.

"It's a good idea to go home," Brian said, knowing that it would be better for her to die at home, surrounded by her family and friends, than alone in the hospital. He was not certain that she understood, that she knew she had terminal cancer.

"You know, Father, I always feel better when you visit me," she said. "It is important to have hope that God will help."

"Yes, it is. It's always important to have hope."

"Yes. It is good to see you." She smiled broadly.

"I bring you the love of your friends in the parish," he said. "Alberto and Elba and José and Carlos and Maria Martinez. And others, many others."

"The same from me to them," she said.

In the next bed a woman slept soundly, snoring. Across the room an old woman sat on the edge of her bed, babbling. Brian and Maria sat in silence for a few moments; the smile did not leave her face as she stared at him.

"Do the doctors speak Spanish?" he asked.

"Only one. Not mine."

Brian did not want to introduce the subject of cancer. He knew that terminal patients were justifiably angry at the one who issued the declaration of death. He knew, as well, that if he brought it up and left, her loneliness would be excruciating. He sat, without speaking.

"I need treatment for my bones," she said. "I know that. I have a disease."

"Yes," he said. "What does your doctor say?"

"He says I have lesions. I know what it is. I had cancer of the womb. Now I have more of it. They're afraid to tell me. I've asked five times. No answers. I'm not angry. I know what it is. I'm not afraid."

"You're not?"

"No. I believe in a larger power. I have hope in God, no matter how much time I have. I have cried, but no more. I

146

see others here, the sick ones with cancer. I see them cry. No more. Not me."

"I think that God is intervening in our lives all the time," Brian said. "I'm not even sure that would be a miracle. Things go on and things do happen, and in a lot of it I see God intervening."

"I do, too," she said.

"God did not save humankind in one stroke, where all of a sudden death was eliminated and sin was eliminated, but He did it by sending Jesus, who would share in suffering and who would be the victim of the very things that people were trying to be saved from. Jesus, by dying on the cross, was showing victory over suffering, not by eliminating it but by going through it. He was victorious by rising from the dead."

"Yes, that is true," Maria said.

"We see only a small section of existence in this world, on our planet. A Christian can see beyond all this to something more. You know, all priests have said that we have our Good Fridays, but we also have our Easter Sundays," Brian said.

He sat beside her bed and offered a blessing for her, his hands interlocked in front of him. The woman, again in the fetal position, faced him on her side, her eyes closed, and prayed with him. He touched her head when he was done, paused, leaned over, and kissed her on the cheek.

He said good-bye, and she waved as he left. As he walked toward the elevator, he resolved that she must not die here, but at home with her family, where she would get the love she deserved. He would talk to her friends in the parish about arranging that. While he had heard of people surviving cancer, he did not believe that she would. He knew that God had miraculous power, but he did not believe that she would live.

In the car on the way back to the rectory, he thought about dying and the way it can overwhelm people to the point where they cannot see any hope in the midst of evil. You can't know how good God is unless you know how evil the devil is: that concept—of the personal power of evil called the devil—was cropping up again, he had noticed. There was now a version of the Our Father that altered "deliver us from evil" to "deliver us from the evil one."

I don't believe that the devil implanted that cancer in that poor woman. But I do believe that God can help her—to endure, to defy an early death, even to accept death if that is to be her fate.

Brian drove north on his way to see an old pastor he had been meaning to visit, a man who was living in a home for retired priests in Riverdale.

The retired pastor's story had touched Brian. He was a man of tainted generosity. It was reported that he had squandered the parish funds, more than $800,000 in ten years. He had not been an able manager, but he had been a caring priest. He had given money to parishioners in need. At Thanksgiving he gave away turkeys and one-hundred-dollar checks. He bought hundreds of portable electric heaters with Church funds and gave them away during the coldest days of winter. Eventually, the parish had to turn to the archdiocese for support. Not long after that, the pastor retired.

Brian found the pastor in his room and greeted him. The old man looked up and smiled; he was in a wheelchair.

"How are you?" Brian asked. He was not there to talk, but to listen.

"Reasonably well, considering my age. Seventy-eight," the pastor said. He was gaunt and his white hair had thinned to a few uncombed wisps.

"What I miss," he said to Brian, "is to see other scenes, to meet other people. Here, the priests are in the toddling stage again. Well, I guess the Church marches on. I hear from the underground about what's going on out there. Neighborhoods change. You can't go around at night. I hear that. You know, all my life I was a parish priest. I was thankful to God to be a priest for so long. I've been a priest for fifty-seven years. Some of my classmates have gone to heaven. Some are still around. I say mass every day. I read; I do a lot of reading.

"You probably don't remember this, but there was a time when a priest could walk on the streets in the middle of the night and no one would bother him. Now, if you go on a sick call, you'd better bring the police along.

"I guess parish life is never dull. That's why I did it for so long. A parish priest is a parish priest—wherever you find them. I have no ambition to go anyplace now. I've been everywhere I wanted to go. Ireland. The Holy Land. Canada, a couple of times. I'm content to stay put. Someone said, 'Old age is an achievement.' And I agree."

"I'm looking forward to it, as an achievement," Brian said, smiling. "And I expect you to be around when I get there, so we can share some good stories."

Brian got up and left, patting the man on the shoulder and saying good-bye.

Brian walked down a dark corridor, past a dining room where old priests sat and ate in silence. *Regression. It's back to the seminary for them. Dark halls. Traditional. And devastating. It's wrong to put old people together like that. Even if young priests just came up to eat with them, to link them to the outside world, that would be better.*

Fall

"No minister can save anyone. He can only offer himself as a guide to fearful people."

FATHER HENRI H. M. NOUWEN
The Wounded Healer

"Does this affirmation of what is Catholic in time and space, depth and breadth, mean that you have to accept more or less *everything* that has been officially taught, ordered and observed in the course of twenty centuries?"

HANS KÜNG
in *The New York Times*

18

As September began, Hurricane David devastated the Caribbean, became a tropical storm, and headed up the Atlantic coast to New York. It rained heavily and cooled the air. Walking along the puddled streets, Brian stepped into a sidewalk pothole and twisted his ankle; his limp inspired sympathetic comments from fellow priests and parishioners.

It was the week that the Incarnation school—grades one through eight—opened. The eighteen teachers (including one former nun) were present, as was the principal, a Sister of Charity named Maureen Dunn. But fewer than half the students showed up on opening day; the strong winds and rain kept three hundred of them at home.

Brian woke up on that first morning of school to discover that the wind had swirled through his bathroom window and had sent a variety of bottles crashing to the floor. He had slept through the noise, but wasn't happy about what he found. He cleaned up the broken glass, had breakfast, and went around the corner for a quick tour of the school.

He strolled through the building. He knew all the teachers (only one had resigned after the previous term) and was pleased to see them again. He realized that they were grossly underpaid and greatly appreciated their love of teaching.

He peeked into classrooms, went into some, and spoke to the children.

"Well, how was your summer?" he asked a first-grade class. The children waved their hands in the air, giggled, and screamed for attention.

"It was very boring," one tiny girl in pigtails responded.

"Really?"

"Definitely. I'm glad to be back in school."

"What's your teacher's name?" Brian asked them.

"Miss Phillips," several responded in unison.

"And what's my name?"

"Missus Phillips," one laughing girl squeaked.

"No," Brian said, laughing.

"Father," one boy yelled, waving his hand in the air.

"Father what?"

"Father, that's all," the boy said.

"Father O'Connor," Brian instructed.

"Father O'Connor," the entire class shouted.

In the fourth grade, he asked the class where they had gone during the summer. The children were eager to respond; they jiggled in their seats and happily shouted their answers.

"Fire Island."

"Florida. Walt Disney World."

"Adventureland."

"Santo Domingo."

"Puerto Rico."

"Far Rockaway."

"Cuba," one small boy hollered. Brian looked at him and remembered reading in a magazine that Cubans who went home to visit were deplored by right-wing Cubans living in New York.

"You have family there?" Brian asked.

"Yes," the boy said. "We visited them."

"They were well?"

"Oh, yes. I liked being there."

In one of the fifth-grade rooms, a student who knew Brian waved at him when he entered.

"And how are you, my friend?" Brian asked.

"You should go on a diet," the boy snapped, smiling.

"A diet? Me?" Brian grinned.

"Yes, you."

As Brian left the room, he could hear the boy call *"el gordito,"* the fat man. It didn't bother Brian; he lived with his girth and never minded the children's jokes about it.

In a second-grade classroom, Brian tweaked the nose of a Dominican girl in the first row.

"We are going to collect noses," he notified the class. "We are going to take them away. Then, if you want another kind of nose, we'll be able to give it to you."

The students giggled.

"Yes, that's what we plan to do. Actually, we'll write names on each one we take, so they don't get lost." The children laughed louder.

"When you leave the room, I'll inherit a shambles," the teacher, an attractive young blonde, whispered to Brian.

Brian moved on from room to room. He loved the children, and their warm response to his presence reinforced that love.

He walked into a third-grade room and spotted a chubby boy standing in front of the class. Brian went up behind the boy and circled him with his arms.

"There is no more beating of children in the school," Brian announced in mock seriousness. "There is no more of what we used to call corporal punishment. I cannot beat any of you, no matter what you do." As he spoke, he poked the boy in the stomach. The boy wheezed with laughter.

"That's true," Brian continued. "I cannot do that." He slapped the boy lightly on both cheeks. "I do that just to give him good color in his face, that's all." The boy laughed and collapsed simultaneously. Brian tapped him on the head and allowed him to retreat to his seat.

He asked a sixth-grade class where they had spent their summer, and one boy said, "India."

"India. You were lucky," Brian said. "I wish I could have gone with you."

"You couldn't," the boy said seriously. "You're too heavy."

"Too heavy?" Brian exclaimed in mock anger. "You could have put me in a trunk."

"They don't make trunks that big," the boy said.

"They do, they do," Brian responded. "Okay, maybe next time you'll remember me."

Moving from room to room, up and down three flights of stairs, Brian kept busy. He mentioned the large number of missing students to a sixth-grade class.

"Maybe some are at home watching TV," one girl said. " 'Laverne and Shirley' are on in the morning."

"In the morning, too?" Brian asked.

"Yes. And 'The $25,000 Pyramid.' My father gets up at six so he can watch 'The Little Rascals.' "

"But you're here and that's good," Brian said. He saw an unfamiliar face. "I see there's a new boy in the class. He must be smart because he's sitting with four girls." The boy didn't respond; the girls giggled.

Brian knew most of the students by name; it was a sign of his interest in them, as they realized. His friendship with the children was ongoing as they passed through the school on their way to high school and, he hoped, college. He felt this most strongly with the eighth-graders, most of whom would leave the Incarnation school for the public high school in the neighborhood. He wanted them to succeed.

FALL

The eighth-graders were reaching for sophistication. The girls wore makeup and dressed to attract attention from the boys, who were happy to provide it. The school had its uniform rule, familiar to many generations of Catholic school students, but there were ways to flash one's identity.

"This is your last year here," Brian reminded an eighth-grade class. "Then it's on to high school. Do a good job in your final year and you'll be ready for high school. And after that, you'll be ready for college. And then you'll get married and have children and come back to see old Father O'Connor, I hope."

The class looked up at him and smiled affectionately.

In his final stop, a fourth-grade room, Brian spotted a boy he knew, a hyperactive boy whose parents were having trouble controlling him.

"Aha! Frankie. There you are," Brian shouted.

The boy smiled at him. They shook hands and Brian tapped him lightly on the head.

As Brian moved toward the door, the teacher, young and eager, accompanied him. He asked her if she knew about the boy's problem. Yes, she did, and she was keeping an eye on him, to give him special help whenever he needed it.

"He's a good kid," Brian told her. "But his parents are having a tough time dealing with him, with that constant energy. He has learned how to take things apart, but he hasn't learned how to put them together again. And that includes his own sense of self."

Brian moved down the stairs toward the exit. A tall, stocky boy named Ernie greeted him, and they shook hands. Brian grimaced in mock pain and commended the boy on his strength.

Brian headed back toward the rectory. Whenever he spent time with the children he ended up feeling better. There was a directness in their manner that made it easy for him to communicate with them. They responded to affection with affection, and they had an unwavering sense of loyalty to those who treated them with love and respect. He planned to see them often in the months ahead. Some he would lead to their First Communion, and others to confirmation. It would be his pleasure.

Back at the rectory, sitting in his rocking chair, he thought about First Communion. It was an important moment because it celebrated the fact that a child, in the second or third grade, had reached what the Church termed "the age of reason." In that moment he could inspire the children to understand that what appeared to be bread was the body of Christ. And his success would be evident in those children who continued to receive communion as they grew older.

In the past, First Communion had meant wearing a white gown or a blue suit and attending a mass specifically designed for First Communion. Now, children could attend mass with their family on Sunday and receive First Communion then. To prepare them, Brian explained the rite in religion classes, showed them the communion wafer, and allowed them to taste it, all without ceremony.

Brian smiled. He remembered that in the past the nuns often told the kids that if you chewed the Host, you were breaking the bones of Jesus. By his time, children were told that it was acceptable to chew it.

Confirmation was the next major step, the sacrament that took place when a child reached "maturity," in the seventh or eighth grade—the equivalent of a Jewish bar mitzvah. For Brian, it too was special; the spirit received in baptism was kept alive in confirmation.

The growth and progress implicit in the sequence —baptism, communion, confirmation—were vital for Brian and represented a gradual coming together of man and God. It was that unity that motivated Brian in his own spiritual life and in his encouraging the children to find what he had found: the productive peace that Christ provided.

19

During the next week Brian began to teach at both a funeral school in Lower Manhattan and at Montclair State College in New Jersey. It gave him the opportunity to put his knowledge of thanatology to use; he taught about the nature of grief, about death and dying, and about customs of death in major religions. He enjoyed the interaction with his classes, the chance to help them deal with the dying, and he appreciated the modest income both teaching posts provided.

With the resumption of the religious education programs and the Hispanic cultural activities after the summer break, it was a busy time for him. Most of Brian's friends in the priesthood were also at work.

Every Tuesday night, usually after 10 P.M., when the day's chores had been taken care of, a group of priests from the 1971 class at the seminary met to talk about their lives, to gossip, to exchange insights, and to seek and receive advice. The practice began the year before ordination, when they all were deacons in various city parishes; they would meet to plan their sermons for Sunday and to discuss theology. Later, when they felt more secure about their offices, the meetings took on a different tone. They were a time to be mutually supportive.

After a day that had begun before 7 A.M., they could sit in a quiet room and relax, be frank about their worries. It happened every Tuesday in one of the priest's rooms at rectories throughout the area.

They came from all parts of the archdiocese from a variety of jobs. Some were parish priests in the devastated Bronx: Tommy Thompson (two years older than the others and a former coworker at Incarnation), Dennis Sullivan, Pat Carroll, and Larry Quinn. Kevin Madigan worked with alienated Catholics in Manhattan. Bob Ritchie was the director of the Catholic Youth Organization, within the diocesan hierarchy. Don Sakano worked for Ritchie and studied for his master's in social work at Columbia University, where another classmate, Paul Dinter, was the Catholic chaplain. Jim Flanagan worked in a parish in Little Italy in downtown Manhattan. Dennis Keane was in an affluent suburb north of the city. John Quinn taught in a Catholic high school in White Plains.

From the varied experience represented, they brought insights, complaints, advice, and concern to the Tuesday-night gatherings. As a group, sitting around a large table strewn with cheese and crackers, cans of Tab, bottles of wine, or ice cream (each priest had his own style of serving; Brian preferred ice-cream cakes), they were open, cordial, affectionate, funny, and occasionally baiting. There was a spirit of collaboration; their experience at the seminary bound them together. Knowing that they wouldn't get to bed before 2 A.M., they did not attend the meetings out of a sense of obligation. They came to combat loneliness, to maintain a sense of unity that all cherished, and to keep each other informed about the workings of their Church.

The members of the group were more alike than different; they could achieve a consensus without lengthy debate.

FALL

They cared about the poor and their plight. That was the primary thrust of every meeting: how could they, parish priests, get the archdiocese to meet the needs of the poor, to rid itself of deception, inefficiency, incompetence, and achieve that end? It was a continuing concern.

Some of the talk was small. Brian noted that he was teaching a course in statistics at Montclair State: "I can't balance my checkbook and I'm teaching statistics."

Then he told a story about a parishioner:

"This old, sad woman was taken to the hospital with a dozen things wrong with her. She belonged there, but you know what those places can be like. I got a call from a snotty administrator. The woman had to go. They couldn't keep her. They were not a nursing home. 'You do what you have to do,' I said. 'But then I'll do what I have to do. I'll have a reporter and a photographer there when she's out on the street in a wheelchair and we'll see what happens.' They kept her."

Later Brian recalled an evening at a dance held in the school auditorium. The wife of one of the Dominican men in the parish was having a marvelous time. She asked Brian to dance and began clutching him, rubbing against him.

"Am I turning you on?" she asked Brian. "I want to."

"You're turning me on and I don't want to get turned on," Brian responded, holding her at arm's length. As Brian told the story, the others smiled, laughed, taunted him.

They talked about times at the seminary, which Paul Dinter sardonically called "Dogoodie." Dennis Sullivan, Pat Carroll, and Jim Flanagan remembered professors they had humiliated or liked, pomposity they had deflated, rituals they had scorned. They gossiped about the archdiocese —who was leaving the priesthood, why, who was being transferred, who had made a fool of himself. Larry Quinn and Kevin Madigan talked about their assignments and the conflicts they faced.

Brian mentioned that he still felt, as he had for a long time, that the Catholic school system was a drain on the finances of the archdiocese. At Incarnation tuition was forty-five dollars a month. The fee for religious education for public school kids (commonly called CCD, for "Confraternity of Christian Doctrine") was only ten dollars a year for an entire family. As a result, he said, school attendance was going down and CCD attendance was going up. In the eight years Brian had been at Incarnation, he told the others, school attendance had gone from 1,200 to 600, while the CCD program had done the reverse.

The group talked about the impending visit of the Pope to America, the ravages of the hurricane on the families of parishioners from the Dominican Republic, a scandal in a local parish in which the pastor, guilty of wenching, among other "crimes," was allowed to remain in his post while a priest, his primary critic, was transferred. The consolation was that the woman the pastor kept in the rectory was persuaded to move out. The indecisiveness of Terence Cardinal Cooke (sometimes called "Cookie") came up, a perpetual theme at the Tuesday-night gatherings.

For the most part, the members of the class of '71 were idealists, seeking to change the Church's stance on a number of issues. The task was difficult, in some cases impossible.

"If nothing has changed by the time I'm forty," Paul Dinter said, "I'm going to get out." Serious, intellectual, sensitive, Dinter was working on his doctorate in theology at the Union Theological Seminary and was Catholic chaplain at Columbia University. He dealt with his frustrations by writing Herzog-like letters, many directed to the archdiocesan brass.

No one disputed Paul Dinter's feelings.

Wednesday mornings were difficult for Brian, a price he paid for his loyalty to the Tuesday-night meetings.

If he had an early mass, he would have to respond to the nagging call of his alarm clock, shower, shave, and appear alert before an eager congregation.

He would get through such mornings, such masses, with a burst of energy held in reserve for these times. Afterward, he would slump in his chair at the dining-room table; others had eaten and gone their ways, and he could be alone. Occasionally, a rectory guest would join him for a cup of coffee.

On this one Wednesday morning he found himself with a layman from another city—Jack Evans, a stockbroker from Connecticut who was in New York on business and staying at the Incarnation rectory. This was common—Incarnation was known to be hospitable. Evans was a Catholic, an old friend of Jack Barry's, and Jack had invited him to spend the night.

"How do you feel about all the changes that have taken place since Vatican II?" Evans, a tall, slim, dignified man, asked.

The subject awakened Brian. This man asked reasonable questions.

"Do you know much about what's been going on since then?" Brian asked him.

"Just vaguely," Evans said.

"Well, for one thing, the Church always taught that it didn't matter who administered the Sacrament or how well it was administered, so long as it was administered."

"Brings back childhood memories of dull Sunday sermons," Evans said.

"That changed in Vatican II. There is much more emphasis on the fact that people have to be prepared to understand what they're doing. To do it sloppily is worse than not doing it at all.

"The mass was stressed as the summit, the source of all Christian life. In the past it was in Latin. Now, it's in the vernacular. In the old days the priest would have had his back to the people for the whole mass. And there was very little preaching. It was as if the priest was in private meditation and the people were doing their own thing. Now the congregation participates. Priests go to school to learn how to preach and how to communicate. And those changes in the mass have made it more pertinent for the people."

"I don't find myself in church as much these days as I did when I was a kid," Evans said.

"Confession has changed, too. Rather than going into a confessional box and confessing your sins in the dark to the priest and being given absolution, it was felt that there should be a room of reconciliation and that the confessor should be encouraged to sit in front of the priest. If the person did not want to be identified, he could kneel in front of a screen and go through the traditional confession.

"Communion has always been a part of the priest's life. But now, on Sundays, the lay people bring communion, too. Of course, the important part of the mass that is never done without the priest is the consecration, taking the bread and then praying over that bread and changing it into the body of Christ. The communion that the lay people give, without the priest, are wafers that have been consecrated at a mass by a priest.

"Marriage has also changed. It used to be perfunctory, going through the gestures. There would be little involvement of the congregation or the couple. We've been encouraged to produce different ceremonies within the framework suggested by Vatican II. The couple can choose the prayers they want the priest to say, and they can make up their own petitionary prayer. There are about five or six different options.

"Confirmation has changed a lot. In the past the bishop used to slap the people coming up, as a sign that they had to suffer. Now, he doesn't. He shakes their hands. The bishop shows up once a year to do the confirmation. But when we have an adult baptism, I can give that person confirmation at the same time."

Evans sipped his coffee.

"Want a piece of coffee cake?" Brian asked him. "We've got some in the pantry."

"No thanks," Evans said.

Brian got up, cut a slice of coffee cake, and brought it back to the table. He munched it in silence for a few moments. He didn't worry about calories; few priests did. Rectory food inspired priests' stomachs to swell against their belts. At Incarnation the priests did not wish to offend the kind, plump Dominican cook by suggesting that her meals were too high in calories. Instead, they would diet from time to time.

"The vestments have become more ornate, too," Brian said. "They're much nicer. In the old days they were just simple, ugly-looking fiddlebacks. Now they're long and flowing and in many good colors. They can vary from church to church; there's not just one that's acceptable. In some of the black churches, they've gone to very African designs and colors."

"Do you have to wear your collar all the time?" Evans asked. "I've seen some priests without it."

"We used to have to wear it at all times here in the New York archdiocese. They were very strict about it—even on your own leisure time, you wore it. But now it's not enforced. And we can relate to the community in a better, more human way without wearing the collar every minute of the day."

"Pope John was the force behind many of those changes, wasn't he?" Evans asked.

"Yes. And the funny thing is that when Vatican II began, there were very few people in the Church who agreed with him that the Church had to extend herself. He said, we have to throw open the windows. We have to reach out. We can't be isolated. He knew that the realities of the world were affecting the Church. And as the Vatican Council went on, the others began to appreciate John's view.

"Interestingly enough, one of the significant break-throughs was the passage of a document about religious liberty. Its essence was that the spirit of God moves not just through the Catholic Church, but through other churches. Up to that point the Catholic Church had always said that it alone had the truth of God's revelations.

"Vatican II gave priests not simply a political conscience —they've probably always had one—but it gave them the freedom to voice their views. It destroyed the monolithic view of the Church. If you asked the Pope, the Pope gave you the absolute finished statement about the Church's position. That image was destroyed by Vatican II. On so many issues now, you know that the seven hundred million Catholics in the world have varied opinions, not just one opinion.

"The Vietnam war was a perfect example. Many of the American bishops were in support of the war. And you had, at the same time, dissent from the younger priests. Some of us wrote to Cooke to disagree violently with his support of the war, and he asked us to come down and see him, which we did. He gave us two and a half hours, and he went over our letter with us and gave his own position. We still disagreed, of course, but if we had done that with his predecessor, we would have had no hope of getting his attention. There weren't any repercussions, either. Fifty years ago, if we had done that, we would have been in the Fiji Islands now. Instead, we all went back to our parish work. Maybe that says something, too, about the way the Church has changed in my time."

Evans got up from the table and headed for the front door.

"Thank Jack for the hospitality. And thank you for the good conversation," he said to Brian.

"Anytime," Brian said.

20

The next day Brian had a 10 A.M. funeral in the church. More than 150 funerals passed through Incarnation each year, friends and strangers. In this case it was a funeral for a woman Brian knew.

He had last seen Patricia Morgan on a ward at Columbia-Presbyterian Hospital, after her daughter had phoned and asked Brian to visit her. She had smiled and cried, alternately, while he spoke with her. He had hoped that she would leave the hospital and return home. She never did.

Thirty of her friends and relatives were in the church. Brian, in long, flowing white vestments with an embroidered red cross, read from the Old Testament: one day God would send a savior to "destroy death forever." He read from the Gospel of St. Matthew: "Blessed are they who show mercy. Mercy shall be theirs."

He spoke of the grief and sadness that all feel on the death of a friend. He referred to a theme from St. Paul —citizenship in heaven, the final journey to the fullness of that citizenship.

"We cherish our life, our family, our friends," he said, his voice booming throughout the spacious church. "Yet we are pilgrims on earth. The end of life on earth is not the end. She knew that she was going to die, but she knew that God would provide for her. When we pray for her, we pray for ourselves. No more tears, no more suffering, no sin. There is no death in God's kingdom. The body that contained her life on earth is finished, but her life has been remade. She can share the gifts of God's spirit, the promise of Jesus, the glorified spirit of Christ."

He prayed for peace among nations, for victims of injustice, for the abolition of hate. He prayed to God "to take our sister to paradise." Two altar boys assisted him, and an unseen tenor sang.

Tom Leonard and Jack Barry walked in and sat not far from Brian; when the deceased is known to several priests of a parish, they can be present during the funeral.

"May Christ be merciful in judging our sister," Brian said. He spoke of "the promise of immortality," with his arms outstretched. "And so Father, we bring you these gifts," he said, preparing to bring communion to those present.

"We praise you, Christ our Lord, from whom all good things come."

Everyone recited the Our Father, and Brian brought communion. "May our sister come to the banquet of life Christ has prepared for us," he said. "Let us pray for ourselves." The church became silent.

Brian recited the Irish blessing and joined the procession down the center aisle to the street. An altar boy carried a tall processional cross, Tom Leonard sang, and the coffin was borne by the pallbearers.

Brian joined the family in the hearse. As it moved along the streets of the parish, passersby made the sign of the cross. Inside the limousine, one of the dead woman's daughters spoke: "Doctors, hospitals, nurses, tests. When my time comes, let me just fall down on the sidewalk and let that be the end of it. Don't call a doctor for me."

"Maybe they ought to sell a medal that reads 'Don't Call Doctor. Don't Get Medical Aid,' " Brian suggested.

"Amen," the daughter agreed.

When the limousine and the hearse got to the cemetery, the eight mourners, all the women in black, gathered at the graveside to listen to Brian again.

"We turn to Him in our time of need. . . . We now commend our sister to the Lord. . . . Bring our sister to the joys of heaven. We pray to the Lord. Comfort us in our sorrow. Let our faith be our consolation."

Each mourner placed a flower on the casket. In the limousine on the return trip, no one spoke. Brian grasped one of the daughter's hands.

At such times, after Brian had put another Irishman to rest, he thought about the deceased. He and Patricia Morgan had spent time together over the years he had been at Incarnation, and then he had seen her decay and disappear into the ground. Such moments invariably took him back in time to recall his own parents. Their deaths had not been easy for him to accept.

When he returned to the rectory that day, Dan Cherico was there, sitting on Brian's sofa, shuffling through papers in his attaché case.

"Another funeral?" Dan asked.

"Yes. They bring back memories," Brian said.

"And grief," Dan said softly.

"I've dealt with grief," Brian sighed. "I'll continue to have to deal with it. You know, when my mother died, the worst thing was to go back to her apartment. And it was hard for all of us. We all grew up in that apartment. My father died in that apartment, in 1957. But this was worse. We cried and we remembered all the stories about what had happened there as we went through Mother's belongings.

"And we had to realize that the house would be dismantled. As soon as we started to do that, I started to cry very, very strongly, I even got hysterical. As did John and then Kathy and Maureen. The four of us, for hours. It was unbearable.

"I realized how my mother's death affected me, and I was very conscious of it. My father's death affected me in ways I wasn't really aware of. The night he died, he gathered us all around before he went to bed and told us that he wasn't going to be around much longer. My mother kept on saying, 'No, no, he's tired.' But he went around and he spoke to each one of us. I remember being awakened for it. He was saying good-bye. He told us that things were provided for.

"A couple of hours later, I remember waking up. John was in the room and said that the emergency squad was there and that Dad was having a heart attack. He died right there, at home. I could hear him saying that he loved everyone and he planned to return, that everyone be well and he knew we were small, but we'd manage.

"In a way, I think I'm going to grieve all the time for my parents. My father certainly was the head of the household, the provider, but my mother took over after he died. She worked and she held it all together.

"Her own philosophy, really, was very much like that of a number of people at Incarnation parish. They're hard-working people and at times they are self-sacrificing for the sake of others, for the sake of the kids. She loved that.

"At my father's funeral, she introduced me to a lady, saying that this woman was telling how her husband died and how she had eight kids and how she managed. The woman said to my mother, 'You're going to manage, don't worry about it.' That woman had a picture of her late husband over her fireplace. And when the husband died, she just looked up and said, 'You son of a bitch.' She kept cursing at the picture for about three years for leaving her with eight kids and no money. My mother got a kick out of that. The woman said to my mother, 'Just make sure you put your husband's picture in the living room and you look at it every now and then and say, "You son of a bitch." It will make you feel better.' "

"Surviving under stress by letting your anger out," Dan said. "That's what that story is all about."

"Exactly," Brian said. "She learned it during her life, and she must have passed it along to me."

"Good student," Dan said.

"Good teacher," Brian responded.

21

In the new rite of marriage devised at Vatican II, "Christian couples . . . nourish and develop their marriage by undivided attention, which wells up from the fountain of divine love, while, in a merging of human and divine love, they remain faithful in body and in mind, in good times as in bad."

For Brian, celebrating the sacrament of marriage was a pleasure. He enjoyed talking to couples planning marriage. And there were rules to appreciate. He knew that a Catholic cannot be married in a civil ceremony and remain within the mainstream of Catholicism.

He was familiar with the procedure. The woman's place of residence determined the parish in which the ceremony took place. The priest asked both parties if they practiced the faith, if they partook of the sacraments, if they were church-going. Then he arranged for them to attend three classes: one by a priest on the theology of marriage, one by a physician on the biological aspects, and one by a group of married couples about marriage as experience.

Brian knew that marriage could be a separate sacrament or be celebrated within a mass. It was the only sacrament in which the priest was not the minister; the couple was, with the priest present as the official witness for the Church.

It was as that witness that Brian married a couple on a cloudless Sunday in September. They were special. His cousin Elizabeth Mockler was marrying Kenny Terzi, who worked for her father at one of his Irish pubs. The father, Brian's uncle Frank, had, by hard work, considerable grit, and a tireless spirit, made his money at his two pubs and an Irish gift shop in Queens. As a wedding tribute to the couple, he was giving them a house and an elaborate ceremony and reception.

Brian drove to St. Anne's Church in Garden City for the 3 P.M. wedding. The church, well lit, air-conditioned, modern, and spacious, was very different from Incarnation; in Brian's mind, the comparison was resolved in favor of Incarnation's Gothic spirit.

But the setting didn't matter to Brian. What mattered was the joy of the celebration, the bringing together, under God, of two young, compatible people.

When he arrived at the church, he knew that the wedding would be a memorable one.

More than two hundred people of all ages attended —women in long dresses, men in dark suits. Two long-haired priests from Ireland, one newly ordained, both family cousins, were among a group of Irish clergy who had come to America to serve in a parish in Biloxi, Mississippi. They looked like road-company Beatles.

The organ music reverberated throughout the church. The bride, arriving with her parents in a white Rolls-Royce, wore a long white gown and clutched a bouquet. She joined the family in its procession down the main aisle as the music swelled.

There were three readings, one from the Old Testament,

two from the New Testament. The first two were read by women, cousins of the bride; Brian read the third, "God Is Love," from St. John. He followed that by remarking, "My relatives were the ones who told me, 'Please make it short.' " In his sermon he spoke of Cervantes, of Don Quixote—the quest for what ought to be, not for what was.

"The victims of hurricanes, a policeman killed, this is what life is about now for the majority of people," he said. "Yet, the marriage ceremony is about what life ought to be. In marriage, you work together so that two can become one, a reflection of the union between Christ and His Church. Life has its difficulties, but those difficulties can be dealt with in the vow of love. Every minute of their lives, Bette and Kenny will have to renew their vows. Like Don Quixote, they will strive to attain the ideal. They must not forget to strive for that ideal. We should reflect, in our lives, the presence of Christ. The bride and groom today are ministers in the sacrament of marriage. They minister to each other."

He questioned the couple.

"Have you come here freely and without reservation to give yourselves to each other in marriage?"

"Will you love and honor each other as man and wife for the rest of your lives?"

"Will you accept children lovingly from God and bring them up according to the law of Christ and His Church?"

The couple joined hands and answered. Then they declared their consent: "I promise to be true to you in good times and in bad, in sickness and in health. I will love you and honor you all the days of my life."

The Our Father was recited and Brian brought communion to the newlyweds and to those who moved forward to receive it. Two singers sang a popular song, "The Twelfth of Never."

In the back of the church, a young couple and their infant son, in long white gown, awaited the child's baptism and watched the wedding party disappear into their cars, after the throwing of rice and the taking of pictures.

It was 4 P.M. when Brian drove to the reception at Antun's, a sprawling catering establishment. He saw his brother John, John's wife, Anne; his sister Maureen and her husband, Jim; his sister Kathy and her husband, Bob. Immediately, the O'Connors formed a cluster over drinks and hors d'oeuvres.

"Great wedding," Maureen said to Brian.

"You mean I was great?" Brian asked, smiling.

"Of course," Maureen said with a laugh.

"Done any other weddings lately?" John asked.

"Sure," Brian smiled. "And one that didn't happen."

"Cold feet?" Kathy asked.

"That's funnier than you know," Brian said. "One night a couple of people came from a wake and asked if I could come over and say prayers. When I got there, the wife of the deceased had a veil on and wanted me to marry her to her dead husband. She said that she'd been taught that if you weren't married in the Church you were living outside the Church.

"They had never been married in the Church. She had been after her husband to rectify that, but then he died. She was obsessed. She'd go to hell, she told me, if they weren't married in the Church. She had rings she wanted to exchange with the corpse. I explained that it was in God's hands and that God was merciful. The Church couldn't do anything for her. She wasn't happy about that."

"Do you ever turn anybody down when they come in to get married?" John asked.

"Not often. When they're too young, when they haven't been around enough to make a judgment about what a good marriage is all about, I tell them I don't think they should get married in the Church.

"One woman I know who was married at city hall

reminded me the other day that I had refused to marry her in the Church. She was sixteen then. Too young, I thought. Now her kids are four and two and she wanted to have a church wedding. I was happy. They're ready for it now."

The banter went on. Brian remembered the time he had been invited to a banquet and had gone with a friend.

"We arrived, went into a room full of people, sat down, and ate dinner. It was terrific. I kept waiting for the speeches we had come to hear. They never occurred. It was a bar mitzvah. When I realized that, I got up and tried to get out, red in the face. But the father of the boy came up and told us to stay. He was delighted that a priest was there."

"Well, you're at the right place at the right time today," Kathy said.

The reception came to an end. The guests sat down and the dinner began. A band played "My Blue Heaven," "Baby, Won't You Please Come Home," several Irish waltzes, some early rock classics (e.g., "Teen Angel"), Italian songs for the groom's family, an Israeli rouser, and a string of pop songs.

The dancing was frenzied. Brian tried it once, with one of the bridesmaids, then retreated to dinner: soup, salad, roast beef, zabaglione with fresh strawberries, coffee, wedding cake. Waiters hovered to refill glasses gone dry.

The hours passed, but the din did not diminish. The two young Irish priests spent considerable time on the dance floor, their long hair flapping around their ears. Brian mingled, chatting with cousins he didn't see often. He spotted a Puerto Rican man, engaged to one of Brian's cousins, and they conversed in Spanish; it made Brian feel like he was back in the parish.

At 10:30 P.M. Brian began to feel weary. He knew that the party would go on until morning, ending with breakfast, but he had a mass to celebrate early. He walked around the vast room, thanked his aunt and uncle, said good-bye to his brother and sisters, kissed his grandmother.

FALL

He hadn't had much to drink. He had smoked one cigar and sipped one cup of coffee, both exceptions to his usual habits. He was tired, but pleased by the day's events—the wedding, seeing his relatives, the festivities, and the good meal. He drove back to Incarnation, pulled into the parking lot behind McGonnell's Funeral Home, locked the car, and walked across the street to the rectory. He was back home.

22

"How was the wedding?" Jack Barry asked Brian at breakfast, not looking up from the newspaper.

"Good. Very good," Brian said. "And very expensive. Nothing wrong with that if you have the money, I suppose."

"Right," Jack said.

"But I think about all those people in the parish who couldn't even consider such a wedding. They would rent a hall and bring in home-cooked food and have a wonderful time."

"Sure," Jack said. "But you went to an Irish wedding and that's different from, say, a Dominican one."

"Of course," Brian said. "One of my friends went to a wedding that was both. They served slabs of butter, already sliced. The Dominicans picked it up, slice by slice, and said it was the most wonderfully smooth cheese they had ever had. The Irish cringed. Nobody was right or wrong. Just cultural differences. That's how it is in this city."

"It sure is," Jack said, peering at Brian over the *Daily News.*

Brian sipped a glass of milk. The long oak table separated the two priests by several yards. It was 9 A.M. and quiet. Sergio and Ken had gone to their jobs. Tom Leonard was in his living room, working through a pile of letters, bills, and miscellaneous papers.

Brian finished his milk and took the small elevator to his rooms. He picked up his notes for the first CCD class he would teach in the new semester that afternoon. It was for the public school kids who would flock to the Incarnation school after their day of regular school for the additional instruction. His group was from the neighborhood junior high school, and they could be unruly. He read his notes and tried to prepare for the class.

Brian knew that the Catholic Church in America had serious problems. Mass attendance was down. Catholics were joining non-Catholics in support of birth control and divorce—despite pronouncements to the contrary by the Catholic hierarchy. At a time when 25 percent of Catholics spoke Spanish, many priests and bishops did not. The Catholic school system, often on the edge of bankruptcy, was losing students to the public schools. Brian wished that the schools could be closed and the money used for other Church-sponsored community programs.

Yet he understood that if a positive force existed against the wave of changing attitudes, it was the CCD program, the primary way in which the Church taught its doctrine to nonparochial children. Allied to the Catholic schools' own religious education program, it was the Church's way of instilling a respect for God in the young.

Once rigid, dogmatic, and predictable, the CCD system had recently altered its approach to try to increase its appeal to the new breed of children, to entice them and hold them as loyal members of the Church.

At Incarnation the CCD program began with the six- and seven-year-olds; the Paulist textbook, *Come to the Father*, was coupled with the teacher's ability to inspire, with several aims.

The teachers, most of them lay people (aided by priests and nuns when schedules permitted), attempted to awaken the sense of God, to initiate children in prayer, to teach the progressive discovery of God's calls in life, and to implant the fundamental religious attitudes: filial adoration, loving trust, thanksgiving to God, and respect and love for others.

In guiding the teachers, the instructional material quoted from Gesell and Erikson and adhered to common sense: "The child can be introduced into the world of faith only in communion with adults whom he trusts and by whom he feels he is loved."

The goal at the beginning was "not so much to explain religion to him or to teach him *about* God as to help him to *discover* God at the heart of his daily experience. . . . For example, we do not say: God *is* this, or God *is* that. Instead, we say: 'God the Father *gives, loves;* Jesus *says;* the Holy Spirit *helps* us.' "

The textbook stressed the use of common skills —painting, singing, mime, prayer—all to understand and celebrate the New Testament. "We should not force the child to pray if he is not so disposed," the instructions pointed out. "We cannot make a child pray any more than we can make him love. . . . The child is no more able than an adult to pray at any given time. Children should never be obliged to pray when they do not seem ready for it."

In the long run, the CCD program acknowledged, "Parents remain primarily responsible for the Christian education of their children." Meetings were encouraged between parents and CCD teachers (known as "catechists"), at home or in school, to discuss spiritual progress. Teachers invited parents to join in some classes; children were introduced to priests and nuns.

The first-year CCD classes concentrated on a series of

accomplishments: the value of silence; body control leading to relaxation and total response; rhythm as liberation and discipline; learning to listen, to see, and touch; the importance of friendship.

Other aims included: teaching God as the source of all life; the beauty of nature (and praising God for it); prayer leading to a relationship with God; visiting the church; the importance of the Gospels ("the Good News") as a way to know God better, to strengthen the child's trust in God, and to appreciate God's gift of "our ability to think, to work, to love"; and Christmas as the feast of joy and love (and the role of the Virgin Mary).

For very young children, Jesus was a human being. "Jesus grew up, like each of us. . . . All Jewish boys like Jesus would learn to read and write, just as you do," the CCD teacher could tell her class.

For children who could not grasp the nature of the Holy Spirit, CCD texts had an explanation: "The fact remains that He is a *person*, as real and living as the Father and the Son. . . . To know who the Holy Spirit is, we must renounce our desire to delineate his features."

The teachings of Jesus were passed along: "Love one another as I have loved you." In loving, CCD teachers told their small students, children reflect their friendship with Jesus. Charity was a form of love to inspire students to become better persons, forgiving persons. Along the way, CCD presented the death and Resurrection of Jesus, the hope of life after death, the mass as the celebration of the risen Jesus, and the Church as the family of God's children (celebrated in baptism). The meal aspect of the Eucharist was held for the second year of CCD; the younger children could not easily grasp that mystery.

For first-graders in CCD, the concept of Father, Son, and Holy Spirit was introduced, without explaining the mystery of the Trinity; it was given simply to "awaken this sense of unity and a consciousness of their living presence with us." More elaborate explanations would be withheld until the children were old enough to deal with them.

The CCD program was the Church's first important contact with children in a position to grow up as devout Catholics. It was designed for students whose public school education left a religious void that their parents wanted filled. As a result, the CCD classes lacked the precise sense of decorum that Catholic schools displayed. The students did not sit still in their seats, obedient to the demands of the teacher and respectful to visitors, as Catholic school students did.

Brian understood that. He did not teach the youngest CCD students; he was assigned to the junior high school group—sophisticated, skeptical, questioning, less responsive than the students he knew so well at the Incarnation school.

One afternoon in late September, Brian began the new term for CCD students. The students slumped in their seats, chewed gum, whispered to each other, and, much of the time, listened to him. Younger children he could make laugh, and when they stopped laughing, they would resume listening. With the older students, he felt that he could best maintain control by being serious.

"This year we're preparing you for confirmation," he announced. "It's when you receive the Holy Spirit in a special way. When we get closer to confirmation, we're going to talk a lot about the Holy Spirit. But for now, does anyone know what the word confirmation means?"

"Make a deal," a buxom fourteen-year-old girl said.

"Okay, or keep it, or make sure. The sacrament of confirmation is to confirm what happened to you when you were baptized. We'll talk about that. And about service, doing something for someone else."

Logically, intensely, he drew the members of the class

into the discussion. He pointed out that "anyone who is a student, a disciple of Jesus, a Catholic, is supposed to do two things: to come to mass on Sunday to thank God with all his brothers and sisters, and to serve other people, because that's the way Jesus helps others." He stressed the meaning of confirmation as an indication of growth and of assuming responsibility.

When the session ended, Brian led them in a closing prayer: "In the name of the Father, the Son, and the Holy Spirit, amen. Oh God, our Father, we thank you for the gifts you have given us. We pray that you will help us to grow in more ways on the inside, to have a heart that reaches out to others. Amen."

As soon as the last word had been spoken, the students got up and raced for the door. One of the boys slapped Brian's outstretched palm as he passed, then headed toward the stairs. Brian smiled.

It was after 5 P.M. and Brian was both tired and hungry. He felt that the first class had been a successful one; there was much more to teach them, but there would be time to do so. He wanted to read an article about the Pope's upcoming visit.

23

Pope John Paul II came to New York in early October. On the day of his arrival, Brian was scheduled to teach the opening session of his new course at the funeral school: "Philosophy of Death and Belief Systems," academese for comparative religion. The students, for the most part, were high school graduates studying to earn their state licenses as undertakers. Brian was the resident thanatologist at the school.

The streets were barren in Manhattan that morning; thousands of police were visible everywhere, guarding the Pope's route. Brian didn't risk driving; he took the subway downtown, taught the course, and took the subway back to Incarnation.

He got back before lunch and turned on the television set. The Pope was at the United Nations, speaking of peace and justice and the dignity of men. Brian sat on his sofa and stared at the screen.

Tom Leonard strutted in wearing his monsignor's black cassock and a bright red sash. Tom looked formal and uncomfortable, and he and Brian laughed simultaneously;

Tom rarely wore the cassock, considering it a pretentious throwback to another era. They sat down together and watched the Pope.

At 12:30 the buzzer rang for lunch. Without pausing, Brian and Tom got up and went downstairs, Brian switching off the set as he passed it. The conversation at lunch was concerned with their involvement in the Pope's visit. Tom and Jack Barry were to serve in the sacristy at Yankee Stadium prior to the mass that evening; the sacristy was the Yankee locker room. Brian wasn't planning to participate, although some of his classmates would be there. He preferred to remain a spectator.

During the afternoon Brian watched the Pope's progress, from a reception at the UN to a stop at St. Patrick's Cathedral. In the late afternoon he wolfed down a sandwich and a soft drink, attached his collar, and went out into the gray light.

At the stadium he passed through a gate and strolled out onto the field to find his seat. It was 5:30 P.M. The Pope was scheduled to appear for the mass at 8 P.M. Brian sat and waited, greeted priests he knew, and stared at the workers on the stage, wondering if it would rain. He could feel a sense of anticipation rising within him.

At 6:12 P.M. the stadium lights were turned on, mock sunlight against a threatening sky. A workman vacuumed the steps to the altar on the baseball infield, smoothing out the red carpet covering the floor of the structure erected for the mass. The choir rehearsed; it was a massive group, dozens of singers from throughout the archdiocese propelling the sound of Bach to every corner of the stadium.

"We're thirteen minutes late," a voice boomed from the public address system.

Three thousand policemen roamed the area inside and outside the stadium, their walkie-talkies crackling, their eyes attentive. Vendors sold pennants and peanuts and papal medals. The devout of all ages, from infants to the old and infirm, entered. Priests tidied up around the altar, beneath its yellow canopy. Nuns, priests, brothers, deacons, and armed forces chaplains made their way to their seats.

"Take your seats in the proper place, *now*," the PA voice instructed.

By 6:45 P.M. there was a crowd the Yankees would have envied; one priest estimated at least eighty thousand in the stands and on the field. The field began to take on the elements of a pageant, a celebration, a show of spiritual strength.

"Is Sister Christine here?" a nervous nun asked a policeman.

"There are twelve thousand Sister Christines here," the cop replied.

A speaker explained that communion would be brought into the stands and field seats by priests and deacons; each one would carry two hundred Hosts. True believers were urged to "receive quickly and with a minimum of movement."

In an alcove above the box seats, two policemen and their wives observed the scene.

"Frank Perdue is here," one policeman said to the other. He pointed to the field where the mayor of New York, Ed Koch, had made an entrance.

The time passed without a hint of frenzy. Preparations continued. The seats around Brian filled. A crowd was standing behind a fence on the field.

Brian looked around the stadium. The Vicar of Christ had come to New York; the leader of all Roman Catholics in the world had come to him, and thousands of others. He felt excited, touched by the experience. He knew that some of the Pope's conservative views clashed with his own, but for the moment he stood and gazed around the stadium and felt proud.

At 8:20 P.M. the orchestra on the field began to play. Police with videotape cameras made a final pass through the crowd near the altar, recording the faces of those present for security reasons should anything go wrong later. At 8:25 P.M. a voice ordered: "Clear the warning track."

One policeman turned to another and mentioned that even before the mass had begun, kids outside the stadium were selling copies of the free program for fifty cents each.

The cheering rose and fell. The crowd was amiable, reasonable, well behaved. Brian looked at the priests around him: old pastors obedient to the rule of the Pope, moved by his entrance into their lives; young, radical priests who resented what they termed the Pope's restrictive traditional viewpoint. Despite their objections, the young priests found themselves drawn up into the increasing momentum of the evening. They would withhold their dissent for a few hours and listen to the Pope.

Finally, in right-center field, a large door opened and a truck emerged with the Pope atop it, waving. The truck moved slowly around the track. The music became louder, its throb joining with the cheering, clapping, whistling. Flashbulbs popped throughout the stadium. The Pope, in white vestments, got off behind home plate and led a procession from first base to second.

A non-Catholic cop said: "Those Catholics sure know how to put on a show." Onstage, the Pope kissed the altar. The mass had begun. His accented English echoed throughout the stadium: "May Almighty God have mercy on us, forgive our sins, give us everlasting life."

He prayed: "Fill the hearts of all with the fire of your love. . . . May we secure justice and equality for every human being . . . a human society based on love and peace."

Helen Hayes read from the Book of Genesis; she looked trim and prim in her long skirt and white blouse. She played to the large audience and did not falter. The audience was respectfully quiet; at times, the sound of a passing subway train could be heard. Other readings followed, including one in Spanish. Clouds of incense rose toward the canopy.

In his homily the Pope stressed his message of peace, "what Jesus offered His apostles after His Resurrection." He referred to "a world that is anxious about its own existence," and stressed the value of peace and justice as the way out of that anxiety.

Don't turn away from people and their needs, he implored, God's love inspires us to cure the ills of the heart. He pleaded for Catholics to help "those most in distress, those who are poor, those who suffer ills of hunger, neglect, unemployment, despair." His voice was strong and firm.

He talked about the generosity of the United States and urged his audience to "be faithful to that tradition." He reminded his followers that "the poor are your brothers and sisters in Christ." He attacked consumerism, self-interest, sexual promiscuity, the abuses of power. What was needed, he said, was "a new enthusiasm and a fresh determination."

He spoke slowly, deliberately, and the PA system did not distort the sound of his voice. He told the parable of the rich man and the beggar, Lazarus, noting that the rich man was not condemned for being rich, but for being insensitive to the needs of the poor man. "Christ demands openness to our brothers and sisters in need," he said, his voice rising in intensity, "to the poor, the underdeveloped, the disadvantaged—more than benign attention."

His fervor drove him on: "Do not be afraid. Open wide the doors to Christ . . . Jesus Christ Himself, our justice, and our peace. Amen."

The choir sang "Holy, Holy, Holy." The audience recited the Our Father. Communion was brought to all corners of the stadium. The sound of Bach's "Jesu, Joy of Man's Desiring" soared into the air. And the mass was over.

Brian had sat through it all, listening, trying to assess the Pope both as leader and man. What had taken place seemed a long way from his parish, just a walk away from the stadium. The audience, so scrubbed and middle class, did not seem to include many of the poor the Pope had stressed he wanted to help. Brian filed out of the stadium to return to Incarnation, knowing he would not forget this evening, but wondering exactly what it meant.

Back at the rectory, he sat with Tom Leonard and discussed the experience.

"It was a special mass for me," Brian said. "And almost all the priests I knew who were there felt that. Sure, I know that some feel that it didn't accomplish any great thing, that it was more a glorying in the triumph of the papacy than the papacy as servant. Yet at the end every one of us was standing on our chairs yelling '*Viva il Papa.*' There was something about the man, about seeing him up close, that had an effect on me. It was his look. He looked directly at us. He didn't have that glazed look. It was penetrating, communicating."

"I got that feeling, too," Tom said.

"His homily was a good one," Brian said. "He made a clear statement about justice and peace. He didn't hesitate to criticize us for consumerism and for eating up the resources of the world. He was saying that we have to pay attention to our world."

"He seemed to be in touch with the people," Tom noted. "He wiped the brow of a young priest and kissed him on the forehead and hugged him."

"You know, Cardinal Cooke once gave a speech to us on the morale of priests and attributed our problems to bad manners. We didn't wear the collar all the time and we ate ice cream on the street and we were heard saying damn or hell.

When I came back afterward, it was hard for me to relate his words to reality. I didn't have that problem with the Pope. He was approachable, human."

"Do you feel changed?" Tom asked.

"Not exactly. More like a married couple celebrating an anniversary. Reaffirmed rather than changed. The Pope didn't change the substance of the problems we face."

"He's not Pius XII, is he?" Tom said.

"Pius XII was a recluse, very quiet, very much the scholar," Brian said. "Of course popes differ. John XXIII was with people, rather than sitting at his desk and writing an encyclical, or figuring out some intellectual doctrine. He was busy communicating and doing it rather well. His body image was not the body image of a superstar. He did not give the impression of being wrapped up in the intellectual world to the detriment of the emotional response. He affected me, especially those years when I was in high school. I could tell that he was a warm, empathetic kind of person. Someone you wouldn't mind sitting down with. He was very much the parish priest.

"Paul VI went back in certain aspects to Pius XII. He leaned toward that strict intellectual approach. But the world was changing and he was anxious to adapt to it, yet not give away too much. You felt that he was struggling, especially with birth control.

"John Paul I was the thirty-day pontiff. Dan and I met him when we were in Italy. We were staying in Venice and we went to mass at the church where he was patriarch. We were impressed with him. He was celebrating the mass alone with no one around him.

"It was about a year before he became Pope. There was no rumor that he would ever be Pope, but we were aware of the fact that John XXIII had also been patriarch of Venice. I remember that during the mass John Paul I came out to the middle aisle and spoke for about twenty minutes. It was a very decent sermon. He wasn't harping on the negative; he was being positive. Afterward, he went out into St. Mark's Square and we talked to him. He was friendly, knew people's names and asked about their families. Later, it was very easy for us to see him make the leap from parish priest to Pope.

"The present Pope, well, it's confusing to see where he's headed. He's following a tradition of pressing the flesh and being out there with the people. And yet I think he wants to backtrack on a lot of issues. At this point, he could have great influence. Since the Vatican Council, the emphasis has been on the national Church, through the national organization of bishops—instead of each diocese having a lot of autonomy. That gives the Pope more power over all the local churches. John Paul II may have a tendency to try to bring things more into a monolithic form than permit matters to surface at their own level—but with some confusion. He may want to be in total charge. We'll find out."

"We certainly will. And soon," Tom said.

"I'm ready," Brian said, smiling.

"I hope you are," Tom said, smiling back at him.

24

The next day the Pope left New York after a series of widely covered appearances. He continued his American tour, his conservative opinions reported in all their detail. The Pope affirmed the Church's stand on celibacy, declaring that "priesthood is forever," eliminating the possibility that he would be generous in allowing priests to join the laity should they choose to do so. He came out in opposition to premarital and extramarital sex, to divorce, to artificial birth control, to abortion, and to the ordination of women.

Brian listened, watched TV, read the newspaper reports. He was disappointed. He had not expected the Pope to become a radical, but he had hoped for more flexibility, for more attention to the problems of the American priests.

Later that week Brian did the one thing that might minimize his growing irritation; he spoke to the second-grade classes at the Incarnation school. The little children always cheered him up. He went to the school at 10 A.M. to talk about God and about friendship. The little girls in their red-plaid jumpers, the boys in their blue pants, white shirts, and ties, greeted him exuberantly. As Brian entered the first of the two classes he would speak to, he noticed an announcement scrawled by the teacher on the blackboard:

Our News:
Today Is Thursday
Father O'Connor
Will Visit Us.
Let's Have a Good Day.

Brian stood in front of the class and smiled.

"The Pope was at Yankee Stadium," he reminded the class. "Why?"

"That's the biggest place," a small boy volunteered.

"Right. They wanted to have a place where a lot of people could watch the Pope say mass. Who's the Pope?"

"John Paul II," a smiling black girl said.

"John Paul II. What is a Pope supposed to do? What's his job?" Brian asked.

"To go and visit all the people," a delicate voice piped up.

"Anything else? Well, a number of us were able to be there as he was saying the mass and then he spoke to us. But today I want to talk about baptism. When they were bringing your baby cousin into church, what did they want the priest to do to your baby cousin?"

"Baptize him," several shouted.

"Yes. Who brings the babies to the church? The Pope?"

"No, no," a serious boy said. "The parents do."

"Okay. The parents bring the baby to the church. They say to the priest that they would like to have the baby baptized. What does that mean? What does the priest do?"

"He pours water," a girl said.

"What does that mean?" Brian asked.

"Holy water," the girl added.

"Does anyone know what *that* means?" Brian asked.

"I remember when I was baptized," a boy said.

"You were one year old when you were baptized," Brian told him.

"I was zero," the boy said.

"You were zero? How can you be zero years old? What do you look like when you're zero?"

"Like nothing," the boy said seriously.

"So you have to wait until you look like something before they can baptize you. Otherwise we would baptize people all day who are zero years old, which means they're nothing."

"I want to be baptized again," a girl in pigtails said.

"You can't be baptized again. You can just be baptized once," Brian said, barely suppressing a smile.

The girl continued: "When I was a little baby, the black thing that is on the belly button from the little babies, it took me twenty days so it could fall off and my mother had to take me to the doctor and my little baby cousin, it took her ten days, and my baby brother it took thirteen days."

"My goodness," Brian said. "You know a lot about that. Do the rest of you know what she's talking about? It's the thing between the baby and the mother, the thing that gives the baby food and nourishment. When the baby is born, mother and baby are separated." He turned back to the girl. "So it took you a long time for that to fall off. My goodness.

"Getting back to baptism, when you're a small child, maybe two months old, the parents bring you to a priest. He pours some water on you and says, 'Maureen, I baptize you in the name of the Father and of the Son and of the Holy Spirit.' What does that do? Well, it takes away what we call sin, in the sense that we now become a friend of Jesus. We become a friend of Jesus in a very special way. Has the child done anything wrong? Has the child committed a sin, the little small child? No, the child has done nothing wrong. What it means is that we all have to become friends of Jesus, because if we're friends with Jesus, it means that He will be close to us and He will help us. So when a child is baptized, the parents are saying, I want my child to become a friend of Jesus.

"The first question the priest asks the parents is what

name do you want to give to your baby. And they answer. After that we read from the Bible and we read about Jesus, and then we take the water and we pour the water on the baby's forehead and we baptize the baby. In the beginning we didn't pour water just on the forehead. We used to put the baby in the water completely. Now why would we do that? What happens when you go down and put your head underwater? Can you breathe?"

"No, you drown," a boy said.

"You drown. Right. But they weren't baptizing young children. They were only baptizing people as old as I am. Am I old?"

"No," a little girl said, giggling.

"How can you tell if a person's old? How can you tell?" Brian asked.

"The people who are young, they have no lines on their face," another boy observed.

"Right. That's one way. What's another way?"

"Old men have beards," the girl with pigtails said.

"They have gray hair, too," a boy added.

"That's me. Gray hair. I'm getting old," Brian noted. He resumed his baptism story. "When you come up after you've been underwater, you can breathe again and it feels as if you're alive. So when we baptize someone, we want to show that we now have new . . . what's the word?"

"Life," a boy hollered.

"Life. We now have new life within us. The life of Jesus. We want to have Jesus to help us so that bad things don't happen to us, or if something does happen, He will always be our friend. Now, what we want to do this morning is something special to show God we are His friends. But we have to be nice and quiet. We're going to have people come up here in a group. We're going to stand around in a circle and I'm going to ask you the same question: Do you want to be a friend of Jesus? And each one of you can answer in your own words. You can say yes or you can say something else. Yes, I love God. Yes, I want to be a friend of Jesus. It's up to you."

The children moved forward in small groups. Brian asked the question to each: Do you want to be a friend of Jesus? When all the groups had responded, he said, "May Jesus always be your friend, and may He always be a special friend of this class."

He left the class, repeated the message in the second classroom, and walked back to the rectory. There was an innocence about those children that moved him; they had not been corrupted. He hoped that his effort, impossible to track through time, would enable them to be virtuous, to believe in God, and to act upon that belief in their everyday lives, not simply in church on Sunday. He wanted them to appreciate the value of prayer.

Dan Cherico was tidying up Brian's room when Brian returned.

"I can't afford to pay you the minimum wage," Brian said.

"I think of it as philanthropy," Dan said with a smile. "Where were you?"

"At the school, talking to the little kids. Second grade."

"What about?"

"Being good, being a friend of Jesus," Brian said.

"Does that ever make you think back to when you were a kid?" Dan asked.

"Sometimes. I remember in grammar school, very early in grammar school, praying. I wasn't praying for anything specific. I just knew it was the experience I wanted to build my life on."

"I've always felt that it was important to integrate prayer into one's life," Dan said.

"True. In the beginning my prayers were compartmentalized, divorced from what I was doing when I wasn't praying.

But now I see it as part of what I'm thinking, what I'm feeling, what I'm doing. Prayer as an offering to God. It's not the words or phrases or ideas that matter, but the purpose. To build up God's kingdom."

"I suppose a lot of people think that prayer is the answer to all the ills of the world," Dan said.

"Some people feel that way, yes," Brian said. "They become overly religious, figuring that the more holy they become and the more they pray, the more their problems will go away. But the bridge between feelings and prayer isn't there. You can't use prayer as aspirin.

"Once a person can talk about his feelings honestly, he can put them into his prayer life. In talking to God in prayer, the important thing is to ground it in reality. Anger, jealousy, selfishness, all those elements not normally brought up in prayers have to be integrated into praying. Accept the feelings and make them a part of your prayers, rather than deny them. The very act of praying is a dialogue with God."

Dan got up and went to the bookcase. He picked out a copy of George Bernanos's novel, *The Diary of a Country Priest*, and opened it.

Dan pointed to a passage and Brian read it:

How can those who know nothing about it, who pray
little or not at all, dare speak so frivolously of prayer?
A Carthusian, a Trappist will work for years to
make of himself a man of prayer, and then any fool
who comes along sets himself up as judge of this lifelong
effort. If it were really what they suppose,
a kind of chatter, the dialogue of a madman
with his shadow, or even less—a vain and superstitious
sort of petition to be given the good things of
this world, how could innumerable people find until
their dying day, . . . sheer, robust, vigorous,
abundant joy in prayer?

"Yes," Brian said, "I can appreciate that."

"Read the last line," Dan suggested, then read it aloud: "An odd sort of dream, an unusual opiate which, far from turning him back into himself and isolating him from his fellows, unites the individual with mankind in the spirit of universal charity."

"Amen," Brian said.

25

It was the first Friday in October, the day for communion calls. Brian left the rectory by 9:40 A.M.

He walked across the parish, entered a dark apartment building, and went to a first-floor apartment. The door was not locked; he pushed it open and proceeded down a long, dark hallway. He could see Mrs. Esposito, the old Italian woman he had seen before, moving toward him.

"Oh, Father, is no good," she sighed hoarsely. "No good. I think I die now. I cannot walk, cannot sit, cannot see good. I think is time to die."

"No, no," Brian said gently. There was something about the woman that touched him. She was not simply old and sick, as many were; she was, in some profound way he hadn't defined, vulnerable.

He followed her into her living room.

"Glad to see the Pope," she said, her mood shifting. "I want to kiss his hand. Very nice Papa. Everybody like him. But, Father, I don't go to confess." Her guilt troubled her.

"You don't have to. You haven't done anything wrong," Brian said, touching her lightly on the shoulder.

He recited communion in English; she prayed in Italian, her hands held high, clasped in front of her face. He placed the Host on her tongue. She shook—an emotional spasm—and began to cry. Brian stood above her and stroked her head in silence.

She stared up at Brian, tears on her cheeks. Then she spoke. "I don't like what I see on TV, putting the Host in the hands. It's bad. No like."

"Yes, that's the new way," he told her. She grimaced. "But when I come here, it's the old way," he said.

Leaving her apartment, he heard her in the distance: "You take care, Father. You work too hard." He smiled and moved on.

He went from apartment to apartment, greeting his parishioners, offering communion, praying. His last stop was at a tenement apartment shared by a middle-aged Irish brother and sister. There was a candle and a crucifix on a small table close to where the woman sat beside a window. She had been watching the young men loitering in front of a noisy Latin record shop across the street.

"My brother's in the hospital," she told Brian solemnly. "A little redness around the eyes, that's what he had. He didn't pay any attention to it. He went for his usual doctor visit and they put him in the hospital. He's been in for three days. They're taking tests. He says he feels good."

Brian didn't comment.

"You know, Father, we're moving."

He hadn't known.

"Yes, we are. Up to 214th Street, in Good Shepherd parish. We had enough. The elevator here keeps breaking. We can't walk, me the way I am at my age, and my brother because of his heart condition. He has a heart condition. The new place is on the first floor."

"Well, I wish you luck," Brian said. "I wish you very good luck."

"I want to thank you, Father, for coming over so often. You know, Father, the Church did many wonderful things for me."

"We hate to lose you," Brian said, heading toward the door.

On the street he thought about seeing many of the same people again, coming back to do communion calls in November. He wished he could spend more time at each call, but Fridays were busy days. Perhaps it was enough to be the visitor, to satisfy their wish to assert their faith. Those in serious trouble could find him at any time in the rectory.

He was grateful for the richness of his schedule. It held off one of the priest's most pernicious enemies, boredom. Back in his living room he thought about that boredom, a negative force that was debilitating, attacking incentive and corroding faith. It was like the pain that could set in after a priest had celebrated mass many times, had heard so many confessions, had brought communion to thousands. It was important to him to find joy in life, because boredom, unopposed, could wear a priest down, could cloud the purpose and meaning of life.

He recalled a story he had heard in the seminary about the building of the cathedral at Chartres. The workers were carrying bricks. The first worker, when asked what he was doing, answered, "I'm carrying bricks." A second worker, asked the same question, said, "I'm building a building." A third, joyous and energetic, replied, "I'm building a cathedral." Brian appreciated that man's sense of purpose.

When Dan Cherico arrived for lunch, Brian reminded him of the Chartres story, then said, "Some priests don't even want to carry the bricks."

"If you want to be holy, you have to be human," Dan

said. "So therefore you make mistakes. To the extent that you are human, to the extent that you are vulnerable, that's the extent that you can be holy. So if you're not tempted, there's no sense being holy. You have to see your options. Harry Stack Sullivan said the unexamined life isn't worth living. You have to look at what's there and then choose what you want. So when the woman who is very seductive comes in, if you're attracted to her, you should admit that to yourself. I think the good priest is able to do that and say, yes, that would be wonderful. But I've chosen *this*. And because I have chosen this, I'm not going to do that. For different priests, different problems become serious. For some, ambition is a greater problem than booze, women, or gambling."

"True," Brian said. "It's not always the big three."

"Today, many people catch themselves before they develop a drinking problem," Dan continued. "And there are ways to get around having an affair. But ambition is one of the few things that a priest can act on legitimately and get praised for.

"Ambition generally leads to moving up on the hierarchical scale, and if you feel that having power will help you, and if you feel you have the ability to manage people, you're going to want to climb. Now, what price do you have to pay to climb? I think many priests have made personal sacrifices to climb, only to find out they haven't gotten where they wanted to get, or it wasn't worth it.

"For example, the priest who works very diligently at raising funds gets to be pastor of a parish only to find out that the parish is not the one he raised the money for. It's changed its ethnic population and he can't stand the group that's there now.

"Or he's moved up to become a bishop and he has nothing to do with being a priest anymore. He's an administrator. He has no contact with people. And yet, if he wants to stay in that club, he has to continue to act like an administrator."

"I never think of myself as a bishop," Brian said. "I remember when I was a deacon in the last year at the seminary, a bishop sat me down one day and explained to me what I could do to become a bishop. He said I had the intelligence and the background, but that I also had a few rough edges which I could straighten out with his suggestions and I would then be bishop material. That was one of those moments of insight for me when I realized that if this was what his life was all about, his life was not for me. So I think that was a good lesson for me, not to have that kind of ambition. The ambition I have is connected with parishes, not the objective most priests aim for. Parish life is always the lowest rung on the ladder. But that's not how I see it. It gets me close to the people, and they matter most."

Dan nodded. "In the late twenties and thirties, no priests in the archdiocese could work exclusively in any one job if it didn't include living in a parish. Everyone who worked in the chancery office had to work in a parish as well. You could teach, but you lived and worked in a parish."

"Everyone had to be a parish priest," Brian agreed. "Even if he happened to spend some of his time doing some specialized work. Under Spellman it became specialized. When you got an office position, that was it. That was your job. You were no longer the parish priest."

"I think that one third of the priests in the diocese were involved at one time in specialized ministry," Dan went on. "I think, too, that the honorary title of 'monsignor' has been for many—especially the old-timers—a source of envy. If they achieved the title, they felt they had arrived.

"Even ten years ago, there were a certain number of parish priests who looked to certain Westchester parishes as plums—well endowed, middle class. But that's all changed. There are no places in the archdiocese today that are really plums. There are some places that are better than others.

"Working in an office at the chancery gives you freedom. You work from nine to five. Parish priests work twenty-four hours a day, seven days a week. They are available. You may take a day off, but you're not free after five, and you don't have summers off the way teachers do.

"You know, I think when someone says, 'I want to be a bishop,' it's like saying, 'I put in ten years in an Hispanic parish and now I want to take it easy in the country.' No one is going to knock anyone for saying that because there's no self-deception involved. But in most cases, I think, there is."

"Especially the ones who are most adamant in condemning people for even thinking ambitiously," Brian said. "They themselves secretly would give both arms to be a bishop. But at the same time, they condemn the hierarchy. Given the chance, they would coopt on any basis in order to get ahead."

"Sure. Look at this house. Look at Tom. I think Tom would want to be a bishop because I think he sees the direction and vision he would like to give. I think Ken would love to be a bishop, too, because of the trappings and the kind of respect that goes with it. Sergio would want to be a bishop to have the power vis-à-vis Rome. He would want to be a bishop to change the notion that the world has of Catholicism. Jack would want it because it would give him power and freedom."

"What troubles me most is the false piety that comes out of ambition," Brian said. "Do anything at any cost to get ahead. They may have started out very simply as parish priests who were effective. But then the piety sort of came, because it was expected. The bishops' club is the most exclusive club in the world. If you're going to break into it, you have to put on the veneer of what a bishop is supposed to be. It means you dress a certain way, you flaunt piety."

"If I were a bishop," Dan said, "I would only wear

starched white shirts. I would have my shoes shined twice a day. I would grow my hair a bit longer, but not too long. I would always smell antiseptic. I would go to the right country club, one that catered to the Catholic WASP type."

"You would cultivate all the bishops throughout the United States," Brian added.

"Yes, you'd have to cultivate the kind of person who has similar ambitions or who has already arrived. I would get an office job. I would get involved in a situation where I could get attention, the kind that makes the Church look good. I would associate with the Cardinal. I would try to go to as many activities as I could where he was present, and I would ask all those asinine questions they ask so he knows they're there. I would write an article or two for the secular press about how wonderful the Catholic Church is and how wonderful the hierarchy is and how God is good and buses go down the street and subways are underground. State the obvious. It's sad. I know some great pastors who should have made bishop. They didn't."

"I really can't think of anyone who made bishop because he was a good pastor," Brian said. "I have heard about people who were good pastors, but who were made bishops for other reasons. Either they were rectors at the seminary or they were known to someone in Rome."

"On the other side of the coin, I know a number of ex-priests who, if they had stayed, would be bishops because they were the type. They were the climbers. They woke up one day to what had *not* happened to them and were shocked, and then they left.

"It's all complicated. Most priests are unprepared for the real world. There's a saying that 'Man cannot receive an answer to a question he has not asked.' In the seminary the real questions are never posed. I remember a student asking our ethics professor, who later became a bishop by the way, 'What do you do when a woman comes in to the rectory and is crying because her husband has left her?' And the professor said, 'You reach into your pocket and you take out an unsoiled handkerchief and you hand it to her.' That's the response you'd get from most seminary professors and priests. When the obvious thing to do would be to get up off your butt, go around the desk, sit next to her, hold her hand if necessary, and even risk putting your arms around her. It may not be appropriate, and more often than not it's not necessary, but if it is necessary, you should feel free enough to do it. Those kinds of questions were never answered satisfactorily in the seminary. So many priests are frigid. Yes, they are. I think this is why you see them loosen up so much with a couple of belts in them. It's great to see priests at dances, where they may dance every dance, but have no other contact with women. Their inhibition breaks down, but then they catch themselves. They're very uptight."

"True," Brian said. "You have the tradition that the head of personnel calls you up and you're expected to move in three days with no problems, because the kind of attachments you had should be something fully under control. The intangibles aren't supposed to matter, only the tangibles."

"Most priests I know are very attached to tangibles," Dan said. "If they work in poor parishes, they're attached to their vacations as escapes. Or their night at the opera. Or their day in the country. Those become sacred, and they grow out of proportion. There are priests who go in for expensive clothing, expensive suitcases, expensive jewelry, or expensive cars. Or the best booze, or the food in the rectory is elaborate and costly. Or they amass book upon book for their library.

"I don't say it's the majority. But even those priests who have no attachment to physical things, the typical good priests, have to have the opera or the theater or something. You enjoy coming to our house, right? But if there's something happening that's important in the parish, you don't come. That's something you don't see too often."

"I really care only about the basic things, that they be taken care of," Brian said. "Beyond that, really, I'm not attached to anything. I'm not concerned about clothes, as long as they're clean."

"And yet you enjoy beautiful things," Dan observed.

"Yes, I do."

"There are a lot of people who have no interest in beauty because they don't like it. You like it."

"Maybe I'm well adjusted," Brian said with a smile.

"Yes, you are. That's so. I think that the well-adjusted priest is that individual who gets lonely, depressed, frustrated, horny, angry, hungry, tired."

"All in the same day?" Brian asked, teasing his friend.

"Same hour even. And realizes that the thing he shares, the thing he has to give his parishioners, is his humanness. He suffers from all the same foibles that everyone else in the parish does. He is no better, no worse. He excels in only one thing. He has been trained to preach, to celebrate the Eucharist, to administer the sacraments, to share God's love through example, through listening, through creative giving. His main objective in life is to give the world more than he's taking from it, to show love in a variety of ways to a variety of people, never to develop a coterie of people in the parish whose needs become more important than the needs of others. He works diligently at preparing himself to preach and to celebrate the Eucharist, to administer the sacraments. He is, in fact, a well-rounded, healthy person who goes to theater and movies, who goes out to eat, who talks to strange people, who takes a hand at doing lots of things."

"One other thing I would add is that the priest be someone who is able to lead people to a deeper understanding of their own lives," Brian said. "In doing that, he sets himself up as an example to others. He's continually in dialogue with his own God, to come to a realization of God's purpose in his life. By acting out that realization in his preaching from the pulpit or in his daily life he would enable people to do the same thing in their own lives."

The lunch buzzer sounded.

"End of conversation. Time to stuff ourselves," Dan said, getting up and heading for the elevator.

"Yes, I continue to be a well-rounded person," Brian said, laughing, and followed Dan to lunch.

26

The voice on the telephone belonged to the son of one of Brian's older parishioners—a German woman named Helga Schmidt—and it transmitted the son's concern for his mother's well-being. The son did not live with her, but he had talked to her on the phone and the conversation had depressed him. He told Brian that she was becoming "strange." Brian assured him that he would check on her.

"Like all good Catholics, she lives on the fifth floor of a walkup," Brian joked to Tom Leonard as he headed out to see her. "Worse than that, she believes that her first husband has eaten their three children—no small feat because they're all grown—and she wants him to vomit them back to life. She may be over the edge. Her son thought it would be a good idea if I feigned a service in her apartment to declare the kids dead for good and to assure her that they were given a good Christian burial. He may be over the edge, too. I'll find out."

The old woman's husband, her second, greeted Brian at the door. The woman, wrapped to the neck in a thick pink blanket, sat meekly on the living-room sofa. She spoke in a faint, squeaky voice. Brian sat down beside her and tried to dent the gloom that surrounded her.

"Are you feeling well?" he said.

"I take all kinds of medicine," she said.

"And your children?" he asked.

"I called my daughter and she's alive," the woman said. "I'm very happy." She began to cry.

"You have a good husband," Brian began.

"I'm trying my best," she moaned. "I would just like to go outside once in a while. I'm supposed to see a priest today."

"I'm the priest," Brian reminded her. "You just get a little confused. We all do. Don't worry about it." He sat down beside her on the sofa and began stroking her forehead.

"I'm very happy to see you, Father," she sighed.

"And I'm happy to come here. Don't worry about anything. It'll all be okay. You don't have to come to church. I'll always come to see you, and I'll be happy if I know you're not worrying."

The husband explained, slowly and patiently, that he needed help to care for her. Perhaps someone might come in and watch her for an hour a day while he did their shopping? Brian assured him that he would find someone to help; he would ask one of the CCD students to be of service.

Brian said a prayer for Mrs. Schmidt; it was the first time during the visit that he referred to God. He shook the husband's hand and went out into the chilly October air.

A few blocks away he found the apartment of Maria Flores, the young woman dying of cancer whom he had visited in the hospital. Her sustaining faith moved him; he wanted to do what he could to support that faith.

When he arrived he was greeted by her six-year-old daughter, Teresa. The girl hugged him, giggled, and ran off, her immaculate red dress billowing in the wind she created. Maria asked Brian to sit down. She talked about her radiation therapy, the chemotherapy she was getting daily. She showed Brian a cross and a line, made with indelible ink on her left arm, where the radiologist targeted his weapon against the spreading cancer.

"It makes me vomit," she told Brian stoically, in Spanish. "But I have no pain." Teresa ran into the room and jumped into her mother's lap; she made faces at Brian and laughed.

At a prayer meeting at Incarnation the previous week, Maria had testified to the power of her faith to overwhelm grief at the prospect of an early death. She reminded Brian of that.

"I am ready for my own death," she told him. "But my family isn't. My husband can't handle it. I'm trying to prepare everyone for it." Brian allowed her to go on. Drawing on his knowledge of thanatology, he knew how important it was to her for him to listen. Later, if necessary, he would counsel her husband.

"You know what, Father? A few days ago my doctor looked at me and he told me that I was 'normal' again. A miracle, he called it. But I know that what I have has gone from one side of my body to the other and that if it goes to my brain, it is all over for me. I didn't know what he meant, so I asked him if he was a Catholic, and he said that he wasn't, he was a Protestant. But he believed in miracles, too. I told him that I believe in God. I have faith."

"Glory to God," Brian said softly and spontaneously.

She sat in her chair, looking worse than she had in the hospital, while Teresa ran over to Brian, hugged him again, and ran off to play in another room.

"It is good to pray," Brian said.

"Yes," Maria agreed.

He stood up and said a prayer; Maria clasped her hands, closed her eyes, and joined him.

When it was done, he stared at her momentarily, then

averted his eyes; he did not want to make her feel self-conscious. He kissed her on the cheek, said good-bye, and moved toward the door.

It is terrible, what is happening to her. Can it be God's will?

He had one more call to make. A sick woman, Mrs. Mendoza, had asked Brian to come over to anoint her.

The sacrament of the anointing of the sick can be traced to the words of the Apostle James: "Is there anyone among you sick? Let him bring in the presbyters of the Church, and let them pray over him, anointing him with oil in the name of the Lord. And the prayer of faith will save the sick man, and the Lord will raise him up, and, if he be in sins, they shall be forgiven him."

It was, in the past, largely reserved for those near death and was commonly called "extreme unction." The Second Vatican Council altered that: "Extreme unction, which may also and more fittingly be called 'anointing of the sick,' is not a sacrament for those only who are at the point of death."

The forehead and the hands are anointed with oil—once olive oil, now any vegetable oil blessed by the bishop during Holy Week. The effect, for the believer, is to take away sin, strengthen the soul of the sick person, remind him of divine mercy, and restore health if God believes that a cure would be to the person's spiritual advantage. It encourages the patience to bear suffering, the pain of ill health.

When Brian arrived at the apartment, Mr. Mendoza, an elderly man smelling of liquor, greeted him. The apartment was small, dark, filled with belongings. Brian had been there often before to visit Mrs. Mendoza, who was dying slowly of inoperable cancer. This time she was under a quilt on the living-room sofa, a serious expression frozen on her face. Brian spoke with her in Spanish as the husband stood solemnly in the doorway to the room. Then Brian began the sacrament, in English.

"Let the peace of Christ come down upon this house and all who live in it," he intoned.

He reminded the woman that Christ had restored the sick to health. She nodded. He led her in a confession of her sins.

"Lord have mercy," Brian chanted. The woman joined in.

He read from the Gospel of St. Matthew about Christ curing the centurion's son. "This is the Word of the Lord," he said. He asked Christ to comfort the woman with His love and mercy. "Lord, hear our prayers. We are laying our hands in your name with blessed oil provided by nature to serve the needs of men."

From a small silver cylinder, Brian dipped oil on his fingers and placed it gently on the woman's forehead and hands.

"Ease the suffering of our sick sister and make her well again," he said. In unison, Brian and the woman recited the Our Father. From the edge of the room the husband joined them.

"This is the lamb of God who takes away the sins of the world," Brian said, giving the woman communion.

He prayed for her "lasting health in mind and body." Then he made the sign of the cross and turned to leave.

"Good luck with the doctor," he said. "We'll be hoping for the best."

Mr. Mendoza escorted him to the front door. "I hear you're not well, Father," he said. "I hear you have some pain."

"Just my foot," Brian told him. The man had gotten the word about Brian's ankle. "They tell me I'm putting too much weight on it," Brian said, smiling and patting his stomach. He was not a priest who felt self-important, but he was pleased that his parishioners cared about his fate.

On the street he thought about the Mendozas. *He's so devoted to her. He can't bear to see her deteriorate and for so long. Now he needs a couple of drinks to get through each day. Too bad. A nice man. I wonder if I would react the same way to such stress, such anguish. He's doing the best he can.*

27

For a priest, the days can be indistinguishable. It does not matter that tomorrow may be Wednesday; what matters is what must be done on that day. For Brian, the seasons called attention to the passing of time. October was nearly over, and he recognized the cool winds of fall, their whispered warning of the coming of winter. Soon he would have to buy a warm coat; then he would celebrate Thanksgiving and Christmas. But he could not think so far ahead. Events in the present commanded his attention.

John Paul II returned to Rome, but the impact of his visit was felt by all priests. At the Tuesday-night gathering a few days after the Pope had left the country, the subject was on their minds.

The meeting that night was held at Archbishop Stepinac High School in White Plains, north of Manhattan, where classmate John Quinn taught. It was a chilly, rainy night, but Quinn had a warming feast ready: several pizzas, soft drinks, wine, beer, and ice-cream cake. The priests met in the living room—long, spacious quarters filled with leather furniture, down the hall from the rooms in which the resident priests lived.

Seven old friends from seminary days made it to White Plains. It was a long ride from some of the parishes, and several regular members of the group decided to stay at home out of the rain.

Dennis Sullivan of the class of '71 was curate at Saints Philip and James in the North Bronx; it was in a middle-class area, less agonized by violence and suffering. Witty, dry, and undeniably Irish, Sullivan brought a sense of humor to bear on his work.

Pat Carroll, a large, chubby, amiable man, had grown up with Brian; he was administrator of St. Thomas Aquinas in the South Bronx, one of the archdiocese's most devastated areas.

Bob Ritchie had clung to a youthful, athletic appearance better than the others; he was without the protruding stomach that rectory food almost always guaranteed. Blond, blue-eyed, and outgoing, he was the archdiocese's choice to be director of the Catholic Youth Organization. He worked in the chancery high rise on the East Side and lived with a dog named Brian in a rectory in Harlem.

Larry Quinn, serious, brooding, idealistic, served as curate at St. John Vianney church in the North Bronx; he was seeking a transfer.

John Quinn, no relation, didn't have the temperament for parish work; he was a contemplative, scholarly man. He did what he did best: he taught history and religion. A reticent man, he was a listener; he did not participate in the dissemination of small talk.

Dennis Keane, tall, handsome, boyish, did not deal with the gritty problems of the inner city, either. He was curate at Our Lady of Perpetual Help in Pelham Manor (and teacher of religion at the local Catholic high school). He rarely heard Spanish spoken in his parish; most of the others heard it daily and spoke it fluently.

FALL

The conversation immediately centered on the Pope's visit.

"When he arrived, when he was here in New York, I loved him," Dennis Keane said. "Then he moved on, and by the time he was ready to go back to Rome, I had started to hate him."

"I know, I know," Pat Carroll sighed.

"He was zinging us wherever he went. Birth control. Divorce. Sex. Everywhere," Keane elaborated.

Bob Ritchie had distributed communion in the upper deck at Yankee Stadium. He noted that he had felt like a popcorn vendor, passing a pile of Hosts down a long row of communicants.

Brian had heard that when it was over, the unused Hosts were returned to an area behind the Yankee dugout and placed in a pillowcase for later use. However, Brian told the others, he had also heard that someone had knocked the pillowcase out of a priest's hands and had spilled the Hosts all over the floor.

"It doesn't matter," Dennis Sullivan said. "They probably picked them up and used them at local churches that Sunday. 'Here's a Host from the Pope,' a priest could say, and the parishioner would scream with joy."

Sullivan repeated a story he had heard from a nun whose brother was a cop. "While all that was going on at Yankee Stadium, the cop gets called to one of those Holy Holy Jesus storefront churches, and when he gets there, this woman doctor of divinity is hollering. She tells him that there's a crazy guy with a machete at the altar. The cop draws his gun and says he's going in to get him. 'Oh, no, officer,' she says to him. 'We don't spill blood in the house of the Lord.' 'Well, what do you want me to do?' the cop asks her. 'Nothing. Let me handle it,' she says, and she marches down the aisle to the altar where the crazy is waiting for her. When she gets close to him, he slashes at her with the machete. She turns to the cop and screams, 'Shoot the motherfucker.'"

THE PRIEST

There was talk about wearing the collar at all times in bad neighborhoods. Some priests felt that it offered protection; others wondered if it did. Keane, now in his affluent suburban parish, had just bought his first black suit; he hadn't needed one as a teacher in a Catholic high school. Larry Quinn said he hadn't worn his collar in weeks; he got by in slacks and shirts in his parish. Some parishioners, he felt, were intimidated by the sight of the collar; he wanted to relate to them without seeming superior.

The subject shifted to gossip about newly assigned priests, wayward pastors, diocesan politics, death.

They all remembered a pompous, pious priest who conducted prayer meetings. "His prayers must bore God," Sullivan said. "We love you, we love you, we praise you—that's all he says."

Another priest they knew had been found dead in his room; the body had been there for several days. He had led a strange life, but a sincere one, trying to minister to drug addicts. Once he had conducted an exorcism to drive out the devils from a drug treatment center. It had tarnished his reputation, and his career had deteriorated.

"What did he die of?" Brian asked.

"We don't know. They're doing an autopsy," Carroll responded.

"I saw him not long ago," one of the other priests remembered. "You know, back in the seminary we thought he was mystical. In those days he seemed spiritual, distracted, on a different road from the rest of us. Now all he seems is weird."

The conversation came full circle, back to the Pope.

"Did you see those guys in Philadelphia in their cassocks?" Brian asked.

"Yes, when the Pope spoke they stood up and cheered."

"That's Philadelphia," Brian observed.

The hall clock chimed. It was 1 A.M.

Brian yawned. "Time to go," he said. The others got up slowly and made their good-byes to John Quinn. They all rode the elevator to the ground floor, then walked to their cars in the parking lot. Under a gray black sky, with a drizzle coming down, Dennis Sullivan did a precise imitation of John Paul II—smiling, waving his arms, blessing a multitude. Then they got into their own cars and were off to their parishes.

Heading back to Incarnation, Brian reflected on the Tuesday-night gatherings, how essential they were to his life. They enabled him and the other younger priests to let off steam, to maintain their solidarity, to discuss their common problems. And at the heart of the meetings was that enduring friendship, so important in combating the latent loneliness in a priest's life.

28

Brian stared at his lunch. There was a large mound of corned beef hash on his plate, topped by two overpoached eggs. He ate slowly. Sergio and Ken were at work, as usual, and Jack Barry had gone off on a mission of his own, destination unknown. Tom Leonard sat beside Brian, poking at his hash, suffering the tragedy, however minor, of the eggs. He appreciated Brian's weariness after the late night with his classmates, so he kept the talk to a minimum.

Jack Barry was back after lunch, in time for a staff meeting that Tom had called. Tom didn't like meetings, nor did Brian or Jack, but there were matters to deal with. The group gathered in Tom's living room. In addition to the three priests, there were three nuns: Sister Maureen, the school principal; Sister Laura, an Ursiline nun who headed the CCD program; and Sister Teresa, who had taught in the CCD program for several years.

At thirty-seven, Sister Maureen was a veteran of the Catholic school system; she had taught at several schools, including Incarnation's, and had returned to serve as principal at Tom's invitation. Short, stocky, assertive, she spoke with a hard-edged wit. She had survived a malignant brain tumor years before—some had termed it a genuine miracle—and was determined to rule the school, whatever the challenges. She did not wear the habit of her order, the Sisters of Charity, preferring conservative skirts and blouses.

She opened the meeting by declaring her frustration about the fact that the school copier was broken. "I think I'll put it in the alley, so someone can steal it," she said with a smirk.

Tom had other matters on his mind. He wanted to talk about offering double species—bread and wine—at communion, instead of just the customary bread. The custom was being revived by the Church; it had been common in the past, then abandoned in favor of simply offering bread.

"At other parishes, teams bake the bread," Brian said. "And they use as many as ten chalices. It's all well coordinated. Should we go that way?"

"Perhaps. But there's the logistics of getting people in and out. It's a problem," Tom noted.

"You'll have accidents," Jack predicted.

"Well, if children can taste the wine at home, they can deal with it in church. The parents can help us," said Sister Teresa, the only nun present in a habit.

A native New Yorker, Sister Teresa had spent many of her fifty-three years ministering to the poor. She did it always in the gray habit of her order, the Society of Helpers (there were fewer than ninety in the United States). She worked with Brian in the CCD program; there was a fondness between them.

She wore the habit, she had told Brian, because "it makes us more available, more public. People can approach me, knowing who I am and what they can expect from me. It enables me to help people." Thin, pale, ethereal in manner, she was bound by a strong devotion to her faith. It was a faith that Brian admired as genuine.

As she spoke, he remembered listening to her talk about

221

her decision to become a nun. "There was that sense of joy that you had found your birth," she had told him. "We always said, you sign a blank check and the Lord fills it in as you go along." On another occasion she had said to Brian, "A good priest is primarily a man of God, a man of prayer given to God. And if he is that, he's going to give himself to others, because you cannot give yourself to God and be selfish. People sense that love of God."

Her words had moved Brian. Now, seated beside her in Tom's living room, he looked at her with conspicuous affection.

Tom's voice interrupted Brian's thoughts. "We have material for both parents and kids from the diocese," Tom announced. "We need Eucharistic ministers for our English masses. We have five or six for the Spanish. Let's get more."

"Make an announcement for them to come to see the priests about it," Jack suggested. "People might come. People we might not think of, who are over eighteen."

"Young college students might be good," Sister Teresa said.

"We could train them in three classes," Brian said.

"Let's set the beginning of the year, or maybe February first, as our target," Tom suggested. "Laura can do a plan for the kids, and Teresa for the adults. We can buy the chalices at the Metropolitan Museum. I hear they have some lovely ones in pewter. We'll need six or more. They must be a hundred dollars apiece, at least."

"That's costly," Brian said.

"Yes, but we don't have much of a choice," Tom said. "And don't forget to tell the adults about the hygienic aspect of it. And remember to tell the kids not to laugh."

Sister Maureen told the others that it would be wise to have priests visit school classrooms several times a month. She was forceful.

"I know that your time schedules are crazy, but I feel

strongly about your presence," she said. "They should know you away from the altar."

"Yes, we really ought to be there," Tom agreed. "How are we doing on the CCD program?" he asked.

"We can use a fourth-grade teacher on Wednesday, from three-thirty to four-thirty," Sister Maureen suggested. "Perhaps one of the school's teachers could do it." She nominated two candidates.

"One of them lives near here," Sister Teresa observed.

"She's new and wouldn't have a tired attitude," Sister Maureen added.

"You know, I'm ashamed at the lack of young people at mass," Sister Teresa digressed.

"At the Spanish mass there are tons of them," Brian said.

"I mean little kids, not teen-agers," Sister Teresa explained.

"I think that the teachers—to get back to them—are confused about our new approach. They don't know we're not as rigid about right and wrong as we used to be," Sister Laura said.

She was tanned from a sojourn in Mexico and was wearing a yellow Mexican cotton dress and sandals. In early middle age, she lived with other nuns in an apartment a short drive from Incarnation and she commuted by car to her work in the parish. A soft-spoken, modest woman, she enjoyed working with the children in the CCD program.

"You know, even if people aren't living a strict moral life, they want the Church to tell them what to do," Brian said.

"What's new at school?" Tom asked Sister Maureen.

"Well, first of all, I'm thinking of resigning," she said, smiling. "No, not really. I'm pleased with the way things are going. Of course, we have a gas leak in the cafeteria and the school could blow up. But there is a sense of calmness about the place now. Really."

Tom informed the others that the car raffle—to raise

money for the CCD program and the school—was going well. Books of tickets had gone out to students and parents. The money was necessary, he said, because new blackboards were needed for the school, rooms needed painting, and he anticipated enormous fuel bills in the winter months ahead.

"There's a dance coming up this Friday," Brian said. "Watch out, there might be trouble at the school that night. I'm opposed to selling tickets at the door because then you get older kids from the public schools, kids maybe nineteen or twenty, and they can get drunk and unruly. The last time we had to call the cops. This time we need chaperones, plenty of them."

"Okay, find some," Tom said.

"I like the idea of those once-a-month meetings with the teachers," Brian said. Sister Maureen had proposed such meetings so that the faculty could get to know the parish priests. "It's absolutely useful and good. The priest could meet with the teachers of the grades he teaches religion to, and that would be excellent."

"Yes, it's agreed, Brian. We'll do it," Tom said.

"Fine, just fine," Sister Maureen said with a smile.

"The meeting is adjourned," Tom announced.

Thanks be to God, Brian thought, as he rushed out of the room, two steps behind Jack. Formal discussions, even when essential, made him weary. Brian favored action. He would rather be doing his work than talking about it.

29

The days became chillier. The sun disappeared earlier; daylight gave way to darkness. Brian kept on the move by confronting parishioners' problems in the rectory, visiting them in their apartments, spending time in hospitals and nursing homes, baptizing children, marrying couples, burying the dead, hearing confessions, celebrating mass. His life moved in small, familiar circles.

After more than eight years at Incarnation, he had come to realize that he would have to accept a transfer. He wasn't quite ready to do so, although he knew that the move was inevitable. In the past a priest was simply told to move; he packed and left within a few days. But the Church discipline to command such moves had deteriorated. Now it was a matter of a phone call to the priest from the director of priest personnel for the archdiocese with a suggestion for the priest to consider.

Such a phone call came on a windy, cold day in late October. Would Brian consider leaving Incarnation for a post at a church in the South Bronx?

He didn't like the idea, but he didn't say so. He was polite. Yes, he would investigate it and report back.

He left the rectory, got into his car, and drove to the parish. Everywhere he looked there was devastation —empty lots where buildings once stood, burned-out shells of tenements once fully occupied, now empty except for loitering drug addicts and people in hiding. The neighborhood stores were boarded up. An evacuation had taken place.

The parish's old church stood in the middle of the squalor, like a bomb-proof remnant in a German city after World War II. It had few parishioners, Brian knew, although several activist priests still lived in its rectory, hoping to energize the neighborhood against all odds.

Brian parked across the street from the church. He stared at the desolate panorama. In his final year at the seminary he had spent time in such a place, working the streets; he remembered this neighborhood, although he did not recognize it now. The changes were terrifying.

Mother Teresa, who won the Nobel Prize for her work with the poor in India, wouldn't accept such an assignment, he thought sardonically; she was a saint and he was not.

He drove back to Incarnation and phoned the director of priest personnel. He told him that he'd rather not make the move, not *that* move. The director agreed; yes, it was a depressing place, tough to survive there. *Then why did he ask me to take it? Someone had to take it, that's why.*

Brian's problem—where to go from Incarnation —remained unresolved. Some priests, faced with the impossible burden of living out their careers in such a tormenting parish, fled the life of a priest entirely. That was not an alternative for Brian.

He did not want to spend his life running bingo games, worrying about the solvency of a parish at the expense of the problems of its parishioners. He had not been ordained to do that. A priest had to maintain his sense of purpose and not permit himself to be distracted.

When he viewed his future, it seemed indefinable. He knew that it was vital to maintain his spiritual life, his friendships, and family ties. In his role as a priest he differentiated between constancy and fidelity, stressing the latter, the opportunity to fulfill God's will. Although he had chosen to do that as a priest, he realized that there were alternatives, such as social work, the Peace Corps, VISTA. Fifty years ago, to serve in that way, you could only be a priest or a nun; today there were other choices.

He was determined to face the problems that plagued the Church, rather than flee from them. For example, he recognized that there was a relationship between the Church's opposition to birth control and lower mass attendance. If in a vital area like birth control the Church was telling people that it was against God's law, then it should come as no surprise that many disobeyed such a law. And that disobedience became a progression, a path away from the Church, from attending mass and practicing the faith. Brian agonized over the Church's stand on birth control, but he was not certain it would be altered. "We'll have to wait for the next Pope to find out," he had said to Dan.

Brian was willing to wait, in the hope that change would come.

Brian was tired. The rectory phone had rung at 4:30 A.M. and he had answered it.

"Do you mind talking to me while I release my seed?" a man's voice had said.

"Go fuck yourself," Brian had shouted, hanging up.

He told Jack Barry about it at breakfast.

"Are you sure it was an outside call?" Jack asked.

Brian laughed, but he was still tired. The conversation

shifted to the death of the priest who at forty had died alone in his room, the priest who had ministered to drug addicts. Brian wondered if they had converted him. Whatever the case, it was a tragedy. "A fine, fine man," he bellowed to no one in particular.

After breakfast he managed a cheerful phone conversation with a young Italian woman who taught in the CCD program; she was going to get married, she told Brian, and she wanted him to officiate. He was pleased.

After that came a call from his aunt, his father's brother's wife; his uncle Pat, who was in a nursing home in the Bronx, was not well. Could Brian visit him? Of course.

Brian had not seen his uncle in several years; Pat was a recluse from the rest of the family, a man who liked to drink and be by himself. Brian realized that Pat might die, and he didn't want to wait for that to happen. He drove up to the Bronx.

He couldn't find the nursing home. Four passersby gave him faulty directions. He grumbled. Finally, he found the place. His aunt was in the lobby waiting for him, and they went up to his uncle's room.

Now in his seventies, Pat lay in the fetal position beneath the white sheet. He stared at Brian, then clutched Brian's hand tenaciously. Brian wanted to take off his coat, but he couldn't; Pat would not release his hand.

"We'll pray together, okay?" Brian asked.

"Yes," Pat mumbled.

"Oh, Father, how good it is to see you," Brian's aunt said.

Brian got out of his coat, held his uncle's hand again, touched his head lightly. Then he prayed.

"May the Lord Jesus show you His mercy," he chanted. "May He give you comfort in the midst of your sickness. May Jesus protect you in body and soul."

He recited an Our Father and prayed for a cure. "I'll

remember you at mass," he told his uncle, who stared blankly at him. "And I'll be dropping by to see you again. Yes, I'll be back."

Brian knew that Pat might not last long. The old Irish were vanishing. Family friends were going one by one, the past shredding away. He hadn't been as close to Uncle Pat as he had to other relatives, but he was sorry to see him curled up in the nursing home bed, almost incoherent. The day, which had begun badly, seemed to be getting worse.

His weariness mounted all day. He needed a nap, but there wasn't time for one. He sustained himself until evening when, still exhausted, he drove up to Dunwoodie to speak to a group of priests who were attending a residence week at the seminary. They had come up for five days to listen to a variety of speakers discuss matters of pastoral concern. Brian, whose background in thanatology was known in the archdiocese, was scheduled to lead a discussion of "Ministry to the Sick and Dying."

The sixteen priests in the room, several of them pastors, had been ordained between 1950 and 1960—all were older than Brian. They assembled in a small lounge in a wing of the seminary, seated in chairs lining the four walls. They wore cardigans, sports shirts, and the customary black pants, socks, and shoes. They looked like golfers in limited mourning. Brian was the only one wearing a collar.

He slipped it off, stuck it into his shirt pocket, hung his jacket on a chair, and began.

"The whole modern movement in regard to the care of the sick and the dying is usually dated back to people like Elisabeth Kübler-Ross. She began to teach a group of seminary students at Cook County Hospital in Chicago. At that time she was a physician. Later she became a psychiatrist. She was very concerned with the fact that there was no one really taking care of the needs of the dying in that hospital. There was a conspiracy of silence. Her premise was that you could talk to someone about their own death. You just had to know how to listen first."

He explained the five stages of a person's adaptation to death, as Kübler-Ross defined them: disbelief, anger, making a bond with God ("If I live until my daughter graduates, I'll submit to death"), depression, and acceptance. He pointed out that not every patient proceeds through all five stages.

"She told doctors and those of us who deal with the dying that we had lost the power of laying on of hands, actually touching a patient. It's the first thing you should do when you visit a patient, she said."

One of the priests interrupted. "I find that doctors shirk the responsibility of telling patients they are terminal. Is that common?"

"Unfortunately it is," Brian responded. "Remember, in medical school they were taught that the ones who died were their failures. They're not trained to handle death. The natural reaction is to run."

"Brian, you were saying that it's important to make contact. Always?" a dapper-looking priest asked.

"Almost always. Do what I do," Brian said. "While introducing yourself, take the person's hand or make some sort of physical contact. Then, listen.

"That's vital. A very good friend of mine has had two cancer operations. He's a doctor himself, and the only person who related to him in the hospital, the only one who would spend time with him, was the charwoman, the woman who came in to mop the floors. Doctors came in, but they didn't have time. Friends didn't have time. But that charwoman would come in every morning and ask him how he was and he would say 'lousy' and she would ask why and listen to him.

"You are saying to the patient, 'I'm here and I'm willing to listen and to help. There's nothing more important for me right now than being with you.' You can do the small things. Peel fruit. Rub the patient's back. Put down the side rail on the bed. People in a bed with the side rails up feel as if they're in a coffin."

One of the priests leaned forward to ask Brian's advice. "I recently had a case where a kid was hit by a car and died," he said. "The father went into a rage and put his fist through a wall. The mother was crying, but she had faith. I didn't have the words. I didn't know what to say."

"The best thing might be to say you don't know what to say because what has happened is so terrible," Brian said.

"You can sound like a Pollyanna if you start talking about the eternal life," an older priest observed. The discussion was getting lively, with more priests joining in.

"I had to tell four children, ages eight to thirteen, that their father had just been killed in a car accident," another priest said. "And when it was all over, the family thanked me for my kind words. I had never said one word. I had just stood there and cried. Sometimes that's all you can do."

"Yes, it's important to be there. Just to be there," Brian said. "The parish priest should be there for the dying, even though there are a lot of other priorities in the parish. That should be a top priority."

"But if somebody in your parish dies, Brian, and you have to break the news, how do you do it?" a tall, spindly priest asked.

"Usually they'll get the message from your expression and your attitude before you say anything," Brian replied. "And you'll get a message from them as well.

"When my mother was dying of cancer, in the hospital one day she said to me that the doctor did the tests and she was sure he'd tell me what they revealed. The next morning I came in and she said, 'I guess you saw the doctor,' and I said I had, and she said okay. That was it. She was telling me that she knew she was dying. She knew that if the test results had been favorable, I would have said so.

"From that point on, we had permission to bring her Harvey's Bristol Cream, which she liked but would never drink because it was too expensive. And we'd bring her Carvel ice cream and she'd eat that three or four times a day. She knew what was happening. She was counseling all of us to accept the fact that she was dying."

The other priests nodded in appreciation of what he was telling them. Brian realized that his visit was almost over. He had a final point to make.

"The greatest thing we can do for the dying is to escort them on the journey," he said. "You bring them to the point where they can continue alone. Then we've fulfilled our own Christian mission."

The priests lingered while Brian put on his jacket and headed for the door. On the drive back to the rectory the subject of death remained in his mind. He thought of his uncle Pat, wondering if he could pull the plug on him if that seemed appropriate. No, he couldn't contribute actively to killing anyone. He might withhold medical help to a terminal patient if that help would only prolong agony. It was a subtle and troubling distinction, not always easy to recognize. He knew that he would rather see a relative die at home in two weeks than languish hopelessly in a hospital for months. *Between two depressing alternatives, one is always better than the other.*

30

The winds of November carried a cold message, but did not bring much snow. Brian was grateful for that. There was a bit of annoying slush one day, but he bought a pair of rubber boots and got through it. When the clerk in the shoe store asked him if he wanted to use his clerical tax exemption on the purchase, Brian told him, "No need to. These are for me, not for the Church."

More and more he thought about his uncle Pat in the nursing home in the Bronx. The image of the man, curled up beneath the white sheet, returned. Brian decided to visit him again.

Pat seemed more alert than he had during Brian's previous visit. He spoke without prodding from Brian.

"Where are you?" he asked Brian.

"I'm at Incarnation," Brian said. "But they'll be getting me to move soon. You look good, stronger than before."

"No," his uncle grunted.

"Not so strong, eh? But actually you're doing better, Pat, you are," Brian asserted.

Pat told Brian, haltingly, that he was worried that the nursing home would close and he would have to be moved. It was a common fear, Brian knew. He told Pat not to worry about it, that it wasn't likely to happen.

At Pat's request, Brian cranked down the bed. Pat stared at the ceiling as they chatted. Brian could understand Pat today—another sign of progress, however temporary. Then Brian said a prayer. "Guide him in health and faith," he said.

He held Pat's hand and gazed at him. It did not appear to Brian that Pat would survive, but he felt that some sort of miracle, possibly minor and not wholly remarkable, had occurred. A miracle in the form of a remission.

He left the room and headed toward the elevator. *For the Irish, death is taken seriously before it happens. That's why we call the obituaries the Irish sports page.*

He returned to the rectory in time for lunch; he tried to do that whenever possible because it had a stabilizing effect on him—a return to the center of his life.

He got a phone call from a woman he knew, a parishioner.

"My daughter says she wants a divorce," the woman said sadly. "Will she be thrown out of the Church?"

Brian knew that some uninformed Catholics assumed that a Catholic couldn't get a divorce. As a result, many divorced Catholics stopped coming to church.

"We believe that marriages ought to be saved whenever possible," Brian told the woman. "But if a divorce is the only way out of a bad situation, we don't oppose it. The problem arises when remarriage becomes a possibility and the couple wants to be married in the Church. That's why we advise people like your daughter to have the marriage annulled, if she can."

"How do you get that?" the woman asked.

"You need proof that the marriage, from its roots, was not valid. You know—dope addiction, alcoholism, abuse. Something that prevented a full commitment. You have to prove that in a Church court. If you can, you'll get the annulment."

"I see. I see," the woman said. "I'll let you know if we need more advice. Thanks for what you told me."

"I'll be here if you need me," Brian said.

He went to his car and drove to Cardinal Spellman High School in the Bronx. In the school auditorium, neatly dressed priests all in black sat obediently while Terence Cardinal Cooke spoke to them about the archdiocese's annual fund drive.

Brian was with two of his classmates and had trouble paying attention as the Cardinal droned on. The drive, Cooke said, "was enabling the loving service of the Church to continue." He read a prepared statement, then talked about the declining number of priests ("There is a widespread decline, but we do not know precisely why").

"The best action a family can render," he proclaimed, "is to give a priest or nun to the Church. It's more valuable than money." There was nothing quite like "the joy of serving the Lord and His people . . . all the way."

Brian fidgeted.

The Cardinal talked about the visit of John Paul II in glowing terms, then turned to the fund appeal itself. In last year's appeal, he said, more than $6,700,000 had been pledged and more than 95 percent of that received in cash. This year's goal was the same, and he urged the priests to "do your best and follow the campaign plan. That's all we ask."

He thanked various people for their help during the previous drive, including "the secretaries; they kept us all in very good shape." Several priests suppressed a laugh. The Cardinal went on to promise that more of the money raised would make its way back to the parishes. "The heart of the Church in New York is in our parishes," he said.

A thin, pale, self-effacing man, he did not inspire enthusiasm among those present. They listened, but only patiently.

He went on to remind them that the annual operating expenses of the archdiocese came to more than $500,000,000. "With God's help, we will succeed again, even in these times," he said, turning the podium over to a professional fund-raiser who was supervising the appeal. The fund-raiser, glib, slick, and persuasive, made his presentation. Afterward, the Cardinal encouraged questions.

Brian continued to fidget.

One priest suggested that it might help the appeal to stress the archdiocese's work in the field of education. The Cardinal agreed. Another priest noted that stressing education might injure the appeal. The Cardinal nodded.

"There is something beautiful about how the poor donate," the Cardinal said. Brian grimaced.

The Cardinal thanked all the priests for their loyalty, affection, and service. He prayed for their well-being and ended the meeting.

It was late in the afternoon and Brian bolted from his seat, walked out of the school expediently, and got into his car. He appreciated the need for fund-raising by the archdiocese, but his distaste for meetings and boring presentations had made him edgy. The Cardinal was a pleasant man, he thought, but not a flamboyant leader. He drove back to the rectory alone, glad to be returning to the parish.

Several days later, on the Monday before Thanksgiving, Brian conducted a celebration in the school auditorium for more than one hundred third- and fourth-grade students. He stood in his white vestments in front of the rows of seats as the children quietly filed in. It was chilly in the large room; there was something wrong with the school boiler. The children smiled at Brian as they took their seats. They had brought with them a variety of canned goods to be given to the poor; the fact was, many of *them* were poor.

"May we have hearts that are thankful," Brian prayed. "This is a special day to thank God for all the things He has given us."

Several children marched forward and displayed artwork they had done for the occasion—drawings of a turkey, the harvest, the Creation. One had made a poster: Indians Were Pilgrims' First Good Friends.

"As a way of showing the many things we thank God for, we want to give and help others," Brian said. The principal, Sister Maureen, read *The Giving Tree*, a children's tale by Shel Silverstein, to make the point that Brian had stated. When she was done, Brian told the children, "We are most happy when we are giving, right? And God, or Jesus, is happy when He gives to us."

The children sang their praise to the Lord, then Brian chose four of them to join him in another prayer. "God's love is without end. Praise God all you people. Thank Him everyone. He gives us His love and His light."

The children held hands as Brian read from St. Luke, about "a man who became a very good friend of Jesus. Once a group of lepers asked Jesus for help and He cured them. One thanked Jesus and praised Him, and Jesus asked, 'Where are the other nine?' The others forgot to thank Jesus. Who would you rather be—one of the nine, or the one who had thanks in his heart for God? Has God helped us?"

"Yes," the children shouted in unison.

"That's why we're celebrating Thanksgiving," Brian told

them. "Now we will help those who don't have what we have. Let's put the food on the table."

Row by row the children moved forward and placed their gifts of food on a long table, touched an open Bible, and returned to their seats.

"God our Father we thank you for all things you have given us," Brian said. Everyone recited the Our Father. After a final song, "Somebody touched me . . . It must have been the hand of the Lord," the children filed out of the auditorium.

As they passed Brian, he patted them, poked them, stroked them, kissed them.

"Hi, Father!" a little girl in pigtails shouted.

"Ah, my good friend Emily," Brian said, holding her hand.

"Hey, Father, want to play football with us?" a skinny boy asked.

"Afraid not, Jimmy, I'm not fast enough," Brian said.

"Okay, then come and watch," the boy said.

"That's a good idea," Brian said.

When the last child had gone out, Brian surveyed the room momentarily, recalling the experience with satisfaction, and moved out of the school to the street.

Christmas

"Our Heavenly Father said mankind was the salt of the earth, son, not the honey. . . . A true priest is never loved, get that into your head. And if you must know: the Church doesn't care a rap whether you're loved or not, my lad. Try first to be respected and obeyed."

GEORGE BERNANOS
The Diary of a Country Priest

"Faith demands certain renunciations, but not the renunciation of intelligence, exploration, spiritual and cultural renewal, profound social concern and the defense of one's inner integrity."

THOMAS MERTON
A Thomas Merton Reader

31

Winter had come to stay. The winds were no longer temperate. They were chilly and strong, and Brian had to wear a warm down-filled jacket on his rounds. His spirit, however, remained warm. He had spent Thanksgiving Day at his sister Maureen's; the eastern branch of the O'Connor family had gathered at Maureen's for the feast and for the gaiety such occasions inspired. Brian felt revived.

It was the first Friday in December, and for Brian that meant it was time again for communion calls. It was a sunny, cold day, and he felt energetic. He collected the Hosts he would need and was out of the rectory by 10 A.M.

He went from block to block, apartment to apartment, bringing parishioners closer to their Church: "Lamb of God, you take away the sins of the world. . . . Happy are we who are called to this supper." The faces and the names and the problems, he knew them all. Mary and Jack and Emily and Mrs. Esposito and Josefina and Nina and Tony and all the others. They waited patiently for him to arrive, and they were grateful to see him. Mrs. Esposito handed him a donation for the Church. "Please, Father, for you," she said. "You very nice to me. God gonna help you."

Although the communion rite he brought to the parishioners was identical for all of them, he tried to think of them as individuals, with distinct backgrounds and differing problems. It was his way of lending dignity and identity to their lives. He did not believe in applying inflexible rules to their existence, telling them that they could do this and couldn't do that. He had a name for his philosophy: personalism. He tailored dogma to the needs of the people he comforted. He was not interested in labels: homosexual (what some fellow priests termed "a touch of lavender"), birth-control user, abortionist. His personalism told him that while there were natural laws, such laws had to be resilient. There were immigrants who stole because their boss didn't pay them enough, who stole because their kids were starving.

The air had turned even colder. He turned up the collar of his coat and stiffened as he headed directly into the wind toward the rectory.

He passed a young girl talking animatedly to a tall black man. A cocaine deal, he thought. It offended him. As a realist, he knew that such things went on around him. As a man of faith, he hoped such self-destructiveness could be countered by a belief in God. It was a perpetual struggle, but he did not flinch in the face of it.

He moved faster; the wind had become painful. It would get colder now, he knew, and then it would be Christmas. If he could help solve *some* of the problems his parishioners brought to him, it would be a worthwhile holiday. Maybe, he thought, he could improve the quality of just a few lives between now and Christmas. He would try.

When he got back to the rectory, he opened the envelope Mrs. Esposito had given him; it contained fifty dollars. "I don't believe it," he said to himself, feeling both guilt and gratitude. "That poor woman."

It was time for lunch. Ken Smith was there, home from his job. A priest Ken knew in Massachusetts was preaching to throngs, people who came to hear him from all over the country; the priest had become a faith healer. There was some evidence of cures he had inspired. Ken did not doubt the possibility.

"Do you doubt it?" Ken asked Brian.

"Well, there are miracles with a small *m*," Brian said. "An alcoholic who suddenly turns around. A conversion. Enough of that to say I believe in miracles. Having meaning and purpose all of a sudden, where it didn't exist before. I would regard that as a miracle, a sign that Jesus touched that person."

"And what about miracles with a capital *M*?" Ken asked.

"Mother Teresa was teaching in a middle-class girls' school and was on a train to Darjeeling when she had a vision," Brian began. "She felt that Jesus spoke three sentences to her, telling her that she should stop teaching and should work with the poorest of the poor. She went back to Calcutta and founded her religious order. The rest of her life had structure. I can appreciate that."

"What about in your own life?" Ken asked.

"Well, toward the end of my time at Cathedral High School, I had a very strange thing happen. I broke out with something. I don't know exactly what it was. It wasn't a rash. It was more like a fungus. It was on my arm and my leg, and it was painful and I wasn't sleeping. They really couldn't figure out what had caused it.

"I went into an intensive period of praying and reading the Bible. I felt more determined, very close to God. And the rash did eventually disappear. It was a very religious moment."

"A miracle?" Ken asked.

"Maybe, maybe not. But it brought me closer to God, and that's what is important," Brian said.

"True," Ken nodded. "But do you believe in faith healing?"

"Yes. When we read the Bible, when we see Jesus curing people and laying His hands upon people, that touch caused a physical cure. Today people wonder if those cures really took place. I say they're a real sign of the presence of God's kingdom. Why can't that be true today? If we believe that God can intervene in a very unusual way, that everything is possible with God, there can be that miracle. There are cures that can only be explained that way."

"So you do believe that it is possible to cure people by faith?" Ken asked.

"Yes, I do. But that must be amended a bit. I wouldn't want to give a person the impression that if he isn't cured, it's his own fault, the lack of power of his own faith. It would be a matter of accepting God's will and not putting Him to the test."

Ken had brought a cold back with him. He sniffed and blew his nose.

"Can you cure this?" he asked.

"Sure. Take two aspirins and go right to bed," Brian said. "You'll be better in the morning. I promise."

Ken laughed, got up, and headed for his room.

"And remember," Brian said, "if you're not better tomorrow, it's not my fault or your fault or God's."

"I understand," Ken said with mock solemnity. "I understand."

In early December he received two pre-Christmas "gifts." Montclair State College offered him the chance to teach two courses, including the one on death and dying. A call from the archdiocese headquarters invited him to teach a course at the seminary on "Ministry to the Sick and Dying" for priests preparing to assume the role of pastor. Brian was flattered and pleased—not only would he be able to put his knowledge of thanatology to work, but he would be earning some extra income. The prospect perked up his spirits during the pre-Christmas season, a time when activity increased and exhaustion always seemed imminent.

One rainy evening Brian went to the school auditorium to introduce fifth- and sixth-grade CCD students to penance, their first confession. They had been taught about the process of bringing their sins to the priest and receiving absolution; this night, they would participate in it.

At 7:30 P.M. Brian stood near the stage of the school auditorium in his white vestments with a purple stole. He greeted students and their parents.

First he spoke of the beauty of the sacrament, in both English and Spanish. Then he led a procession from the school to the lower church, carrying a lighted candle. In the church parents and students took their seats. Near the altar a banner was posted: God's Plan—You Are All Brothers. Walk as Children of Light.

Brian led them in prayer: "Granted that we may meet Jesus this evening." A hymn was sung in Spanish. Brian explained the use of the Christ Candle, which he had carried: "It is the light of Christ guiding us." He read from St. Paul, with the help of two children who read portions as well. Several children read petitions of thanksgiving. Brian told them all that after each child had gone to confession, he or she would return to the pews after attaching a small felt figure of a child to the banner, to symbolize their devotion to each other and to Christ, then each would light a candle.

"There are moments in life when we say no to God," Brian told them. "We say or do something that is wrong. After those times, we say to God, I am sorry." Several children read petitions of forgiveness. "For the times when we want everything our own way," one small boy said, "forgive us."

"We know that God is always ready to forgive us, when we are sorry," Brian instructed. God, he told them, is like the father in the parable of the prodigal son; he read that story while a group of children mimed it beside him. Then Tom Leonard and Jack Barry joined Brian in front of the altar; they recited a prayer: "We too are sinners, but you have chosen us to be messengers of your love and mercy," they chanted.

As music filled the church from a record player, the children chose their confessor from the three priests and lined up. The confession was face to face; the lines were monitored by three CCD nuns and a lay teacher. The children, well dressed and properly behaved, waited patiently to see the priests.

Brian's line was the longest.

When the last child had completed confession and had returned to his seat, Brian returned to stand at the altar. He invited the children to join him, in a semicircle, with hands clasped. He led them in reciting an Our Father. Tom Leonard gave each child a certificate.

After Brian's final blessing ("Guide us and strengthen us"), the children began to file out, singing "Somebody Touched Me." As they did, Jack Barry moved next to Brian and said, "This little kid came in with his mouth curled down and a tear in his eye and he couldn't say a word. I said, 'Are you scared?' and he said, 'Yes, I'm scared.' I told him not to worry. We talked about the Mets and the Jets and he got through it just fine."

There were moments when Jack would suppress his nagging sense of irritation and express genuine kindness.

When Brian got back to his rooms in the rectory on that rainy night, he found a pile of drawings a teacher in the school had collected for him. Brian had spoken of penance to the fourth grade, as well as to the CCD children. He went through the drawings.

"Father O'Connor—Thank you for forgiving me."

"I thank you for confessing me and the way you forgave me. With love. Bye!"

"Thank you for spending the time with me. I feel much better now."

When confession was productive, it converted you from the old way of doing things to a new way—you felt better. Now, thanks to a change two years earlier in the rite of confession, the priest could deal with sin *and* provide spiritual advice, formerly kept out of confession. Brian was pleased, too, with another change. The person confessing could either sit or kneel in front of the priest, instead of remaining concealed behind a screen. The old confessionals were still used, as an option, but more and more people wanted to talk to their priest face to face.

Brian appreciated the value of confession, although he did not go to confession himself very often. He prayed to God, and in that way he spoke directly to God; when he felt he needed the rite of penance, he would confess to a priest in another parish, avoiding the complications of confessing to a priest with whom he lived.

He shuffled through the drawings.

"I thank you for everything you have done. In my confession, I was very happy."

"You are the best father I know."

"I am sorry I did not tell you all my sins. I hope to go to confession fast again. I was really scared. Thank you anyway. I love you very much."

Brian read the messages and smiled. It was after 10 P.M. He walked over to the television set and snapped on a news program. He had not been in touch with the outside world all day, and he missed that. He sat back and listened.

32

The priests administered the sacraments, but the life of Incarnation parish could not be sustained without the support of eager parishioners. Various cultural groups met at Incarnation, and those groups, working diligently to help the Church, had their own leaders. When the Church needed money, it depended upon its loyalists in the parish. When the rectory needed repairs, the priests called on parishioners to help.

Among the leaders Brian respected most, Pedro Tarno held a special place. Active in a variety of community Church groups, Tarno did not wish to lead, but he insisted on being present whenever he could be of help.

Tarno, a Cuban who looked like Omar Sharif—dark, stocky, handsome, with a thick moustache—was born in a small Cuban fishing village in 1945. His father owned a fishing fleet. The family moved to Havana when Pedro, an only child, was two. The father became the owner of several grocery stores and made enough money to send Pedro to the United States in 1961, after Castro had assumed power.

CHRISTMAS

Pedro was not intimidated by his new home. He continued his education, living with several different Cuban families in New York. In 1966 he joined the army and served in Vietnam. When he returned, he got married, fathered two children, and settled down in Incarnation parish. He got a job with an insurance company and made progress in its international division.

By 1979 he had saved enough money to send for his parents; they were allowed to leave Cuba, and Pedro met them in Montreal and escorted them to his home in New York. A few months later, he found them an apartment of their own, near his. With his attractive Cuban wife, Elizabeth, Tarno had managed to make the most of life in Upper Manhattan. His success, he asserted, was due in large measure to his belief in God, his friendship with Brian, and his work at Incarnation.

One evening in December, Pedro came to visit Brian. Pedro had volunteered to help decorate the church for Christmas, and Brian knew that he would do a splendid job and not seek any credit for it. They sat in Brian's living room and talked informally, as friends, about their faith.

"After I emigrated from Cuba, there were moments when I was afraid," Pedro said. "But when I look back, I think religion was my strongest support.

"My faith is vital to me. A relationship with God has to be twenty-four hours, three hundred and sixty-five days a year. Raising a family, sitting down with your work, whatever you do. Religion cannot be just a Sunday thing or a praying thing. It has to be your whole life. There is the hand of God in everything you do."

"It inspires you to participate in life," Brian said.

"Exactly. You know, if my religion was only coming to church and taking communion and going back home to pray, that would not be religion. To me, religion has to be shared. The fact that I have friends who come with me to church, the fact that I get involved in projects, whether it's street cleaning or a party for teen-agers, that's all part of my religious duties. I must be human, in the best sense."

Brian looked at Pedro. He admired him as a very unusual man, one who had integrated his faith into his life.

"I have to tell you that you have a gift, the gift of being human," Pedro said to Brian with conspicuous enthusiasm. "You take a deep interest in whatever concerns other people have, whether it is religion or a physical need, anything that affects their lives. You have to be an excellent person to be an excellent priest. You take a stand. I know where you stand all the time. You tell me. And if there's a point in the Church's teaching which you don't fully agree with, you openly explain your doubts. You are an honest man."

Brian appreciated how demonstrative the Hispanics were, more so than most of the Irish he knew.

"You have had a lot of influence on me," Pedro continued. "To worry about my brothers, to care. I use that word—caring—as part of religion. It's the only true way to express a relationship with God. These are turbulent times. We both know that. Yet the more difficult the living is, if your faith is a true faith, the easier it is to see the hand of God. If I'm walking down the street and I see a couple of junkies under the influence of drugs, this makes it very vivid for me to spread the Gospel, to bring God's message to those people."

Brian knew that Pedro and his family would inevitably leave the parish. Pedro was doing well in his job and he was expecting a significant promotion soon. Brian asked him about it.

"Soon. I expect good news soon," Pedro said.

"And then? Will you be moving?" Brian asked.

"It is possible," Pedro said. "But I've been giving a lot of thought lately about how difficult it would be for me to move to suburbia and find myself in the middle of one of those

Sunday masses, then just walking out of church and saying to the pastor, 'What a nice sermon,' and going home. And maybe coming down for coffee and cake a couple of times a week for some social gathering at the church. A Knights of Columbus breakfast is not Christianity to me. That would not be living religion to me."

"I understand," Brian said warmly.

Pedro got up, shook Brian's hand vigorously, hugged him, and left.

Brian sat alone in his living room, thinking about what an extraordinary man Pedro Tarno was.

Jim Doyle's Irish grit, even in the face of cancer, endeared him to Brian. And Brian was loyal to Doyle, so much so that even on a December day when the cold winds brought pain, Brian set out to visit Doyle in a veterans' hospital in the Bronx. The hospital was not far from the nursing home where Brian's uncle Pat had been languishing; so Brian decided to spend the afternoon first with one Irishman and then the other.

He walked through the drab corridors of the VA hospital until he found Doyle—in pajamas, socks, and a plaid robe—asleep in a five-bed ward. Brian touched him on the shoulder and said his name softly. Doyle awakened and, without moving, looked up at Brian.

"Ah, Father. Ah," Doyle sighed.

"Just wanted to see how you were doing," Brian said. "They were asking for you at the senior center. I told them I'd be dropping in to see you."

Doyle coughed; his body quivered as he sat up in bed.

"It's the coughing that's the worst, Jim, eh?" Brian asked.

"I like to walk, too, and that's getting harder to do," Doyle said. "But it's worse in bed." As if angered by the lung cancer, Doyle sprang out of bed, put on his slippers, and led Brian into the corridor. He darted from room to room, until he found a wheelchair. He got into it and said to Brian, "Let's go for a ride."

Brian pushed the chair into an elevator, and together they went to a chapel on the first floor. Doyle got out of the chair and walked spryly into the chapel. Inside, both men prayed quietly for a few minutes.

Back outside, Doyle decided to push the empty wheelchair around the hallway. "It's good you get some exercise," Brian joked. Then Doyle jumped into it and started to speed toward the elevator.

"You're not operating that wheelchair properly," a stocky nurse warned.

"So take my license away," Doyle yelled, racing after Brian. He shook Brian's hand, made a U-turn, and raced back to his room.

As Brian left, he spotted a hospital chaplain making rounds. He knew the drudgery involved in being a hospital chaplain. They moved from patient to patient with dubious cheer, telling jokes, being lively on purpose, avoiding the serious. "The Irish backslappers," he called them. It was not his style, not even with his own family.

When he got to the nursing home to visit his uncle Pat, he found the man again curled up under a sheet, silent.

"It's Brian. How are you doing?"

"Not too bad," Pat mumbled.

"Want a little glass of water? Sometimes you can get thirsty in bed like that."

Pat nodded. Brian brought him a paper cup filled with water. Pat clutched it, but could not move it to his lips.

"Do they have you doing any exercises? Moving around?" Brian asked. Pat did not reply. "Would it be easier if I got you a straw?"

Brian went out into the hall and told a nurse he needed a

straw. She wanted to know why. Patiently, he told her. She went to get one.

Brian gave Pat some water through the straw. Then he sat beside the bed and stared at Pat. On the music system the Beatles were singing "All You Need Is Love."

"Anything else I can do for you?" Brian asked. "Maybe I'll run around the block for you. It'll help you and me. I'll lose some weight."

Pat smiled. They stared at each other affectionately, without speaking.

"I'll say a little prayer and give you a blessing," Brian said. Pat nodded.

Brian's voice could be heard in the corridor, and one old woman peered in at him as he prayed.

"We pray that your servant Patrick may be helped in health and in faith." When he was done, Brian clutched his uncle's hand, patted his forehead gently, and said good-bye.

Driving back to the rectory, he thought about the two old Irishmen, Doyle and O'Connor. He remembered his father and his uncles, tough fellows who did their best in tough times. There was a sadness that a sentimental Irishman could feel at such moments. Both Doyle and Pat would be gone soon, but Brian would resist the human inclination to forget them. He would remember them. He owed them that.

33

The rectory phone rang at 9 A.M.

"Something terrible," the woman told Brian in Spanish. Her son, José Perez, twenty-three, had been arrested after a traffic accident and had been sent to the Rikers Island detention center pending trial.

"What happened?" Brian asked. He knew the woman as a parishioner, but he couldn't remember her son.

Mrs. Perez told Brian that her son had been driving along the Harlem River Drive late at night when he hit another car. The driver of the other car was injured, and her son had been arrested.

It was another in the unending train of personal disasters that parishioners brought to Brian. They trusted Brian to be both calm and helpful under pressure. In this case, Brian wondered: Did the boy have a driver's license? Did he have insurance? Had he been in trouble before? Were the police leaning on him because he was an illegal alien? The mother could not answer Brian's questions. She loved her son and he needed help, that was her message. Could Brian write a letter testifying to her son's virtues, indicating that he was not a menace to society? It would help during the trial, she told Brian.

Brian withheld a promise to write the letter, but he told the woman he would visit her son. He had not been to Rikers Island since his seminary days, when with a group of seminarians he had visited the place on an indoctrination tour.

Brian drove a winding course through Queens to the bridge leading to Rikers Island. Two Corrections Department guards stood beside the entrance to the bridge. It was raining, an all-day rain, and they were drenched.

"Father, please pray for an end to the rain," one asked. "But don't get us wrong," the other added, "we'd rather be here than in there," pointing across the bridge toward the prison complex.

Brian drove across the bridge, parked, and entered the reception area. Through a window he could survey the complex: a hospital, an adolescent center, a prison, and the Men's House of Detention, where the parishioner's son was being held. Grassy plains surrounded the styleless buildings, and high fences were visible near the water's edge. The East River dashed against the shore, and planes taking off from nearby LaGuardia Airport periodically obliterated conversation.

In the waiting room, troubled relatives took seats and waited to be called to board a bus to the building and the person they had come to visit. A small, emaciated black cat had the run of the room. A painter leaned lethargically from his perch atop a scaffold to dab white paint on the ceiling.

Finally, when Brian was summoned, along with a dozen other visitors, he went through a turnstile, passed inspection, and boarded the bus that went to the Men's House of Detention. He got out and entered the building.

"I'm a priest," he told the captain on duty. "And I'm here to visit a parishioner, José Perez."

"How do I know you are a priest?" the captain said.

"You can call the chancery office and they'll tell you," Brian said, growing angry. He was wearing his collar; it was visible.

"We have rules here. You have to bring credentials," the captain said. Brian, his face red, left.

Back in the waiting room, he raced to a phone and called a Corrections Department administrator Tom Leonard knew. The man said he would try to help. Brian hung up and sat down.

A few minutes later the Corrections Department administrator came rushing in breathlessly. He took Brian off to a secluded corner and tried to explain.

"What do I have to do to get in?" Brian shouted. "It's stupid to do this to me."

The prison's Catholic chaplain rushed over; he had heard, too, about Brian's brush with the captain. He apologized.

"I can't overrule the captain," the administrator told Brian. He was conspicuously nervous. "But if you come back tomorrow, I promise you'll get in."

"They're busting balls, right?" Brian asked.

"Right," the administrator said. "When you come back, bring a letter from Tom Leonard identifying you."

The next morning, at 9:30, Brian was back. He brought the letter from Tom Leonard and, in case he needed it, his passport. He was ready. He went through the reception area, boarded the bus, and arrived at the Men's House of Detention.

The captain who had turned him away the day before now greeted him amiably. Brian was not searched as other visitors were. The point had been made. He was admitted and taken to an interview area, a group of small cubicles with tables and chairs. Two guards sipped coffee nearby. No one else was in the room; so when José Perez was brought to see Brian, they were almost in privacy.

Perez was a good-looking young man. He wore a gray sweat shirt, dark pants, and sneakers. Around his neck he wore a string of rosary beads. He was thin, clean, soft-spoken; as he talked, he stroked his moustache.

They spoke in Spanish. "I weighed one hundred and seventy-two pounds when I got here," Perez said. "Now I weigh one hundred and forty-three."

"The food?" Brian asked.

"Yes."

"When did you get in here?"

"In early September." It was almost Christmas.

"You have a lawyer?"

"Yes, he's working on it. But I can't get out. They won't reduce the bail."

"How much is it?"

"Ten thousand dollars."

"Ten thousand dollars? What did you do?"

"I was going up the Harlem River Drive. It was late. I didn't see the guy in the other car and I hit him. He was hurt. Not seriously. A few teeth knocked out. He wanted to press charges. Lousy luck. The cops got there. You know what? A couple of hours before that, some cop had been shot near there. And they were mad. They called me 'a menace.' Me. They demanded the high bail and they got it, and I wound up in here."

Brian glared. He knew that 85 percent of the inmates were black or Hispanic, and poor, and unable to post bail. So they remained in confinement until they went to trial. Technically, they were innocent, but still they served time, waiting.

"When is the trial?" Brian asked.

"At the end of January."

Brian counted; José would have served five months before going to trial.

"My lawyer feels good about it all. He thinks we can win. But he needs letters from people like you."

"I'll do it," Brian promised.

"It's a crazy place in here. My wife cooked a turkey dinner for me on Thanksgiving and brought it here, and they wouldn't let her give it to me. I get depressed."

"I don't blame you. So would I," Brian said. "What's the cell block like?"

"Not bad, actually. They must know I'm not a criminal like most of the others. They put me in a block for guys who just stay a day or two; I'm the only one who hangs around longer. I'm lucky not to be with guys who spend months here and go crazy."

"Yes," Brian sighed.

"You know, Father, I've never been in trouble before. I don't know why I'm in here. Other people have accidents and they don't get in here. Why me?"

"I don't know," Brian said. "But what can I do to help you?"

"I'm worried about my wife and about my mother and getting that letter for my lawyer."

"I'll talk to your wife and your mother. Don't worry about them. And I'll get you that letter as well."

Brian said a brief prayer for the inmate's welfare, shook his hand, and left.

He went through the exit cycle in a foul mood—out of the building to the bus, to the reception area, to the parking lot. He got into his car and turned the key. He stepped on the gas heavily and the motor roared. There were two thousand men locked up in the Men's House of Detention. How many of them deserved to be there, he wondered. He drove back to the rectory to write that letter, to call the mother, to think about the young man with a suddenly distorted future.

CHRISTMAS

At least the fellow has not cursed the Church for his fate. That happened. People went to mass, prayed to God, then had some bad luck and blamed the Church. The rewards for a good Christian were not always received in this life; yet he was not one to ask suffering parishioners to accept their pain. Such people had to discover value and importance in their lives; the discovery could minimize suffering. He hoped that José would maintain the strength of his faith, that he would have a skilled lawyer working for him, and that he, the parish priest, would be able to help.

34

Incarnation's charismatic renewal prayer groups met regularly. The Spanish-speaking group gathered every Thursday evening at 7:30 P.M. in the school auditorium. One of the priests would attend to lead all the members in prayer, but the sessions belonged to the group. The priest did not attempt to dominate them. For Brian, when he did have the time to attend, it was a rare opportunity to be a rewarded spectator—to appreciate and be moved by the exuberance of the group.

The charismatic renewal movement was to be found in many parishes in many dioceses. It was a return to less disciplined, more emotional expressions of faith —something common in many Protestant sects in America, but less familiar to old-line American Catholics. It was popular at Incarnation, particularly among the Hispanics who preferred being demonstrative to being passive in prayer.

On one Thursday evening in December, fifty people of all ages braved the cold to attend. The session began with lively music, Spanish hymns played and sung with the verve of popular songs. Several guitarists and tambourine players provided the music; the congregation provided the enthusiasm.

As the Latin rhythms pulsed, that enthusiasm mounted. The members waved their arms. They prayed aloud. They shouted. They pleaded. They reached out. It was a maze of simultaneous prayers, a polyphonic tribute to God. "Like conversation in the waiting room to heaven," one Dominican man remarked.

"*Gracias, Senor*," they shouted. Thanks, Lord.

The crowd kept growing as the evening progressed. People arrived in midsong and joined in. The leader of the group made various announcements. There would be Bible classes for those interested, and there would be a Christmas party. Scripture readings followed, then moments of silence to reflect upon the readings. One speaker quoted from a Dominican publication for charismatics about the Pope's visit to Mexico and his praise of children: "The youth are my consolation and my force as Pope."

There was testimony: stories about salvation through faith. A woman rose and told about her past—filled with the evils of drugs, the torture of pain and sickness, various physical problems—and how she got through them thanks to God and the charismatic movement. "I became aware of the presence of God within me," she said zealously. Her voice grew louder as she went on, the accents becoming more dramatic. Then her testimony became prayer and others joined in to praise God.

There was a pause for the embrace of peace—each person hugged the one next to him. Then they all sang "Mother Hear Me," a hymn to the Virgin Mary.

Ken Smith was the priest in attendance, and he said a prayer and inspired others to pray spontaneously. One by one they did, each voice bedded in the silence of those waiting. They prayed for the politicians of the world, that they would grow in wisdom and eliminate conflict and find peace for everyone.

They prayed for the fate of the American hostages in Iran, for an increase in priestly vocations, for the health of their families, for the sick, the lonely, the imprisoned. Then there was more joyous music and more prayers.

Brian, returning from a visit with a troubled parishioner, arrived just before the meeting ended. Some of the people stayed to browse through an assortment of books for charismatics. Others dashed off into the night air, waving at Ken and Brian. Everyone smiled.

"It is a good way to spend time," one man said. "With God."

"There is nothing better," his wife added. Hand in hand, they left the school and headed toward home.

Brian spotted Rosita Wein on her way out, came up to her, and touched her gently on the shoulder. At sixty-eight, she was one of the most fervent charismatics in the parish. Short, vital, attractive, and well groomed, she looked far younger than her years. Brian appreciated her sense of spirit. She had been an agnostic who had discovered Catholicism. With that discovery had come a sense of happiness that had been absent from her life.

"You know, Father O'Connor, I am what Mother Seton called a child of the Church. I am in love with the Catholic religion," she said to Brian.

"You are good for the charismatics and the charismatics are good for you," Brian smiled.

"Yes, I'm into the dynamics of prayer," Rosita said. "Psychotherapy in prayer or prayer in psychotherapy, I don't know which. We're into the mystical, the mystical prayer. It is therapeutic. We charismatics receive gifts—the gift of the Holy Spirit. A charismatic is a soul who is chosen by God. You can't restrict God. I have that ecumenical spirit, chosen by God to do His work. Once you become aware of that, it is easier for you to grow spiritually. It's a proclamation. You proclaim that you are the Good News."

Brian hugged her, and she headed out into the night. He remembered then something she had said to him once: "If you don't believe, you're hopeless." He agreed.

35

Tom Leonard had been putting up Christmas decorations with obvious pleasure. Two tall, unadorned pine trees were placed on either side of the altar and green wreaths appeared on the pillars of the church. A decorated tree materialized in a corner of the dining room at the rectory; parishioners would place their presents for priests beneath it, and the priests would put their gifts for each other there as well. The fragrance of pine filled the church and the rectory. Christmas cards began to arrive.

In a celebrating mood, Dan Cherico decided to redecorate Brian's rooms. He chose a Chinese motif, and one day while Brian was out Dan moved the furniture around, brought in Chinese vases, prints, and a large Chinese screen. Brian's reaction was one of astonishment mixed with pleasure; he liked the change, although he wouldn't have done it himself. Dan moved in his own ways, and Brian's customary response was quiet appreciation.

It seemed appropriate on that viciously cold December Tuesday to serve Chinese food to the Tuesday-night regulars who were convening at the Incarnation rectory. Brian went to a neighborhood Chinese take-out restaurant and brought back mounds of assorted food, piled it on the table in his living room, and waited for his classmates to arrive. By 10:30 P.M. five of them had shown up to plunge into the Chinese feast and talk about the state of their lives.

Paul Dinter was there, also Larry Quinn, Dennis Sullivan, Pat Carroll, and Jim Flanagan. Reserved but articulate, Flanagan served at Old St. Patrick's in Little Italy; tall, wide, and studious, he was a conscientious priest and a vital presence at the Tuesday-night gatherings.

The early conversation rambled, as it often did: diocesan gossip, the changing color of Larry Quinn's hair (he had gone on a Caribbean trip and his hair had lightened), Jim Flanagan's poker game to raise money for the parish; Pat Carroll's lack of concern for his excess weight (he was a diabetic). The subject of idealism came up. Had it eroded since their days in the seminary in the face of parish reality? The conversation became serious.

"I don't think that the idealism erodes," Larry said. "When you finally get out of the seminary, when you're liberated at ordination, it is a liberation from that place, that system. The ideals don't disappear. You may have a great frustration in trying to realize the ideals, but what you do emerges from who you are, as opposed to the superstructure."

Jim Flanagan leaned forward in his chair; his girth almost made the spindly chair disappear from view. "You can feel that you're your own master," he said, "whatever the frustrations."

"I don't know that I had to face the unexpected when I got out," Brian said. "Certainly there were a lot of things that I hadn't envisioned would be part of my work. But not shocking things, just matters I wasn't prepared to handle."

"You go into a parish after ordination and you're just

another priest," Paul noted. "The parish has had a succession of boobs, characters, klutzes, and a few pious, good men. You just fall into that long black line. The first crisis is rescuing your personality. I didn't realize that was going to happen.

"In a sense, we lapsed into passive resistance in the seminary. We all had to toe the line to get through. I remember that we had a primary intuition which we were absolutely right about—that once we were ordained and got assigned, they were going to try to divide and conquer us. And we came up with a proposal, which Jim mainly authored—that we be assigned in twos. We didn't want to lose that strong support we had provided each other.

"At the time, no one was really talking about Tuesday night becoming an institution. We were all pious, and it was a Scripture-sharing evening, preparation for the homily time. But the more I think of it now, we realized that it was going to be difficult out there."

"That was a shock for many people," Brian agreed. "Because in the seminary and as deacons, we did things as a monolith. But when you got out into separate places, you got divided. The Tuesday nights have helped an awful lot."

"That may be true," Pat said, "but there's also a kind of sophistication that sets in once you're out in the real world. Nothing will surprise me anymore, not after these years of being a priest."

"There's more to it than that," Jim said. "I think I feel more secure in what I'm doing. After eight years, you have an idea of where things are at. You set more realistic goals for yourself."

"For me," Brian said, "it's where we place our priorities. It's a variation on the brick-and-mortar philosophy: you're not building the buildings anymore, you're maintaining and keeping the shop open."

"You know, one of the men I live with is an eighty-five year-old former pastor," Paul said. "He's my companion in the rectory. I went in last night to have my late supper on a tray, and he sat down and brought me some pumpkin pie he'd gotten in New Jersey. He constantly reminisces, and it's like filling in all sorts of gaps in my own awareness. He's always contrasting the way things are done now with the way they were under Hayes, let alone Spellman. He says that Hayes once said that the last thing a Church is, is a business corporation. He told me that you could go down at any time and see Hayes and discuss your problems. He said he was a father, that's the kind of person he was. But now that old priest is almost afraid."

What Paul had earlier defined as a lack of support from the archdiocese hierarchy was a source of festering irritation to him, inspiring him to speak out, to write letters to bishops. In many ways he spoke for the Tuesday-night group—while the others shared his zealous wish for reforms, they were not as energetic in expressing that wish. When Paul articulated his grievances on Tuesday night, however, the others responded supportively.

"I just thought about the one thing that really did shock me," Larry said. "That was when I experienced firsthand the attitude of the official Church downtown toward the problems in our parish and elsewhere. They really couldn't care less about a community or its suffering."

"Yes, it's too threatening," Jim agreed. "They can't admit the level of rot that is presently in the priesthood—that there are boozers, that there are concubines."

"I think they accept it," Larry said. "That's the problem. I don't think that they really care about the needs of the people."

"They're so busy protecting priests and the priesthood as a kind of all-male, white, middle-class, quasi-celibate institution," Paul snapped.

"They care more about institutions than they do about parishes," Pat said.

"The people around the Cardinal are telling him that the

parishes are still alive," Brian said, "but it's the person who comes along and says they're dying that they don't want to hear from. They would rather hide those people in parishes, so they won't be heard from again. And the in-breeding is such that you don't get to the top in the Church unless you cooperate with them."

The room became silent, except for the sound of eating. The Chinese food had almost disappeared. It was close to midnight, but no one seemed tired.

"You know, I think a poor life-style would attract people to the Church," Paul said. "And if the diocesan priesthood is to have any impact, it'll be because we threw away most of the presuppositions of what it means to be a priest—the clerical style, the idea that we're running one of the biggest and most impressive organizations in society. That was all evident during the Pope's visit. The cassocks, the belly bands, the whole clerical style—as if this were Europe fifty years ago. It's a pageant. Maybe it would be good if it were the last pageant."

"Some of the presuppositions have been destroyed," Brian joined in. "In the past priests wanted to become pastors and run plants—and most of us won't accept that. It's almost as if they can't reward us and they can't punish us. In the past they would reward you by giving you a good parish, meaning a very rich parish. But when you tell them you have chosen to work with the poor, they can't understand that."

"It's an elitist system," Dennis said. "And I don't think our parishioners want us to be elitist. I think all people, poor and middle class, want us to be holy. I've always felt that celibacy helps to set us apart."

"They want us to be holy, yes," Jim said. "They want us to be those things that they either are not or cannot be. And if we're ever going to see any turnaround in the number of vocations, they have to see us doing those things that they cannot do. Anybody can collect the tuition at the school. Anybody can pull the lucky number at the raffle. Anybody can be a monitor at a movie in the school auditorium. What people are seeing us doing, more and more, is secular work. Why should you become a priest, take on celibacy, simply to do things like that? Why should you become a priest when you can see your cousin or your brother-in-law doing that same kind of business just as easily? Maybe we've got to divest ourselves of some of the power attached to all those things."

"We should be dealing with the spirit, not with economics," Brian said.

"You know, if there's something sacramental about my life, it's because it has become my ministry, and vice versa," Paul said. "That doesn't mean I'm trapped in a role. It means that my work and my person are married."

"People do expect a lot from us, and that's good," Brian said. "They expect you to be a good spiritual person, and that means how you live what you are preaching, twenty-four hours a day. They want your acts and your words to be unified, to lead them to a deep and productive belief."

"I really think they expect you, particularly in preaching, to give an interpretation to their lives," Paul said. "There is a tradition of the interpretation of life, the meaning of life, the dynamic of faith. The Church has tremendous resources in that tradition, but they're not used. It's frustrating."

"It's odd, perhaps, but sometimes I feel most despairing when I put myself in the position to pray," Dennis said. "It's hard to explain. I bring to it all the frustrations that I have to live with and the prayer is often despairing. It's a very emotional experience for me."

"I guess I suffer from the Irish quietism," Pat said, smiling. "Standing in the middle of the church with just three people there, or seeing the church in flames and finding out that the school is closing on Monday—that wouldn't bother me. It's my rose-colored approach to reality. But there are two things that are painful for me.

"One is becoming involved in people's lives, getting very close to them, and then, all of a sudden, having them drift out. You're no longer . . . I don't want to say 'needed,' because that implies they use you, but to a certain extent, it is a little bit of that.

"The other thing, quite honestly, has been when a priest I worked with seemed not to trust me. His basic idea was trust nobody and you'll be right. I remember going down to my room and just lying there, saying I don't *believe* that goddamned fucker. I just don't believe him."

"That's not too quietistic," Paul said with a laugh.

"No, it isn't," Pat said, grinning.

"It's Irish," Brian said knowingly.

"Well, I didn't go back and kill him, which is the modern Irish approach," Pat said.

"Loneliness without support, without reciprocity," Paul said. "That bothers me. I think I'm capable of an awful lot in my ministry; yet I've always had the sense that one of the most lonely moments is when you finish a wedding and the couple goes off followed by the wedding party, followed by all the people. And you're left alone standing in the sanctuary. That's poignant.

"And pain. I experienced real pain when I felt that there was no place I belonged, no community I was part of to help me from day to day. I could be living anywhere, and the fact that I live in a rectory surrounded by priests makes it worse.

"Your options are limited. The priest I do talk with is eighty-five. And I listen to him. But he's not going to understand what *my* life is about. It's this lack of support from which loneliness comes that's so painful."

After completing an assault on the last egg roll, Brian joined in. "For me, the loneliness you're talking about is most painful when I am involved in situations where I really don't feel I'm a vital, intricate part of people's lives. That if I did leave the parish, the people would do the same things with their lives that they would have done anyway."

"When you leave a parish, they have to absorb the loss, and so do you," Paul advised.

"I had a funny experience about a year ago in that very context," Pat said. "There was this elderly nun, a parish visitor, standing in the hallway, and she had just heard a rumor that I was being transferred. It wasn't true, but that's what she'd heard. Standing next to her was this Puerto Rican woman who'd been involved in the parish. And the woman said, 'Oh, Father Carroll, we're going to miss you.' And the older woman said, 'Don't worry, somebody else will come.' Just like that. And she was right. Somebody else will come, as I came."

"A couple of years ago," Brian said, "I was on a retreat and the priest who was giving it said that people who are dissatisfied with conditions and who advocate change, who are angry, can't be saints. I disagreed with that premise —that the angry, frustrated person isn't a saint because he can't say 'This is God's will.' I don't accept that."

"In the kind of spirituality we were fed," Paul said, "they took the conclusions that the saints reached after a lot of pain and they tried to make those solutions panaceas. The acceptance of almost anything in life as God's will is a particular use of religious language. It says that after wrestling with pain you can see anything as redeemable. Any disaster can be a moment for grace, can become redemptive. But that doesn't make it any less disastrous or any less painful. The person who never gets angry at people or at God or at the Church is a blob fool. Because if you have no passion for what you're doing, where the hell are you going to go with it? A lot of priests are going nowhere because they have no passion for it. Those priests should leave, as some do. They marry nuns because that's their woman-experience in parishes. The nun may have been the only support the priest found."

"I have heard two priests mention that they left not to marry, but because there was some lack of faith," Brian said. "It wasn't a lack of faith about the existence of God, but a lack of faith of God working through the Church."

"There are other ways to leave," Paul responded. "You get an advanced degree, a job, and you leave. I ran into one of those guys recently. Now he was 'fascinated' by what I was doing. He wanted to come in and talk to me and find out how I was doing. I felt like saying, why the fuck do you want to come back when you weren't interested enough to stay around?"

"Tom Leonard told me that when he had the job in personnel, there were three signs that a priest was leaving," Brian said. "One, he went on for a degree. Two, he bought a small car. And three . . ."

"He lost weight," Paul completed.

"Yes, he lost weight. Well, I did only two out of three," Brian said with a laugh, "so I'll see you all next week."

It was 1:30 A.M. and the priests slowly got up. Brian escorted them to the front door and said good night. He returned to his rooms, looked at the Chinese food cartons, sighed, and cleaned up quickly. He went to bed at 2 A.M. He had the 7 A.M. mass in the morning, and he knew that he would be tired.

36

It was the week before Christmas and Brian had not done any Christmas shopping or sent out any Christmas cards. It was a matter of choice. At Christmas he appreciated the gaiety of others, especially children, and he honored the holiday for what it meant spiritually, but he could not convince himself to participate fervently in the gift-giving frenzy. This was not out of any deep antimaterialism; his disinterest in possessions and dollar rituals was more a matter of habit, nurtured by a childhood devoid of luxury and a life-style that denied superfluous comforts.

In midweek he realized that he wanted his nieces and nephews to have a joyous Christmas, and he wanted to contribute to that; he sent checks to his brother John and his sisters Maureen and Kathy, so they could buy presents in his name for their children. They would know what the children wanted most. Dan Cherico supplied an assortment of Christmas cards for Brian, who then sent out a few dozen only to feel guilty when he received cards from parishioners he had not sent cards to.

More important, there were all the pre-Christmas distractions. The church and the rectory came to festive life. The doorbell sounded frequently, the phone rang. There were parties to go to. Each class in the school would have its celebration; the teachers would go home with shopping bags bulging with presents. Brian liked to drop in to share in the festivities. The teachers would have their own party in a restaurant not far from the parish, and Brian wanted to be certain they knew how much he appreciated their work. He knew that one of the wonderful aspects of Christmas was the opportunity it provided to express gratitude, to participate in the happy moments in the lives of others. Throughout the parish, there would be Christmas trees with sparkling ornaments, window decorations that gleamed at night, and parties, both elaborate and simple. There would be many chances to demonstrate the love that Christmas exemplified.

Brian knew that his time would be limited, as it always was, and the feeling made him edgy. He went to the school auditorium to investigate a report that it had been defaced with obscene graffiti. The report was correct. Brian stared and sighed. The souvenir had been left by someone who attended a weekend dance. A phone had been pulled out of the wall as well. It would have to be repaired somehow, and the teen-agers would have to be taught to respect property. He doubted that such a lecture would be effective; it might be necessary to restrict the use of the school auditorium.

Back at the rectory, the phone kept ringing. Parents wanted to arrange baptisms. Couples wanted to be married during the Christmas season. Brian walked a few blocks to visit a woman with a child in a heatless apartment. They sat huddled together, talking about the landlord's promise to provide heat. The woman shivered; her child was bundled up.

Later Brian's aunt called him to tell him that his grandmother, at eighty-seven, was not well. She was in the hospital. Doctors had diagnosed a malignant abdominal tumor. One of them wanted to operate; the family was not certain it was the wisest move. His grandmother had made it clear that she wanted to die without the anguish of surgery at her age. Brian told his aunt that it would be sane and compassionate to honor her decision. He assured her that he would visit his grandmother.

He heard more confessions from schoolchildren.

"Remember me?" one little girl asked him. "You heard my first confession in the fourth grade. My name begins with a *V* and is the same as one of the states."

"Vermont, how are you?" Brian shouted. The girl giggled.

Brian phoned his sister Maureen to tell her that he'd be up to visit on Christmas Day. It would work out well. John and Kathy and their families would be there, too. Anticipation of that cheering afternoon calmed him. Maureen's house was spacious and it would offer the children the chance to celebrate wildly. The food would be splendid. There would be reminiscences and laughter and the encouragement of familial affection. Brian looked forward to it all. He didn't know what his brother and sister in California would be doing; they were not as close to him as the three in the East.

When Brian got off the phone, a twenty-three-year-old man from the parish was waiting to see him. Brian escorted him into one of the offices and shut the door. The man sat down and began to cry.

"What is it?" Brian asked, concerned.

The man continued to cry.

"What is wrong?" Brian asked.

"I've been out of work for four months," the man sobbed. "I can't find work. And the people at welfare say I have to wait six weeks to get money from unemployment. It's Christmas. My God." He kept crying.

For some, Christmas is a tormenting time; it reminds them of what they do not have. The man's plight touched Brian, but he did not know exactly what to say. He put his hand on the man's shoulder. A pious pronouncement was inappropriate; the man needed a job. He had faith or he wouldn't have come to Brian.

"I have some friends who might help, maybe find something part-time for you now, something better later," Brian said, thinking that he could contact Dan Cherico, Pedro Tarno, and a few other parishioners. "I'll call them this afternoon," Brian added.

The man stopped crying and left.

Brian looked at his watch and walked over to the school for a student Christmas celebration. The auditorium was full. Parents, mostly mothers, sat in the rear. Brian leaned against the back wall and watched. The children were dressed up, wearing their best clothes. The room was decorated with Christmas posters the children had drawn.

The first-grade class, sixty of them, sang, "I'm Getting Nothing for Christmas." They smiled as they sang. The eighth grade performed a play the children had written, a mystery entitled "Did Santa Do It?" The sixth grade described, in serious recitations, "The Real Meaning of Christmas." Jason Richardson, a bespectacled, neat, and serious young black boy, played the piano: "Babes in Toyland" and "O Holy Night." The third grade sang "Jingle Bell Rock," and the second grade performed a nativity play. The applause was substantial, and Brian smiled in admiration. He could sense the anticipation that filled the room, the children's eagerness to respond to the season.

Christmas was on a Tuesday. By the preceding Friday, Brian's nerves were frazzled. The phone kept ringing. The doorbell kept chiming. He kept running, from his rooms to the main floor, from the rectory to a troubled parishioner's apartment, noting baptisms to be performed, weddings to be rehearsed. Despite the demands and the joys of Christmas, parish life had to go on.

That afternoon he sat in his room, exhausted. He held a Christmas card he had had printed years before. It contained a quote he liked, by the nineteenth-century Protestant theologian Friedrich Schleiermacher. Brian read it again, as if to tranquilize himself:

> I cannot but laugh and exult like a child. Today all men are children to me, and are all the dearer on that account. The solemn wrinkles are for once smoothed away, the years and cares do not stand written on the brow. Eyes sparkle and dance again, the sign of a beautiful and serene existence within. To my good fortune I too have become just like a child again. . . . The long, deep, irrepressible pain in my life is smoothed as never before. I look upon all things with a gladsome eye. . . . As Christ had no bride but the church, no children but his friends, no household but the temple and the world, and yet his heart was full of heavenly love and joy, so I too seem to be born to endeavor after such a life.

Christmas. He knew non-Christians who were inspired by its mood and its sense of truce with the anxieties present during the rest of the year. For Catholics, it was pivotal, inspiring, memorable; one could trace one's life from the first Christmas remembered to those along the way to the present—Christmases that honored Christ by loving Him and one's family and friends; Christmases in cramped apartments, in seminary rooms, in suburban homes, in the Incarnation rectory. They all came back to him. *Christmas is a rejuvenation, whatever the pressures.*

That weekend would be frantic. It always got like that at Christmas. And despite the gaiety, he knew that the Christmas blues would be felt by some, priests and parishioners alike. Brian would combat them with Dan, with his brother, his sisters, his nieces and nephews; yet it was undeniable that Christmas could be a lonely time for priests.

He left the rectory, got into his car, and drove to the hospital to visit his grandmother.

She was in bed, tubes in her nose and arm, asleep. Two of his aunts were sitting beside the bed, waiting.

"Should we wake her up?" he asked.

"Yes, she would want to see you," one of his aunts said.

Brian touched his grandmother gently and she stirred.

"It's Brian," he said, softly, lovingly.

"Yes, yes," she said, smiling.

"How are you feeling?" he asked.

"You know, Brian, I must have been a very, very bad girl to live so long," she said.

"You mean you're being punished now?"

"Yes."

"Well, you're not. You've done nothing but good for all of us. It's too bad that you're not feeling better, but you will, you will," he said.

He prayed over her. The prayer was brief, and she stared at him as he spoke. She smiled and closed her eyes. In a few seconds she was asleep. Brian kissed his aunts, leaned over the bed and kissed his grandmother. He waved and left the room.

She is my mother's mother, and soon both of them will be gone from my life. Strong, amiable, hard-working, loving women who had helped shape his life. In years ahead, he knew, they would suddenly leap into his consciousness. But one could not mourn forever. You learned what you could, you remembered them, but you moved on.

It was late afternoon, and dark, but not snowing or freezing when Brian drove back to the rectory. Strangely, the city seemed placid; it had lost its customary frantic edge.

He sat in his room, opened more Christmas cards, made a few calls, and had dinner. Then he joined a group of volunteers Tom Leonard had assembled outside the church to stroll through the parish singing Christmas carols. It was a ritual that Tom enjoyed, and he never had trouble finding others to share it. Young Hispanics, Irish teen-agers, a few boys and girls from the Incarnation school, and several older parishioners were in the group. In his bulky coat and Irish tweed hat, Brian towered over everyone.

The group moved along the streets singing in front of apartment buildings, in English and Spanish. Windows were opened and Christmas greetings were shouted out. Parishioners peered from the apartments down at the singing throng, and smiled. The air was cool, and as Tom fervently led the singing, his cheeks turned deep pink. The group moved along the streets and increased in size; more teenagers joined, including a large contingent from a Dominican youth group that had just completed a meeting. A tall boy showed up with a trumpet and played along. As the singers progressed, people handed out donations or dropped them from the windows, and Tom stuffed them into his parka pocket.

After more than an hour, the group convened in the Incarnation convent, two blocks from the church, for hot chocolate and doughnuts. The retired nuns living there had decorated the dining room with a Christmas tablecloth and green bunting and were standing in the room, beaming, when the carolers arrived. The singers sipped the hot chocolate and the doughnuts disappeared quickly. More carols were sung. By 9:30 P.M. the group was ready to disband, and the convent emptied. The Sisters of Charity said good-bye to the singers and wished Brian a Merry Christmas.

At the rectory Brian made mental notes about what he wanted to do over the weekend. There was a Dominican youth group show to attend in the school auditorium, a wedding on Sunday, calls to make, help to solicit for various parishioners in need. He hoped to get some rest before Monday, which would be a long day, from mass in the morning to the midnight mass for Christmas. He was to offer the homily at that mass, and he had still to write it.

After Monday, he decided, he would feel better, stronger. He would enjoy Christmas Day with his family. The tension he had been feeling was turning back to anticipation.

37

On the morning of Christmas Eve, Jack Barry sat at the dining-room table reading the *Daily News*. Ken Smith reclined on the sofa in his living room, listening to Luciano Pavarotti on his stereo. Tom Leonard ran around busily preparing for the midnight mass.

Brian drove to a stationery store on the East Side and bought Tom a Montblanc fountain pen for thirty-five dollars. He had planned to visit Maria Flores, but then received a card from her from Santo Domingo, saying all was well. He felt good that she had managed to get under the therapeutic sun. Finding himself on the East Side, near the hospital where his grandmother was staying, he went to visit her.

A heavy fog had settled over the city and a light rain was falling. He found his grandmother alone in her room, sitting in a chair beside the window, gazing at Central Park in the haze.

He noticed a sign posted over her bed—Hold Lunch —and pointed to it. "I should have that sign over *my* bed," he said, laughing.

THE PRIEST

They chatted about the family and about Brian's plans for Christmas. His grandmother wished that she could be there, at Maureen's for the celebration, but then she assured him that she would be thinking of all of them on that day. Brian wanted her to know that even if she couldn't be there, they'd remember her fondly in their conversation.

Brian noticed that she seemed to be more alert. "It's better than before, when you had the pain," he said.

"Definitely," his grandmother said. "You know, Brian, I think my regret is that when I could have had a hearing aid when I was sixty-five, I said I wouldn't live long enough to get any benefit from it and turned it down. Here I am, without it, twenty-two years later."

"Well, here you are, that's what is important," he said.

She smiled at him lovingly. He said a brief prayer for her, kissed her, and left.

He drove uptown to the senior center, where a Christmas party was in progress. The dining room was brightly decorated, and when Brian entered, most of those present waved at him.

An old Jewish man was on the stage, speaking about his life in Poland and the importance of believing in God for both Christians and Jews.

When he was done, Brian stepped up to the microphone. "This is a time of year to be grateful for our blessings, for the blessings of God," he said. "That's true whether you celebrate Chanukah or Christmas. We have made a family here at the center, thank God. May the peace of God instruct us all. Our love reaches out. Let us always seek the peace that God has given us in our hearts."

The crowd applauded and Brian headed for the door. It was time for lunch at the rectory.

After lunch Brian went to his room to work on the Christmas homily. He turned on the radio and found a station playing nonstop Christmas music. An hour later he had completed a draft of the sermon, four typewritten pages. He sat and studied it. He would not read it to the congregation; the script would serve as a guide.

At 4 P.M. he visited the church. Tom had decorated it beautifully, in what Brian thought of as Tom's less-is-more manner. Its grandeur wasn't defaced by too many decorations. The two tall Christmas trees near the altar, devoid of ornaments, the unadorned wreaths on the pillars, a simple Christmas banner on the wall near the altar—they all looked splendid. In front of the altar there was a carefully designed crèche of primitive wood and straw, with small carved figures and pine branches surrounded by clusters of red poinsettias. Pedro Tarno had helped put it up. A young boy was cleaning the pews with a broom. Everything seemed ready.

The dinner that evening was exceptionally good: roast beef, browned potatoes, vegetables, salad, homemade soda bread that Tom's father had baked and sent to the priests. It was the priests' Christmas meal; on Christmas Day, they would be off to other destinations, and the rectory would be quiet.

At dinner the priests remembered how they had spent Christmas as children.

"We'd stay home and friends of my mother and father would come over," Brian recalled. "A crowd. My aunt worked in a candy factory and she'd always bring big bags of candy. We'd open our presents Christmas Eve, before we went to bed. It was simple and good and nice."

After the meal Brian went back to his rooms. He could hear Tom pass by below, singing "For Unto Us a Child Is Born." Tom's mood was one of energetic celebration; the sound of his voice cheered Brian. Ken was back at his stereo and Jack was wrapping presents. Sergio had returned from a visit to the Maryknoll center and was considering the midnight mass he would celebrate in Spanish in the lower church, with Jack's help, while Tom and Brian celebrated their mass in the main church. Jack looked up from his pile of unwrapped presents and shouted at Sergio, "None of that overthrow-the-government stuff." Sergio grinned.

By 9 P.M. Brian needed a break. He wanted to share the excitement that was rising up within him. He got into his car and drove to the Cherico house in nearby New Rochelle.

He joined Dan and his family for dessert, wished them all a Merry Christmas, and got back to the rectory by 11 P.M. The Chericos were a lively, cheerful lot, and spending two hours with them heightened Brian's exhilaration.

He could hear the singers and the brass quartet rehearsing. Tom had hired them, spending four hundred dollars to make the mass more memorable. The regular organist would be present, too.

At 11:30 P.M. Brian entered the sacristy. He walked around the room, thinking about the sermon he would deliver, about the holiday itself and its inherent vitality, about Christmas with his family. He put on his vestments. Outside, in the church, he could hear the music welcoming parishioners with the sound of "Shepherds Shake Off Your Drowsy Sleep," "God Give Ye Merry Christmastide," "How Brightly Beams the Morning Star," "God Rest Ye Merry Gentlemen," and other carols. The sound of brass filled the church.

Parishioners filed in out of a light rain into both the upper and lower churches. There were teen-agers in jeans and sneakers, small boys in suits and ties, fashionably dressed women and men, Irish and Dominican, Cubans and Puerto Ricans, Columbians, Haitians, Italians. More than 350 people came to each mass, more than Tom had expected.

The mass in the upper church began promptly at midnight with a procession up the side aisle and down the center aisle to the altar.

Tom, in gold and green vestments, followed Brian and one of the deacons. Brian was in white, with a gold stole. Five altar boys proceeded with them.

When they reached the altar, Tom turned and spoke.

"We come to celebrate tonight the birth of Christ."

Yes, Brian thought, that above all is why we are here.

In his opening prayer, Tom said, "Lord our God, with the birth of your son, your glory breaks on the world. Through the night hours of the darkened earth, we your people watch for the coming of your promised son. As we wait, give us a foretaste of the joy that you will grant us, when the fullness of His glory has filled the earth, who lives and reigns with you forever. Amen."

Two women read from the Bible, from Isaiah and from Paul's letter to Titus. The deacon read from Luke, then Brian delivered his homily.

"Christmas is here again. One could conclude that life is merely repeating itself. We watch the news every night and feel that everything, somehow, sounds very familiar. The names and the faces have changed, but the news is the same. Yesterday's Vietnam is today's Iran. And Christmas is here again.

"This feeling that life is merely repetitious, that nothing new exists under the sun, provides us with the ideal setting for the celebration of Christmas. In the Scriptures there is a clear sense of the vicious cycle of life without God. . . . And yet into that cycle, that monotonous repetition, came a reality that shook humanity to its foundations. God became man. . . . And yet this is the reality we celebrate tonight. No longer is life a mere repetition. Life is now given a clear focus. Now our time on earth leads us forth into eternal life."

He spoke of John Steinbeck's novel, *The Pastures of Heaven*. The town in that novel was filled with troubled people; yet the driver of a tour bus, pointing out the town from afar, saw it as a form of perfection.

"Often when we seek God, we look for Him in quiet,

sedate villages, nestled in the hills. . . . But that is not where He is to be found. He is involved in the life and the problems of each of us. He is incarnate in our flesh, and that is where we must look for Him and find Him.

"The Catholic Worker movement of Dorothy Day brought home that reality in a poster. In it, Christ is pictured as one man among many who are waiting on a breadline, needy men in search of help. There is our God, incarnate in our humanity, incarnate especially in the poorest among us, incarnate wherever the stables of Bethlehem exist throughout the world today.

"It is appropriate that we worship tonight in a church called Incarnation. The spirit of God that is incarnate in Jesus is also incarnate in it. . . . This is the essence of the Christmas story. Our God is not to be found in noninvolvement or in escape from reality, but in the everyday events of our lives, in the everyday people of the world."

He wished the congregation a blessed and Merry Christmas and returned to Tom's side, behind the altar.

Dozens of people moved forward to receive the Eucharist: "the bread of life and the cup of eternal salvation," Tom proclaimed. A collection was taken. The singers and the brass provided more music; the organist played. An Our Father was recited by everyone. The Rite of Peace—the shaking of hands—was celebrated. Tom thanked everyone who had helped, then gave the closing prayer, in the midst of which a car outside screeched past and a trumpet played "La Cucaracha." During the recessional the musicians played "Angels We Have Heard on High."

At the front door to the church, Tom and Brian and the deacon shook hands with the parishioners as they headed out into the night. It was 1:20 A.M.

When the last good-bye had been said and only a few stragglers remained in the church—admiring the crèche, whispering to each other, praying—Brian went into the sacristy, removed his vestments, and came into the dining room where others had gathered.

"I should be tired," he said, "but I'm not."

"It's Christmas," Tom said, beaming.

"That's it," Brian laughed. The mass had been a good one, filled with adoration and meaning, an act of affirmation that had brought him closer to God.

They sipped egg nog—Brian, Tom, Sergio, Jack, several deacons, and two visiting nuns. Ken would return soon from celebrating mass elsewhere in the city. There was a pile of presents under the dining-room Christmas tree, and the priests began to open them—gifts for the priests from the rectory staff and parishioners: bottles of liquor, packaged shaving kits ("And I went out to buy shaving cream today," Jack said), sweaters, shirts, books. Tom liked the fountain pen. Brian admired a small calculator he had received.

At 2 A.M. Brian offered to drive the nuns home; they lived on the East Side, miles from Incarnation. The three of them went out into a light drizzle. Brian got them home by 2:30 A.M. and turned around to head back to the rectory.

He was exhausted, but encouraged. In a few days he would complete the year at Incarnation. The new year would arrive and his life would change. He expected to move on to another parish. His grandmother might die soon, and Uncle Pat and Jim Doyle. Sergio might return to Chile, and they might not see each other again. Pedro Tarno might make enough money to move into a house far from Incarnation. Maria Flores, dying of cancer, how long could she hold out? The children in the school, of whom he was particularly fond, would they make it past the temptations the city presented? The questions had to go unanswered. *When you're tired, if you don't get depressed, you get sentimental.*

The years at Incarnation had been productive. He knew that it was the first stop in the life of a parish priest. He had been strengthened by the experience, by his friendship with

Tom, by knowing his parishioners, by helping them when he could and allowing them to help him with faith, compassion, and loyalty.

When he got back to the rectory, the place was silent. Tom had gone to bed, as had Jack, Sergio, and Ken. The phone was quiet, the doorbell untouched. He went to his bedroom, took off his clothes, put on his pajamas, and sat on the edge of his bed. It was 3 A.M. Before slipping into bed, he prayed for strength and faith and a peaceful world.

Acknowledgments

There's always someone to thank. A journalist cannot pursue his craft in isolation. In this book, all those portrayed are real people. In most cases, parishioners' identities have been disguised to preserve their privacy; a few (Jim Doyle, Rosita Wein, Pedro Tarno, Monique Brown) agreed to be identified. All the people who answered my questions did so with impressive candor. My pledge to them was to be responsible; they asked no more.

When I first embarked on my search for a priest to write about, Brother Edward Walsh of Iona College was particularly supportive. Monsignor Walter F. Kenny, Director of Priest Personnel for the Archdiocese of New York, was gracious and helpful. Tom Leonard, his predecessor in the personnel post and pastor at Incarnation, was a splendid host, astute advisor, and untiring guide, despite the demands of his packed pastoral schedule.

Brian O'Connor never evaded a question and never falsified an answer. His fellow priests at Incarnation—Ken Smith, Sergio Torres, and Jack Barry—were extremely help-

289

ACKNOWLEDGMENTS

ful to me. Brian's seminary classmates, named in the book, were cooperative and frank. So was Tom Schweder of the senior center. Parishioners made me feel at home in their neighborhood; they shared their faith and their frailties with me.

Two editors were invaluable: Don Hutter, for his customary wisdom and patience, and Fredrica Friedman, for her extraordinary attention to detail. My good friend Hedy Weiss and my favorite feline, Lola, displayed exemplary affection and support when I was weary. I thank them all.

D.G.